W9-BAH-343

THE POWERS
THAT BE

GORDON UTGARD

© Copyright 2005 Gordon Utgard.
All rights reserved. No part of this publication may be reproduced,
stored in a retrieval system, or transmitted, in any form or by any
means, electronic, mechanical, photocopying, recording, or otherwise,
without the written prior permission of the author.

Note for Librarians: a cataloguing record for this book that includes
Dewey Decimal Classification and US Library of Congress numbers
is available from the Library and Archives of Canada. The complete
cataloguing record can be obtained from their online database at:
www.collectionscanada.ca/amicus/index-e.html
ISBN 1-4120-6565-8
Printed in Victoria, BC, Canada

TRAFFORD

Offices in Canada, USA, Ireland and UK
This book was published *on-demand* in cooperation with Trafford
Publishing. On-demand publishing is a unique process and service of
making a book available for retail sale to the public taking advantage
of on-demand manufacturing and Internet marketing. On-demand
publishing includes promotions, retail sales, manufacturing, order
fulfilment, accounting and collecting royalties on behalf of the author.
Book sales for North America and international:
Trafford Publishing, 6E–2333 Government St.,
Victoria, BC v8t 4p4 CANADA
phone 250 383 6864 (toll-free 1 888 232 4444)
fax 250 383 6804; email to orders@trafford.com
Book sales in Europe:
Trafford Publishing (uk) Ltd., Enterprise House, Wistaston Road
Business Centre, Wistaston Road, Crewe, Cheshire cw2 7rp UNITED
KINGDOM
phone 01270 251 396 (local rate 0845 230 9601)
facsimile 01270 254 983; orders.uk@trafford.com
Order online at:
www.trafford.com/05-1476

10 9 8 7 6 5

Contents

Author Notes

This book is dedicated first to my wife Linda, my son Mark, and my daughter Emily, each of whom sacrificed greatly in keeping things going on the home front without the head of the household being present. Without Linda's understanding and encouragement, I am sure I would not have stuck it out and thus would have missed the unique experiences and adventures recorded here. Both my son and daughter were extremely understanding of why their dad seemed to never be present for such activities as the high school activities or graduation ceremonies. I do plan on making that up.

Secondly, this book is dedicated to Dr. Pritima Kaushik, a very special individual, who was a well-known and respected ob/gyn physician in Jeddah. Her dedication to her patients and to Al-Salama Hospital was remarkable. She was sometimes misunderstood by her colleagues, but always respected by them. As with all of the other physicians, her life changed dramatically and unexpectedly with the forced taking of the Al-Salama." She, perhaps more than any other, experienced the highs and lows simply because of her attachment to Al-Salama Hospital, where she and other physicians were able to practice a very high standard of care for their patients.

I dislike having to use the first person. But an account of my own experiences dictates the narrative "I" rather than "we" on most occasions. Without the help and encouragement of others, not only would this book have never been written, I would have missed out on the remarkable experiences documented here.

I want to mention the names of a few people that have helped me in so many ways regarding this endeavor. My editor Susan Pittman spent hours reviewing and cleaning up my many mechanical mistakes. I can understand why she was such an outstanding English teacher, although I am glad I was not her student, for I would have probably flunked her class. I wish to acknowledge Boone Powell, Jr., retired President & CEO of Baylor Medical Center, Diane Peterson, Peterson & Associates in Houston, Brenda Walton, Keith Froom, and Dr. Arnold Shipstone of the United Kingdom, and Chirag Dhruve in Australia. All of these individuals took the time to read my manuscript and provided insight, ideas, and, most of all, encouragement to move the manuscript forward. Without these individuals and several others not mentioned, I am sure I would not have prevailed in completing the book. Thank all of you.

Special recognition goes to Trafford Publishing House. Thank you Annette, Laura, and Bruce for your patience, tolerance, and wisdom.

Prologue

After much thought and consideration, I decided that there would be sufficient interest, especially given the events of 9/11 and the recent Iraqi war, for me to write this book. I believe that the events I have experienced first hand during the somewhat recent past are truly unique and should be shared. Never in my wildest dreams could I have imagined beforehand what I would encounter. I have done my best to record my experiences in as accurate a manner as I can. I have also attempted to make this book an enjoyable and interesting read. I must emphasize that many of the events that have been written, although considered normal in the Middle Eastern culture, will seem very unusual to the Western reader. The events are set down as I have perceived them. Sometimes the truth and perception are not always the same. I believe, however, that my work placed me in a unique position to be close to the action and to see and hear things that most individuals would not have had the opportunity to see and hear.

THE POWERS THAT BE is an attempt to demonstrate how the Royal Family sometimes functions when dealing with private business. It is also an attempt to surface the way business is typically conducted within the Kingdom and the culture of Saudi Arabia. Perhaps readers who have worked in Saudi Arabia, specifically in hospitals, may be able to relate to the book more successfully than others. I trust that regardless of one's profession, the book identifies and reinforces certain management principles that are universal. After all, human nature is the same regardless of the location. I have also tried to provide a picture of the rugged beauty of this vast country and the modest nobility of most of its inhabitants. The book indirectly reveals the tremendous influence that oil has had in the development of the infra- structure of the Kingdom. Part of the book provides insight into what actually goes on in the Saudi social environment, contrary to popular belief abroad. The book clearly demonstrates that often circumstances beyond human control determine whether we live or die, become happy or miserable, strike it rich or lose everything. We do not control our lives the way the chess player controls his moves. Circumstances beyond our control, and sometimes beyond our understanding, may well determine our fates. I, for one, look at the adventure of life as traveling down a river for the first time. One never knows what is around the next bend, whether it is calm, cool, deep blue waters or Niagara Falls. I myself do not wish to know in advance. This book is about my experiences and adventures as the chief executive officer of what was at the time the most lavish and modern private hospital in the Middle East, owned solely by one of the richest individuals in the world, and about what can happen to a business in a monarchy. It is also about my experiences as an expatriate working and living in the Kingdom of Saudi Arabia, which I am sure, is shared by other expats. If I am only partially successful in this account in surfacing my experiences and adventures of doing business and living in the "Magic Kingdom", I will have accomplished my mission.

Chapter One

Beginnings

"Nothing ventured, nothing gained."
Benjamin Franklin
(*January 1998*)

We were driving back from a great ski vacation in Vail, Colorado. I had leased a large Lincoln town car to give the family plenty of room for the two days drive required from Grapevine, Texas to Vail, Colorado. Some where between Clayton, New Mexico and Amarillo, Texas, my wife, Linda, asked what my business plan was when we got home.

"I have to contact Barry Weinrebe at the Blue Cross and Blue Shield Association (BCBSA) to see what additional international cities they need completed this year. (He had indicated before Christmas that there were probably a couple more cities in Asian countries that require networking). I also need to contact that doctor in Houston who is trying to launch an international telemedicine network. He claims he has several physicians interested as investors and I believe he may want to use me in promoting the telemedicine network to some of the BCBSA international hospitals I have worked with in the past. I am not sure exactly how I will fit into his plans or how I am going to be paid. It is a long shot, but it may have some potential. The Joint Commission of Health Organizations (JCAHO) International may have another assignment coming up in either Istanbul or Riyadh."

Linda replied, "Why don't you pursue that job at the Blue Cross in Denver? You were gone more than you were home last year. Emily is growing up and you are missing a lot by traveling all over the world."

"If I take the job in Denver, assuming it is offered, will you be willing to relocate?"

"Gordon, I hope you find a job in the Dallas/Fort Worth area like many of our friends? You know that it's important that Emily be able to finish her high school in Grapevine like Mark was able to. Also, I really like my teaching situation. I enjoy teaching fifth grade science. I hope you can find work here in the DFW area."

It wasn't the first time we'd had this conversation.

I had created the proprietorship, UTGARD ASSOCIATES, back in January 1997. At that time, BCBSA (the Association of Blue Cross and Blue Shield Insurance Plans) was developing a worldwide hospital network, and they did not have internal resources to do this job. My employment with Blue Cross and Blue Shield of Texas (BCBSTX) was somewhat precarious at the time because of the merger with the Illinois plan. Through out the entire year of 1996 and part of 1995 I had been exclusively involved in developing the Mexico provider network for BCBSTX. The Illinois Plan (who would become the dominate Plan through the merger) was simply not interested in placing additional resources in to Mexico. By creating a proprietorship consultancy, this provided an entity that BCBSA could contract with. For the next six months my sole client was BCBSA. It was an exiting time for me. Not including Mexico, I had worked in nineteen major cities in ten different countries building hospital networks for BCBSA. But, by August 1997, the work with BCBSA was beginning to taper off. My second client, Joint Commission International (JCI), a subsidiary of Joint Commission on Accreditation of Health Care Organizations (JCAHO), was signed in August 1997. I spent the next four months in Riyadh, Saudi Arabia working with the Kingdom's Ministry of Health on behalf of JCI. A couple of other small clients had emerged that produced a little work, but the backbone of my business was BCBSA and JCI. The business had done much better than I had anticipated, and I had enjoyed being my own boss.

I met Dr. Norman Berkman in Houston in December 1997. Dr Berkman was a prominent internist and quite the entrepreneur. He was involved with a health care telemedicine start-up company and was interested in networking key hospitals throughout the world by telemedicine. The idea was that physicians back in Texas at the Texas Medical Center in Houston could provide second medical opinions to their counter parts anywhere in the world where the telemedicine hook-up was available. This communication mode could also be used for a number of other functions including physicians and nurse's education programs. At the time I first met Dr. Berkman, no way in my wildest imagination could I have predicted that my association with this physician would lead me in to the work experience of a lifetime.

The family arrived safely in Grapevine shortly after midnight, with the familiar sound of Mercedes' excited bark welcoming us all back home. We all hit the bed quickly and were asleep within minutes after the exhausting sixteen-hour drive back from Vail.

"Gordon, wake up, you better call that doctor in Houston. He has left four massages to call him at your earliest convenience."

"Honey, let me have a cup of coffee first. I am sure it can wait until then."

"Hello, Dr. Berkman, this is Gordon Utgard in Grapevine. How are you doing? Great, yes we had a wonderful time on our ski vacation. Do you have any news regarding the telemedicine venture?"

After a short conversation regarding the telemedicine project status, he asked if I might have an interest in a CEO position in a private hospital in Jeddah, Saudi Arabia. My initial response was no thanks, but then I indicated that I might be interested in a three months interim assignment while they searched for a permanent CEO. Dr. Beckman knew that I had been a hospital administrator at a large military hospital several years previously in Tabuk, Saudi Arabia. He was also aware that I had been a hospital administrator at three for-profit hospitals in Texas and Oklahoma.

"Gordon, I want you to know that this is no ordinary situation. I have known this Saudi family, who owns this hospital, for many years. They are the owners of the National Commercial Bank, which is the largest private bank in the world. This is no ordinary hospital. It is probably the most lavish and high tech hospital anywhere in the Middle East. It's not even completed yet. I happen to know that they are looking for a CEO because I serve as their medical contact in the USA and typically co-ordinate their health care when they are in Houston at the Texas Medical Center. I believe that you would be ideal for the job, and I believe you should pursue it. They are looking for an American. I don't think they would be interested in a one to three month assignment, however."

"O.K. Norm, tell me more, do you really believe they mean business, and if so, will they make it worth my while?"

"Gordon, don't worry about the pay. If you land this assignment, you will be well compensated."

"Where do we go from here, Norm?"

"Gordon, let me make a couple of calls. I believe they would want to meet with you either in London or in Paris in the next couple of days. I will get back with you soon."

When he hung up, I turned to Linda, "Honey, you will not believe this conversation I just had with Dr. Berkman. I think the guy is either half crazy or may be he is really on to something. Anyway, I won't be holding my breath until he calls me again. I think I will go down to the park and get in a run before lunch. Let's take in a movie this afternoon since you have to start teaching tomorrow. Emily and Mark both have their own agendas, so I'm sure we won't be missed."

While we were gone, Dr. Berkman had called once again and left a message for me to return the call as soon as possible. At 2 pm I returned his call.

"Hello, Dr. Berkman, it's Gordon returning your call. That was quick. What did you find out?"

"Gordon, they want you to travel immediately to Jeddah to meet with them. They will arrange a special visitor's visa for you within forty- eight hours and would like to see you on Saturday."

"Are you really serious? You know they can't get a visa that quickly. Are you sure this is on the up and up?"

"You must believe me when I tell you that Sheikh Khalid Bin Mahfouz is very influential. If the family wants to see you, I'm surprised that they have not already sent one of their private jets to receive you. Catch the next flight to Houston. Southwest Airlines has a flight from Dallas Love field to Hobby every hour until midnight. I will retrieve the visa application from the Saudi consulate. If you catch the 4 pm flight, I will meet you in the coffee shop at Hobby at 5:30 pm. We will complete the application form there, and I can get it to the Saudi Consulate first thing tomorrow morning. We will secure the visa tomorrow. You will leave tomorrow from DFW at 2 pm on Delta direct to JFK. From New York, you will take Saudi Arabian Airlines at 9 pm direct to Jeddah. It's about an eleven hours flight. You will arrive in Jeddah on Thursday at approximately 5 pm. The Jeddah Intercontinental Hotel will meet you at the airport upon your arrival. I have made your reservation already at the Intercontinental Hotel for Thursday, Friday and Saturday nights. If you will need more time, we will simply extend the stay.

"You are supposed to meet the sons, Abdul Rahman and Sultan Bin Khalid Bin Mahfouz at their private office on Saturday at 9 am. A driver from the office will be at the hotel at 8:30 am to pick you up. Best of luck to you. This could be the best opportunity you will ever have so don't blow it. By the way, another American, Jerry McDuffy, who works for the family will be your contact in Jeddah. If you need anything, Jerry will be available to help. You may want to give him a call. I will fax you his home and office telephone numbers. See you at Hobby Coffee Shop in a couple of hours."

Dr. Berkman's interest in me being the successful candidate was not completely benevolent, for he did stand to gain a substantial commission.

"Linda, guess what? I have to leave immediately to fly to Houston Hobby to see Dr. Berkman concerning visa papers. Then tomorrow I am off to Jeddah, Saudi Arabia to interview for the hospital CEO position. I still don't know what to make of this. Berkman says that this is the typical modus operandus when this family finally decides to act. Well, if nothing more, I will have a couple of days at the Intercontinental Hotel on them. I believe I would like to stay an extra day so I can get in at least one good dive in the Red Sea."

Chapter Two

Encounters

"If you only knock long enough and loud enough at the gate, you are sure to wake up somebody."

Henry Wadsworth Longfellow
(February 1998)

Saudi Arabian Airline flight # 22 departed JFK promptly at 9 pm en route non-stop to Jeddah, Saudi Arabia. The first class accommodation on the modified Jumbo 747 was very nice and the service, as expected, was superb. As I settled back in my comfortable seat shortly after take off, I briefly considered a gin and tonic as I reflected upon the past forty-eight hours. Recalling that alcohol is officially taboo in Saudi Arabia and, thus not served on its airline, I settled for a fruit cocktail drink instead.

Just a couple of days ago I was skiing down the slopes at Vail, Colorado and enjoying the open fireplace at the Marriott Mountain Resort Inn. Now here I was at 30,000 feet on an eleven-hour flight to Jeddah to visit with some Sheikhs about managing their hospital. Life is unpredictable and I was looking forward to the encounter with cautious anticipation.

My mind was recounting the last time I had dived in the Red Sea. It had been in late October last year when I was on assignment in Riyadh working for the Joint Commission International. I had met up with some Americans who were working for ARAMCO (Saudi Arabian Oil Company) in Damman. They had invited me to go with them to Yambu for a weekend of scuba diving. It had been a great experience and was the first time that I had actually scuba dived in the Red Sea. The fish and color of the reefs were astonishing. We had even explored an old wrecked freighter, which had been lying on its side for the past twenty-five years in about ninety feet of water. I would undoubtedly take an extra day to once again dive in the Red Sea even if it was only offshore. These were my thoughts as I drifted off to sleep somewhere over the North Atlantic.

The Moroccan flight attendant awakened me about thirty minutes before landing. I must have been exhausted, for I had fallen asleep about two hours after takeoff from New York and was just now waking up. I reset my watch according to Jeddah time, advancing it nine hours from Central Standard Time. As I completed my mandatory custom declaration card, I could not help but notice the statement: "Warning-Death Penalty to Drug Traffickers."

I saw several Saudi women in first class seating. It is always fascinating to watch these striking young women in their designer fashions line up to enter the aircraft restrooms about thirty-minutes before arriving in the Kingdom. When they emerge, a metamorphosis has taken place. They have changed into their black abayas and their faces are veiled with only their bright eyes exposed. They are about to reenter their native culture where woman are expected to be very discreet.

Going through customs was rather easy with no undue delays. Of course, I was traveling light and had only checked one bag, which contained my diving gear. Customs is very unpredictable. At times it can be quick and other times excruciatingly slow.

The Indian driver at the airport holding up the Intercontinental Hotel sign with my name on it was a welcome sight. We reached the hotel at 8 pm. local time.

I was glad the next day was Friday (their Sunday). Having a day to myself before meeting with the Sheikhs on Saturday, I relaxed at the hotel pool and took a stroll down the sea front. The sea breeze was gentle and the sound of prayer calls brought back waves of nostalgia. I was glad to be where I was.

"Hello, Mr. McDuffy, this is Gordon Utgard, Just wanted to let you know that I arrived safely and I am currently enjoying the Friday afternoon at the hotel. Yes, everything is fine. The flight was quite comfortable and every thing was like clockwork. I am looking forward to meeting you tomorrow."

"I will meet you in the morning at 8:30 am in the hotel lobby, Gordon, tomorrow will be a busy day for you. The people you will be meeting are the decision makers. Sheikh Abdul Rahman Bin Mahfouz, whom we call A.R. is the eldest son of Sheikh Khalid Bin Mahfouz and is primarily involved with the National Commercial Bank. A.R. is only about thirty years old but a mature individual who represents the family well. Unfortunately, Sheikh Sultan Bin Mahfouz, the younger son, who has the responsibility for the hospital, will not be available. You will also meet Dr. Hesham Mehriz; he at one time was in-charge of the old Al-Salama Hospital. His input will be important as he has influence with the Bin Mahfouz family. They typically place a lot of weight on his observations. The third person you will meet is Dr. Rayes Bin Mahfouz. Dr. Rayes has been in charge of the hospital for the past few years, and basically you will be replacing him. Keep this in mind, for I am not sure that he is happy about their decision to employ a new CEO. Regardless, he will be at the hospital in some capacity, and it will be important that the chemistry between the both of you is good. I believe the previous American administrator didn't communicate well with Dr. Rayes, one of the reasons why they are seeking someone else. Remember, Gordon, they have decided to recruit a highly trained professional CEO who will have complete authority and accountability. Don't be fooled by this, however; Dr. Rayes will play an important role in your endeavors if you are the successful candidate. I am just not sure whether he will be a positive or negative influence. He is not one of the direct descendents of the owner Sheikh Khalid Bin Mahfouz. I believe he is a maternal cousin of A.R. You will not be meeting the owner. At the appropriate time, you may or may not have the opportunity to meet him. You will understand more later if you are asked to join the group."

Dr. Berkman had previously briefed me regarding the mission of the hospital. The name of the facility was Al-Salama (good health). Sheikh Khalid was its dynamic owner.

The new hospital was being built to replace the existing Al-Salama Hospital, which had been open since 1987. Sheikh Khalid looked at the hospital as a memento given back to the city of Jeddah as a gesture to the people for supporting him over the years. Its philosophy was entirely different from that of other private hospitals in the city. Yes, efficient management and operations were important, but the key factor was providing the best care possible in the most elaborate and modern facility in the Middle East .The owner anticipated that cash injections would routinely be required, but hoped that would be reduced over time. Still, profit was not the primary reason this hospital existed. Providing excellent private health care services in a superb facility to the citizens of Jeddah and Saudi Arabia was the mission, according to Dr. Berkman. Jerry McDuffy had also indirectly articulated the same during our short drive to the private office.

We arrived at the office on Tahalia Street in north Jeddah a few minutes before 9 am. I still had not seen Al-Salama Hospital, but my curiosity was increasing by the minute. It sounded like the facility was state of the art and more of a palace or a five star hotel than a hospital. The facility was in the final stages of a major construction project, according to Jerry and Norman.

The office of Bin Mahfouz enterprises was quite nice, but not overly elaborate. My first interview with A.R. lasted about 45 minutes. I then visited with Dr. Mehriz and then with Dr. Rayes. Each interview lasted about 45 minutes. The interviews were nothing out of the ordinary. They asked typical questions about my experience, and I provided to them academic responses regarding my philosophy of management and other "BS" that I thought they would like to hear. I quoted some verses from Allen Toffler and Peter Drucker, trying to impress them with my great knowledge of modern management. Like all interviews, ninety percent is the chemistry between individuals and the ability to connect with the other person. It was obvious to me that the head honcho and key decision maker amongst the three was A.R. I felt comfortable in talking to all three, especially A.R. and Dr. Rayes.

It also became obvious to me that Dr. Mehriz was keen to understand my knowledge of information management services and data processing in general. Only later did I learn that he headed up a sister company that was involved in the implementation of a new information management system in the hospital and that the implementation was having serious problems. By the time I had met with all three individuals, it was time for lunch.

Jerry and I drove to a nearby Burger King fast food restaurant for lunch. As we were going, I noticed familiar establishments such as Kentucky Fried Chicken, Fuddruckers, Pizza Hut, and, of course, "the Golden Arches." As I reflected upon the time since my arrival, I thought about how westernized the city really was. I remembered my drive into the city center from the airport. All major advertising signs were in both Arabic and English. Most of the people I met spoke some English. The highway systems, airport, and city buildings were all very modern. It was evident that the infrastructure had virtually sprung out of the desert as a result of the world's thirst for oil. Getting around and communicating here, a half a world away, was much easier than in Mexico, which was just adjacent to Texas.

"Gordon, my feedback is that the interviews with all three gentlemen went well. They wish to meet with you as a group around 5 pm. I will drive you back to the hotel so you can catch a nap before I pick you up at 4:30 pm."

When I returned to the private office shortly before five, I was escorted directly to A.R.'s office where I was offered chai (tea). I sat there about 15 minutes before A.R., Dr. Mehriz, and Dr. Rayes entered the room. A. R. opened the conversation. "Congratulations. We believe you are the right man for the job. We want you to start immediately. As a matter of fact, we would prefer next week if possible. What type of compensation package would you require?"

I was totally surprised that things could move so fast, although I kept my poker face on. I asked if I could be excused for half an hour while I considered their offer.

"Sure, Gordon." A. R. responded, "We understand this is a major decision for you. Take your time. Let's meet again here in about an hour. There is an office down the hall you can use. Feel free to use the international telephone if you need to discuss this matter with anyone back home."

At times Saudis can move at warp speed. At other times it can take forever to get something done. You never know on the front end which it will be.

When I presented my compensation requests, I immediately realized that I must have been too conservative in what I asked for, although I considered it quite substantial. They, as a group, quickly agreed and asked what type of time commitment I could make. I thought about what Dr. Berkman had stated about their not being interested in a one to three month interim assignment. I had decided that depending upon how the compensation negotiations turned out, I would suggest either a one- or, maximum, two-year contract.

"Gentlemen, with the magnitude of this project and what has to be accomplished (they had code named this job search "the Schwarzkopf initiative" after General Schwarzkopf of the American Armed Forces during the first Gulf War), I believe a three-year contract would be appropriate." Everything settled, we all shook hands.

Then A.R. said to me, "Gordon, I want to arrange a meeting tomorrow with the medical staff to introduce you as the new CEO. We will set the meeting for 1:30 pm, after the morning clinics."

Jerry drove me back to the hotel about 9 pm. "Congratulations, Gordon, but let me tell you that this job is really going to be a challenge for you. That hospital has been a can of worms. The building project has been going on for five years. The information management system has been under implementation for the last three years, and the doctors, although they have a good medical reputation, have been running the place and are very much an undisciplined lot. You really are going to have to establish yourself early and show no mercy to bring the place to some type of order. Don't be surprised if the turnout to your introduction tomorrow is lukewarm. They will be looking upon you as a stranger and a threat to their status quo.

"I am responsible for writing the offer letter to be signed by Sheikh Sultan Bin Mahfouz, the Chairman of the Al-Salama Hospital, and you. This document will serve as the official offer until a standard conforming contract can be made. My goal is to get this signed by Sheikh Sultan before you leave. I have been here now for several years and I do not have anything on paper that spells out my agreement. That's not good, and I don't want you to be in the same situation."

"You know, Gordon, you and I are about the only Americans they have employed here in the Kingdom. Sometimes, they simply forget about the details we might expect, such as contracts. The previous administrator, who left about three months ago, had some type of disagreement about his end-of-service package. There was nothing in writing and, thus, only his verbal understanding of what was supposedly offered when he joined. Needless to say, he was not a happy camper when he departed."

"Jerry, you're right. That written promissory offer letter signed by both parties, if not the official contract, is essential for me to have in my hand before I leave Jeddah."

I had already had enough experience in the Middle East to understand that anything like a contract had to be in writing; even then it's not for sure. The Saudis are notorious for slipping out of understandings. An Arab verbal commitment is extremely precarious.

Later that evening as I lay in bed looking at the ceiling of my hotel room, I tried to visualize the meeting with the medical staff the following day. I mentally noted certain comments that I should make, primarily about my excitement and anticipation of working with the medical staff to continue to see Al-Salama Hospital improve and lead the competition.

During the negotiations earlier that day, we had agreed that my start date would be first of April 1998, not the following week as proposed by A.R. Suddenly, my anticipated dive in the Red Sea seemed much less important to me. I had not yet seen the hospital. I had not even discussed the events of the past two days with Linda and the kids. Things seemed to be moving way too fast, but really I had already committed to the Bin Mahfouz family regarding "the Schwarzkopf initiative." I knew in my heart that Linda would support my decision and Al-Salama Hospital would be a very important client for Utgard Associates.

The next day, Dr. Rayes and I were sitting in a trailer outside the main hospital at 1:30 pm. The trailer was serving as a temporary location for the employee cafeteria and also as a conference room facility. Most of the Filipino nursing employees had already finished their lunch and were leaving the trailer. When Dr. Rayes and I arrived, I still had not had an opportunity to tour the hospital facility. It was obvious from the facade that this was not only a massive, but also a lavish, five-star facility. It was also evident that the construction project was a long way from being complete.

Between 1:45 and 2 pm the physicians began strolling nonchalantly into the temporary conference room. They all had on their traditional white coats with the large majority of them being Arabs of Egyptian nationality. There were some Saudi physicians and a couple of female doctors present. As far I could tell I was the only American in the group. They were all polite but guardedly cautious.

Dr. Rayes briefly introduced me as the new CEO and stated that I would be starting on duty April 1st. After the brief introduction, he turned the podium over to me.

As rehearsed the previous night, I spoke about teamwork, dedication, and the importance of developing covenant working relationships. I indicated I would be looking forward to working with each one of them and asked that they give me their support and some time to learn each of their names. The reception was certainly not warm, but rather sterile with a bit of tension. Overall, it was about what Jerry had indicated that it probably would be. A couple of key physicians had failed to show up because of supposedly prior commitments. He had warned me that working with these doctors was going to be about as much fun as swimming in a shark tank. Yes, I was beginning to understand why this project had been named "the Schwarzkopf initiative."

I did get in that Red Sea shore dive early the next day. It was now Monday morning, and my flight back to Dallas via New York was still some twelve hours off. I was cautious and went no more than twenty-five feet deep for only a twenty- minute period since I knew I would be flying soon. I had heard the horror stories of divers that flew too soon after diving and had developed the bends because of the extreme changes in air pressure in a relatively short period of time.

The Red Sea was just as beautiful as ever, with vertical reefs dropping off into the clear blue water. The vivid color of the reefs and the many fish never fail to amaze me. I knew that during the next couple of years, I would be experiencing the wonders of this great diving location many times, *Inshallah (God willing)*.

Chapter Three

Kick-Off

"Any fact facing us is not as important as our attitude towards it, for that determines success or failure."

Norman Vincent Peale
(March—May 1998)

Approximately six weeks later in late March, I was getting ready to leave Grapevine, Texas to begin the assignment at Al Salama Hospital. With my having to wrap up so many loose ends, the weeks had flown by. My other clients had been contacted and understood that for the time being I would be focusing one hundred percent on this new assignment. I had worked through several items with Linda, who would be attending to the details of living alone for awhile. We had several things done to the house that we had been putting off, such as a new air-conditioning system and a new automatic water sprinkler. Hopefully, the replacement of these items would give Linda peace of mind in not having to worry about them. I replaced all the tires on the automobiles and had the cars serviced. Brenda Sanders, my secretary, had been thoroughly briefed regarding the status of the other clients and knew how to reach me. I wanted to continue my work relationship in some fashion with, at least, BCBSA insurance companies and Joint Commission International. Having a fairly good idea of what lay ahead (or so I thought), I really did not know if I would survive the first three months.

We were planning for Linda, Mark, and Emily to visit me in Jeddah during the summer vacation of 1998. Our tentative plans were that they would arrive in mid June and return the first week of August to start back to school. Mark would be entering his final year at Baylor University where he was getting his degree in Mechanical Engineering. Emily would be entering her final year in middle school (8th grade) during the fall.

I had decided to take Delta Airlines from Dallas via New York to Zurich and then on to Jeddah. I knew there was an eight-hour lay over in Zurich that would give me plenty of time to take a train from the airport to the old city. I had done this a couple of times in the past and really had enjoyed it. I would typically place my carry-on bags into the airport lockers and catch the train at the airport to the central station in Zurich. The trains run like clockwork in Europe and especially in Switzerland and Germany. I would get off the train at central station (fifteen minutes from the airport) and rent a bicycle or walk through the beautiful old city. Many of the quaint buildings serve both as businesses and also as living quarters upstairs. Most residents grow flowers on the window ledges that really brighten up the old city. The narrow cobbled stone streets are a couple of hundred years old. After four to five hours and a little cheese, wine, and a light lunch at a sidewalk café, I would return to the airport and catch my flight, either back to U.S.A. or on to the Middle East.

I arrived in Jeddah on Friday, March 27th, having taken my quick jaunt in Zurich as planned. I checked into the Intercontinental Hotel where I had negotiated a good rate for a two months stay. I knew that the first couple of months would be spent almost totally at the hospital. My accommodation needs would be simple: a nice place to sleep, meals, maid/ laundry services, and health club facilities. I planned to relocate to a villa in a western compound by 1st June before my family arrived. Having decided to live in a hotel for the first two months proved to be a good decision. The convenience of the hotel allowed me to focus exclusively on my work. It also provided me the time to look at several western compounds and the villa that was best for me without being rushed.

Jerry McDuffy called me that evening to see how I was doing and if I had arrived with out incident. I thanked him for his concern and he mentioned that a hospital vehicle would be at the hotel at 9am the next morning to take me to the hospital.

"Gordon, I want to wish you good luck on your assignment. You have a monumental task ahead of you. Remember, the first couple of months are critical to your success. Establish your authority early. You won't be hearing from me any more, but feel free to contact me if you need to. My assignment regarding your mobilization is now complete. Please don't think I am being abrupt, it's simply my nature. I'm up to my ass in alligators. The Bin Mahfouz family has got me running in a hundred different directions at once."

"I understand, Jerry. Thank you for every thing you have done. Maybe when Linda gets here in the summer we can get our families together."

"Sure, Gordon, that sounds great. Good luck in your new job."

During the next three years, I would not see or talk with Jerry more than half a dozen times. When I think of that now, it seems rather odd. Jerry's typical blunt New York style and his heavy travel schedule and workload probably kept us from becoming closer friends.

Mr. Syed Mustafa, the hospital administrator, was the first to welcome me to my new office. The administrative offices were located in some temporary trailers right across the street from the new hospital construction. These were the same type of trailers that housed the employee cafeteria and conference rooms. The offices in the trailer were adequate but modest. My office was adjacent to Dr. Rayes Bin Mahfouz's office, with our secretaries in a fairly large waiting room adjacent to these two offices. Syed's office was just down the corridor. The Personnel/ Human Resources office also shared these trailer accommodations. This location would serve as our temporary offices for the next eighteen months.

I was fortunate to have an experienced executive secretary, a gentleman named Mr. Mustafa Cheema. Like Syed, he was of Pakistani origin. He had been working at the hospital for several years and was well acquainted with what was going on and who was who. The previous American administrator had advised me that I would be well served if I could manage to get Mustafa as my executive secretary. His loyalty was his greatest attribute. The same administrator had also told me that one of my biggest headaches would be in keeping the staff from going directly to Dr. Rayes about every issue. Unfortunately, Rayes did not discourage such practices. This became something I had to learn to live with to some extent during my tenure. Mustafa did his best to help control that problem.

My priority for the first six weeks was to meet one-on-one with each clinical and administrative head. I also wanted to build a good relationship with Dr. Rayes during this initial period, and I wanted to become familiar with the building and the construction project.

I turned to my secretary, "Mustafa, let's kick off by arranging the department head one-on- one meetings beginning tomorrow starting at 7 a.m. Let's arrange these early meetings at the Intercontinental Hotel over breakfast. The following meetings should be in my office. We will try to have three scheduled each day, allowing one and a half hours for each meeting. I really want to have enough quality time during these meetings and not be rushed."

He asked me who I would like to see first and than made a couple of good suggestions.

"I believe we should start with Dr. Mohsin Hussien. Let's mix in the clinical and administrative department heads. I would rather not just see one group first and then the other later. Also, I want to have a scheduled meeting for at least half an hour each day with Dr. Rayes.

"Also make appointments with the Director of Facilities on a daily basis so I can get up to speed on the hospital layout and construction program. I am going to leave it to you to manage the scheduling, but please do not schedule any thing after 8 p.m. without checking with me first."

My objective for these meetings was to become acquainted with each department head. I wanted to establish early that I was genuinely interested in their problems and concerns. I also wanted to express my management philosophy and my expectations from the very beginning. I had asked *all* department heads to prepare in writing what they considered to be their five top priority items in advance of our meetings.

"Mustafa, one of my pet peeves is meetings that don't start on time. Encourage the staff to be on time."

I explained what Lombardy time was. When Coach Vince Lombardy, the legendary coach of the Green Bay Packers, told the team that the bus would depart the hotel for the stadium at 10 a.m., that actually meant the bus would leave at 9:55a.m. I hoped such analogies would help foster a sense of discipline and the importance of time.

I anticipated that this requirement by the new boss would not be received well in this culture but *it* was a part of establishing discipline. I was also adamant about establishing specific, measurable goals with specific time- tables so managers could be held accountable. This was something that had not been done in Al Salama Hospital before and would be considered another requirement that the key staff probably would not like about their new boss. All of the department heads had been working at Al Salama for several years in a loose environment (like that of the easy going corner convenience store).

The first week on the assignment flew by. I started each day with the 7a.m. one-on-one meetings and wrapped up in the evening at about 9 p.m. I felt the meetings were going well and I was accomplishing what I had intended. The daily meetings with Dr. Rayes were informative and I sensed I was beginning to build a good working relationship with him.

At the same time I did not have as much of an opportunity to familiarize myself with the construction project as I had intended. I really needed to spend more time in this area in the coming weeks.

Mustafa reported that Dr. Pritima Kaushik, the chief of ob/ gyn requested that she should be scheduled as my last one-on-one. When I spoke with her by phone regarding the scheduling, she welcomed me to Al Salama and wished me good luck.

"I would like to be scheduled last regarding your department head meetings. By this time you probably have been told that everything is fine with the hospital and that all is well. I'm one of the very few who will tell you exactly the reality about the hospital. Believe me, there are many problems. There are lots of worms in the woodwork.

"By the way do you have sense of humor?" she asked?

"I hope so."

"O.K., I am sending you by fax a cartoon that is self explanatory and very much relevant to your new assignment."

Suddenly, I remembered what Dr. Rayes and Dr. Mohsin had said one day about this doctor. She is the only one who will give her true opinion about anything regardless of the situation or ramification.

A few moments later, I received an interesting cartoon on my personal fax machine from Dr. Kaushik. In this cartoon, there were two army generals walking out of the Pentagon in Washington D.C. They had just come out of a meeting with politicians. One General says to another "Give me the battlefield any day. There the enemy wears a uniform and you can at least recognize him." I would find out during the coming months just how accurate that cartoon really was in this environment.

I usually met with Dr. Rayes Bin Mahfuoz each day at 11:30am. During these meetings, I would become somewhat impatient because we would be continually interrupted with both employees and other Saudis coming into his office unannounced. This is a common Saudi custom. You might be discussing a serious business matter with six other people in the room. You might be just getting to an important point when a new visitor enters the office and takes up another ten minutes in polite Arabic greetings and dialogue, thus interrupting the entire proceedings. This is just a way of doing business here, quite frustrating for the westerners, but the norm for the Saudis. A lot of tea and coffee is consumed in these meetings. It would be considered impolite not to offer your visitor such even though he just dropped in.

Many times the interruptions would occur with customary conversations like "Walekum-salam" Dr. Inas El Marzuki, I want you to meet Mr. Gordon Utgard our new CEO." Then the conversation would be converted into a full- blown Arabic discussion, much of which I had no clue of what was being spoken.

Dr. Rayes had headed up the Al Salama Hospital for several years as General Director. Under the new organizational structure, he was the President. On paper I reported to him with all other clinical and administrative functions reporting to me as CEO. In reality, I was in charge and Dr. Rayes was more of a Saudi liaison officer with the title of President. I saw very quickly that this would become a problem if I moved too aggressively here. After all, he had been the General Director for several years, and now suddenly he had a different title and reduced responsibilities.

This somewhat ambiguous relationship between the CEO and President was a source of frustration to both Dr. Rayes and me, though mostly to me. I believe we both knew when to take and when to give; and, as a result, over time we came to trust each other. It was perhaps a little more ambiguous for the employees. There were many occasions when a direct report of mine, who did not like a decision I had made for one reason or another, would go directly to Dr. Rayes to see if he would intervene. The situation would usually unfold as follows:

Dr. Rayes would say, "Good morning, Gordon, Dr. Yousry visited me this morning with a problem. You know he has some commitments in Egypt that require him to go there on short notice."

I might reply, "Yes Dr. Rayes, I am aware of that. Unfortunately, he has allowed two other consultant surgeons off on leave next week on vacation, and if he also leaves then we have to cancel some of the evening clinics. So I suggested to Dr. Yousry that as Chief of Surgery, he should, if possible, wait until the following week. He did not like the suggestion and came to you."

This would be a common occurrence and generally Dr. Rayes would support my position after some clarification. At other times when I could see his point of view made more sense, I would change my position. Many of the staff tried to take advantage of this ambiguity in the decision-making responsibility of the CEO and President. Over time, however, the staff learned that this was not acceptable behavior and it occurred much less often.

The first actual confrontation between Dr. Rayes and me came some six weeks after I had started my work. One of the major money making physicians at Al Salama Hospital was Dr. Magdi Sheikh, Head of the Artificial Reproduction Technology Department. Both he and the Head of Cardiology, Dr. Taher Hassan (both Egyptian by nationality) had been somewhat distant with me and seemed not to be very supportive. After their not showing up for the second rescheduled one-on- one meeting, I sent the following memo to both of the physicians:

Dear Sir,

You were once again absent for our one-on-one meeting. In the future if you are going to be late or cannot make a scheduled appointment, I respectfully request the courtesy of a telephone call to my office advising me of such. Not to do so demonstrates a lack of professionalism.

Gordon Utgard, CEO.

The next day, I received the following memo from Dr. Magdi Sheikh:

Dear Sir,

Never in my professional career as a respected physician has any administrator ever sent me such a curt and disrespectful memo. I will be discussing this with the owner.

Sincerely,
Dr. Magdy El Sheikh,
Head IVF Dept.

The next day during the routine meeting with Dr. Rayes, he brought this subject up and alluded to the fact that both Dr. Magdi and Dr. Taher were two very important physicians for the hospital.

"Dr. Rayes, I completely understand that. But, during the last six weeks I have experienced passive resistance from certain quarters, and these two key physicians and medical staff leaders fall within that segment. If not addressed early, this type of behavior, I expect, will quickly result in the undermining of the leadership. I must have your full support regarding such matters."

Dr. Rayes listened.

A couple of days latter, he and I visited with A.R. and Sheikh Sultan, the hospital Chairman, at the Private Office on a finance issue. At the conclusion of the meeting, A.R. mentioned, "Gordon, I understand you had a little run-in with a couple of the doctors the other day. You know it is critical that you and Dr. Rayes communicate well and work well together for the success of the hospital."

It was obvious to me that Dr. Rayes, or someone, had briefed A.R. on the incident with the two doctors and had slanted the conversation in a negative manner.

"A.R. as far as I know, Dr. Rayes and I are communicating well and working closely together." I then looked at Dr. Rayes and asked, "Do you have any problems or concern regarding our communications?" Dr. Rayes responded that he had none.

I then gave A.R. a brief account of what had occurred with the two doctors. Then he replied, "We did not code-name this the 'Schwarzkopf

Initiative' for nothing. You have our full support and under the circumstances, as you have described it, I believe your action was perfect pertaining to these two doctors. Gordon, they will test you severely. Be prepared. I know that Dr. Rayes will give you his full support in such matters, right Rayes?"

"Absolutely so."

This brief meeting reinforced my authority with Dr. Rayes. For several months afterwards, I would have his full support regarding any such matters.

Our part time Medical Director was Dr. Mohsin Hussien, a Sudanese neurosurgeon. Dr. Mohsin had been at the hospital since the beginning of the original Al Salaam Hospital. He was well respected by his colleagues, both within and outside the hospital; he was known to be a very good neurosurgeon.

I quickly discovered that Dr. Mohsin, as a part-time Medical Director, was not overly willing to provide leadership and discipline in matters that involved the medical staff. I also quickly ascertained that his interest and skills were certainly more in the area of Neurosurgery than in medical administrative matters. As a result, I found myself having to become too much involved in matters ranging from physicians' leave requests to medical problem cases with the Ministry of Health (MOH).

Very shortly after the incident regarding the two physicians who had failed to attend the meeting, Dr. Mohsin and I had the following conversation:

"Dr. Mohsin, I am not satisfied with your involvement with medical administration matters. Do you have time and the interest to be the part-time Medical Director? I need more time and support from you in medical administrative related issues than you are presently providing."

"My first love is my surgery, Gordon. But, I believe that I have the respect and admiration of the majority of the medical staff. I think I am the best choice you have for medical director, even though it is only part-time."

Dr. Mohsin was right. "In the land of the blind the one-eyed man is supreme." He was the best physician on staff available to serve in this important medical staff leadership position.

"Dr. Mohsin, are you willing to discipline the physicians who need correction. Will you be able to fire a physician who is non- productive or who consistently does not follow established policies? Keep in mind that most of these doctors have worked with you and socialized with you over the past years. Will you really be able to be hard-nosed with the colleagues you may have had dinner with the night before?"

He was honest. "Gordon, you are correct. I probably will not be able to provide the type of discipline that is surely needed at this hospital and is what you expect. You probably need to recruit a new full time experienced medical director. I would be able to give background or guidance to such an individual and then would be able to focus primarily on my neurosurgery." We decided that it was important to recruit an experienced western Medical Director as soon possible.

The Finance Director was an Egyptian named Mr. Hani Abul Khair. He had been at the hospital since it had opened. I quickly discovered major deficiencies in his department, one being the lack of a reliable information system that could provide the required financial information. The financial reports were poor. The account receivables were understated. Account payables were out of control. I quickly could see that the financial department was not functioning properly. Much later, I came to know that he was a close relative of a major shareholder of the old Al-Salama Hospital and a close friend of Dr. Mehriz.

After my first three weeks, I decided to engage the consultative services of Arthur Anderson Company to conduct an evaluation of the finance department. The three weeks evaluation had produced basically what I had expected. There were few standard processes in place, and the data being presented was very suspect. Checks and balances were non-existent. Also, the evaluation pointed out the information management system's weaknesses. I had a hard time understanding why, after three years of software implementation by our sister company SDS (Software Data Systems), the implementation had not been completed. Now, I was beginning to understand why Dr. Mehriz had been so interested in my knowledge of information management systems during my interview with him. I was also beginning to question the company's ability to complete the implementation of the oracle-based software, called OASIS.

The Arthur Andersen evaluation very quickly identified recommendations for major and rapid changes within the finance department. Such recommendations included a complete overhaul of the processes in place along with the replacement of several employees, including Mr. Hani.

By the end of the first six weeks, I had completed all one-on-one meetings with the clinical and administrative heads. I had closely worked with Dr. Rayes and had started to develop a working relationship with him that would be as good as possible under the circumstances. I had tried to understand the status of the construction project, but this was one area that I had simply not been able to spend enough time on.

The hospital had some very good things going for it such as its reputation for medical care and the excellent facilities that would soon be available. But, it lacked basic processes and there was very little discipline among its staff. There was the lack of a service attitude, especially in the hotel aspects of care. It was obvious that a new mind set had to be established soon and this was truly a "turn around" situation. The replacement of many of the key personnel would have to occur with new qualified personnel appointed as quickly as possible in many areas. It was also obvious that there was a serious cash flow problem that should have been addressed long before now. When asked what I thought about Al Salama Hospital, my response was to compare it to a corner convenience store that had turned in to a Wal-Mart with the business still conducted as before.

I believe that all work is a process. And there were very few established processes in place at Al-Salama Hospital in the spring of 1998.

I mentioned to Mustafa that we needed to schedule an all staff meeting with dinner to follow. I was ready to present what I had discovered during this "kick off" phase and where we were going to go from here. Also, I wanted to invite the owners and the Board of Directors.

At that time, the only Board members that I could tell existed was Sheikh Sultan, who seemed to have very little interest in the hospital, and Dr. Hesham Mehriz.

"Mustafa, let's schedule the meeting at the Intercontinental Hotel since we currently lack the necessary auditorium space. I will talk with the hotel regarding the cost of the conference room and of the meals. They should give us a good deal based upon my living there for the past six weeks. I have gotten to know several of the staff there, including the General Manager."

The conveniences offered to me by the hotel had allowed me to focus exclusively on Al Salama Hospital. I had been quite happy in calling the

Intercontinental Hotel my home during the past six weeks. The General Manager and I would have coffee every couple of days and discuss the hospital and hotel generic problems. There are many similarities between the two businesses, especially in the service aspect.

All hospital employees were expected to work six days a week. Thursdays and Fridays are equivalent to Saturdays and Sundays back home. The entire time I was associated with the hospital I always worked six days per week and averaged about twelve hours per day. Fridays were very special for it was the one day of rest each week when I could put the hospital out of my mind.

Lufthansa Airline's flight crew used the Intercontinental Hotel for their weekly layovers. The crew would arrive on Thursday morning and would not leave until Sunday late evenings. I got acquainted with several of the Lufthansa pilots and co-pilots while living at the hotel and had an interesting experience at the Red Sea that involved them. The hotel had a beach resort that could be used *by* the hotel guests. Usually, I would take advantage of the beach at least every other Friday. This particular Friday morning, the entire flight crew and I decided to hit the beach and do some snorkeling.

I drove out to the beach early, and the others came by the hotel bus about an hour later. I noticed that the sea was rougher then usual, the wind having gotten up to about twenty-five knots. When the flight crew arrived, I suggested to Captain Monfred Vaeth that perhaps the crew should not snorkel this morning because of the waves. They insisted that they go ahead. I went with them so that at least I could direct them through the narrow channel (about three meters in width) that had been chiseled out of the reef to allow snorkelers to enter the deeper waters outside the reef. That morning the currents were rather stiff pushing the water out of the man-made channel in to the sea. There was no problem going out of the channel but quite difficult returning through it.

Suddenly, Captain Vaeth yelled to me, "Gordon, the strap on my flipper has broken and I can't make any headway against this current. Help me."

When I reached the captain, I could tell he was completely out of breath. He was a big man and not in very good shape for this type of strenuous exercise.

"Monfred, just relax. I am going to get behind you and push you over to the shore."

The hotel had constructed a water break with large rocks. The channel went through this rocky water break and connected the hotel beach with the sea just outside of the reef. I only had to push Monfred about ten meters perpendicular to the channel to reach the water break. It took me several minutes of hard swimming to make headway against the stiff current that was leading back out to Sea. Monfred was no help for he was totally exhausted. When I finally managed to get him to the rocks, he could barely move.

"O.K., Monfred, you must pull yourself out of the water up on to the rocks. You will be battered quickly if you don't."

The waves were breaking onto the rocks and a swimmer simply could not stay there long without being battered. With great effort, I managed to help push him from the waves on to higher ground out of danger. He had come out of this with only slight cuts on his knees and elbows.

Soon after, I again heard, "Gordon, I can't swim against this current, I need some help." One of the flight attendants was having the exact same difficulty that the captain had a few minutes earlier except she hadn't lost her flipper.

"Carla, hang on I'll help you." Fortunately, she was about one third of the captain's weight and I was easily able to negotiate her to safety.

After the episode was over, I became the hero of the moment for the Lufthansa flight crew. That evening they took me out to dinner and we all had a big time. They made me an honorary captain for my great bravery, as they put it.

In reality, it had not been that big a deal. I really did not think at the time that either Monfred or Carla was in any real danger. What really amazed both of them was that I went back in the sea to retrieve the captain's lost flipper, which was floating away. I am a good swimmer and at no time had I been that concerned about their safety, except when they were next to the rocks. I was afraid they would be injured, smashed against the rocks by the force of the waves.

For months after that incident Captain Vaeth called me whenever his crew was back in Jeddah. He always asked me out for dinner with them. Over the next several months, I really enjoyed getting to know the crew better and sharing fun times together.

One of the good things about working at Al Salama Hospital without my family being present was being able to maintain an excellent exercise routine. The first couple of months, with the exception of Fridays, the only thing to do was to work and to exercise. I have never been a big shopper. After a couple of trips to the souq, I had seen all of the gold shops and other unusual establishments there were to see. For those who like to shop and bargain with the shopkeepers, Jeddah has much to offer. The city also has excellent restaurants. Later, after I moved out of the hotel, I took advantage of these restaurants at least once a week.

By the time late May had arrived, I was ready to move out of the hotel into a more family-style environment. I had located a very nice two-story villa in a small western compound called Nueva Andalucia. This executive compound had only thirty-two villas, was beautifully landscaped, and was only about one kilometer away from Al Salama Hospital. The villas were fully furnished, including the silver ware, and had maid services. Other amenities included a small restaurant, a great work-out gym, beautiful swimming pool, modern computerized bowling alley, tennis courts, and all the luxuries one might like to have.

Rentals on all such compounds usually have to be paid at least six months in advance, and Nueva Andalucia was no exception. These were probably as nice as any of the westerner villas in Jeddah. My villa rented for about SR 18,750 per month, at the time, the equivalent of 5,000 US dollars. I remained at the Nueva Andalucia compound for just about two years before moving to another compound.

There were several American families living on the Nueva Andalucia compound. General Motors, Saudi Arabia Ltd. had two American families living there, and the American Consulate had four families there. I knew that Linda, Mark, and Emily would really like the place. At that time, I still had hopes that Linda and Emily would relocate to Jeddah. Emily would have gone to the Continental School, and Linda could have easily secured a teaching job as an elementary science teacher. Mark would have remained in Texas since he was entering his senior year at Baylor University. I knew one thing that would have a significant influence as to whether they stayed or not was where we lived. This location was superb and the villa could not have been better suited for us.

I quickly got to know the families in the compound. One of the rewards of living and working overseas is the chance to develop very good friendships with some people quickly. These friends become your support group and extended family. Every one knows that all are in the same boat, facing the same difficulties and problems associated with living in such a different culture. Within these extended families, life long friendships develop.

As Chief Executive Officer of Al Salama Hospital, I had to guard against becoming too friendly with my staff. Familiarity does, indeed, breed contempt. Thus, the CEO must keep some distance from the others. It is lonely at the top. Because of this and because at first, we had very few westerners at the hospital, my true friends, with one exception, were not Al Salama Hospital employees. Even later when I had recruited several American key staff, we did not socialize very often.

The bi-weekly Thursday night party at the "Brass Eagle" located with in the American Consulate was one of the functions I enjoyed and looked forward to. I was always able to receive an invitation (the Brass Eagle parties were by invitation only) because of my friends from the consulate who lived at my compound. About four times a year, the Consulate sponsored some really nice parties. The Fourth of July bash, the Snow Flake Ball, the Halloween party, were all great fun and well attended. The others were less spectacular but always fun and a good diversion from our day-to-day life in the Kingdom. Walking through the doors of the Brass Eagle was like stepping back into a party back home. The drinks were the real McCoy, the bands were always swinging, and the western girls were decked-out in their tights with their abayas (a black long over coat) left at the entrance.

Mustafa had scheduled the key staff presentation at the Intercontinental Hotel for the evening of May 25th. I knew that this meeting would be extremely important. I had taken the past two months to talk with as many of the key staff as I could in trying to evaluate the situation and develop an action plan. This presentation would serve as the catalyst in moving Al Salama forward. It was essential that my presentation be straight forward, clearly communicating my observations and the action plans that we would follow. I wished to capture their undivided attention and somehow build into their psyche a true sense of urgency.

The hotel had done a superb job of arranging the conference room for the presentation. I had learned that Sheikh Sultan again, unfortunately, would not be attending the meeting. Dr.Mehriz, Dr. Rayes, and I were positioned at the head table. All the staff was sitting in the chairs facing the head table.

I quickly realized that Dr. Rayes was very uncomfortable in such an environment. He sheepishly waited for either Dr. Mehriz or me to begin the presentation. I soon recognized that neither of them intended to do any type of greeting or introduction, so I took the initiative before this hesitation became too obvious. The following represents a taped recording of what I had to say that evening:

INTRODUCTION / IMPRESSIONS

"Good Evening, thank you for your presence. I trust this presentation will give you a clear picture of what my initial impressions are and how I see we should proceed. Unfortunately, Sheikh Sultan Bin Mahfouz, our Chairman, was unexpectedly called out of town and won't be able to join us this evening. He asked that I pass on to you his regards. (I would have to cover for Sheikh Sultan in this fashion many times in the future).

"The purpose of this meeting is to provide you feedback on my impressions during the past two months and to lay out specific major objectives for the hospital during the remainder of the fiscal year.

"During the month of April, I spent considerable time conducting individual meetings with staff at the hospital. The primary purposes of those meetings were (1) to become better acquainted; (2) to deliver insight regarding my management style; and (3) to gain an understanding of your specific goals, challenges, and obstacles.

"As a result of these meetings, certain themes floated to the surface both good and not so good. On the positive side, we are very fortunate that Sheikh Khalid Bin Mahfouz, our owner, desires for this facility to be one of the best hospitals in the Middle East. The facilities are some of the best in the world with the most advanced state of the art equipment. Patients and prospective patients cannot help but be impressed by these excellent facilities that have been put at our disposal.

"The hospital is one of the few if not the only private hospital of this caliber, where the owner is not directly responsible for the day-to-day operations, but has entrusted this to the management.

"Another very positive impression is that certain medical specialties have an excellent reputation in Jeddah and throughout Saudi Arabia. All of the staff I interviewed indicated a sincere desire to increase the positive aspects of the organization and have a clear understanding that such is important both individually and collectively.

"The latest ARAMCO Quality Management Survey has shown remarkable improvements over previous surveys. This is the result of a lot of hard work and really is a very positive development.

"I would be remiss, however, if I did not mention certain themes and observations that all of us need to recognize as shortcomings and areas where attention is required. It is each manager's responsibility to instill a sense of urgency and discipline by setting the example in seeing that our patients' (customers') needs and expectations are being met at the highest level. I sense that there is a certain degree of complacency in the organization that will have a tendency to lower the level of our services to our customer.

"It is my impression that our Saudization efforts may be lacking. We currently only have about 8% Saudis in the hospital workforce and at the beginning of this year our requirement issued by the government was 15%. By next year that requirement goes up to 20%. We must do a better job in bringing additional qualified Saudi nationals into the workforce and providing them with opportunities to learn and become a vital part of our staff. In the near future, the Human Resources Department will be working with all departments to develop a plan and specific goals regarding the Saudization effort at the hospital.

"Another area of concern is the lack of operational in-patient beds that has caused considerable difficulties in meeting the needs of our patients. It is critical that we open-up additional beds as soon as possible to take this pressure off. The relocation of our services into the new facility has many logistical problems. The fact that we are building a brand new hospital in the same location as the existing functional facility causes all types of difficulties and makes it imperative that the commissioning of the facility takes place as soon as possible.

"An area where I believe much additional focus must be placed is in the computer conversion to the OASIS system. The hospital will benefit greatly with the type of information that the new information system will provide. I sense that there may be a lack of urgency with some of the hospital staff in supporting the computer conversion that must take place as quickly as possible. There will always be some resistance to change. Department heads and Chiefs of services must function as a catalyst of change. The computer conversion in a timely fashion is critical to the hospital.

"I sense some lack of discipline as it relates to the financial aspects of the organization. We have been provided a beautiful and very expensive building that is not requiring funding from normal hospital operations. Thus, we are very fortunate not to have to worry about paying down bond interest and principle out-of hospital operations. Even with this advantage over most all other hospitals, we continue to have a serious cash flow problem that must be addressed. This will require direct action and fiscal constraint to fix the problem. We have very high fixed costs and must do what we can to control the variable costs.

"My interviews with the staff have revealed what I perceive as a frustration, some confusion, and some disorganization that is the result of a lack of communication between departments. This has occasionally created a lack of teamwork."

VALUES AND PHILOSOPHIES

"First, I believe that every thing we do must always have our customer's well-being and desires as a base. What I call the "hotel" aspects of hospital care is critical, and for better or worse, will be how our customers (patients) will judge us. If these specific hotel aspects of their encounters with us are not of the highest quality, they will eventually go to another hospital. Because we have a five-star facility, our customers will expect, demand, and deserve five-star services from the moment they enter the hospital grounds. If there is trash on the hospital grounds, this affects their impressions. If our telephone operators are not answering the phone in a professional, polite, and prompt manner, this will have a negative effect. How well the customers are initially received in the reception area will make a lasting impression. How clean the hospital is, how well the food was prepared, and how it was served is very important. How quickly the nurses responded to the nurses' call alarm and when they arrived, if they had a smile on their face and professionalism about them and an attitude that reflects compassion and caring. How well the physician communicates with his patient and informs the patient about post-hospital care is very critical. Patients expect to be informed and rightfully so.

"Our major employer groups such as ARAMCO, Saudia Airlines, and National Commercial Bank have a right to expect and demand top value for the money they are spending on their employees' healthcare. We must be in a position to show these major clients through objective measurements that we are delivering value to them for the money they pay. The old saying that we offer the highest quality of care, without our being able to substantiate that based upon specific measurable objectives with established bench marks will not convince these clients that they are, in fact, receiving the highest value possible.

"Clinics must start on time and hours must be extended where the patient demand is sufficient to justify this. We must take the initiative in these types of matters and not be in a reaction mode. All personnel must be prompt at the clinics so the patients will be seen without undue delay. No one likes to wait, especially if he has a predetermined appointment time. This is a reasonable expectation that must be provided. We must do our best to educate our customers that to better serve them the appointment system for non-emergencies is in their best interest.

"Having a transportation system that consistently is on schedule will help the productivity and morale of our employees. All of the above actions will help us deliver the type of services that are expected.

"A couple of work related idiosyncrasies that I have are that I believe in being on time for meetings, assignments, reports, etc. and that I really don't like surprises. Promptness demonstrates good discipline, and having few surprises demonstrates that proper planning is taking place. These two items are not unreasonable and will go a long way in giving us a competitive edge. An initiative that has already been started to help improve communications is that each morning at 8:15 the senior management, night duty manager and I are meeting briefly to discuss what has occurred during the past 24 hours that needs attention. I call these daily morning meetings our early bird briefings. We will also be having routine department meetings with those departments that I'm working directly with. I will be encouraging more organized meetings to help improve communications. The CEO direct reports will be meeting as a group on the first Wednesday of each month at 10:00 a.m."

TEAM WORK

"There is no other organization that is as complicated, with as many different parts, as a hospital. No one area or department can be an island by itself. Any action or in action by one area is going to have a ripple effect either directly or indirectly throughout the organization. Thus, teamwork, coordination, cooperation and some compromise with our colleagues is essential in providing the customer with the highest possible service with optimum value—value being defined as the point where quality and cost intersect. Teamwork comes from the building of covenant professional relationships that are based upon trust, respect and compassion. This is not possible if we are not communicating with each other. We must communicate, communicate, communicate, especially important with the commissioning of the new facility and the computer conversion going on simultaneously. This is how teamwork is built."

PROCESS

"All work is a process. Generally I have discovered over the years that problems typically arise within and between certain areas of an organization because of a lack of process or because a process is in place that needs overhauling. Virtually all employees desire to do a good job and feel good about contributing positively to a cause greater than they themselves. It seems that problems are usually caused because of roadblocks that result from faulty processes not poor employees. Thus, I am challenging each department throughout the organization to review their work processes and to refine them where necessary working together as a team. Only in this way will we be able to deliver a high value service product to our customers. We will be developing a quality incentive program where employees who can demonstrate genuine concrete cost savings through implementation of new processes or refinements of existing processes will be financially rewarded. We will also attempt to quantify the cost involved with non-conformance to established processes."

KEY OBJECTIVES

"I believe that it is essential that we focus our energies on four certain key objectives for the remainder of the year:

1) We will strive to provide the highest service we possibly can in meeting the needs and expectations of our patients and our customers and provide top value to our major clients.

2) We will complete the computer conversion to the OASIS system throughout the hospital by year end.

3) We will move into the new facility as quickly as various departments and areas are turned over to us by the contractor, realizing that certain services might not be at optimum levels initially. This, of course, is with the understanding that we will not put our patients in harms way by a premature relocation.

4) We will improve the financial condition of the hospital by providing needed financial information and financial controls. I would like to take a moment to discuss this objective since I have already previously elaborated on the other three. We must improve the cash flow of our hospital. A basis axiom of Economics 101 is that when one's outcome exceeds his income, his upkeep is his downfall. This is true for individuals, families, business and governments. Our owner is not looking at this hospital to generate large profits. He desires that the hospital not continue over the long run to require cash infusions, not an unreasonable expectation. He understands that we have very high fixed costs and that it will take some time to achieve profitability. We must be diligent in improving the hospital's financial status and there are only five ways to do so."

INCREASE PRICES

"There is a limit to this, for the market place will decide what the market will tolerate. We must have a good pricing strategy in place and not find ourselves behind the curve any more than we would necessarily want to be ahead of the curve. Two examples of good pricing strategy would be (1) not setting the ER visit fees lower than the Out-patient consulting visit fees to help avoid inappropriate use of our ER services. (2) Establishing a price base such that if at some point in the future some type of government pricing ceiling limits are imposed, we can avoid being "locked in" at low rates."

REDUCE DISCOUNTS

"We have too many employees authorized to give discounts. We will very soon be authorizing only a very small number to have this responsibility. I do not believe that it is appropriate for our physicians to be giving discounts to their patients for a number of reasons. I realize this is common practice today. We must be more aggressive with the insurance companies and employers groups regarding the discounts they are demanded. The level of negotiated discounts with these types of customers should depend upon the volume of business they bring to us, their timely payments, and the lack of administrative hassles they create."

INCREASE UTILIZATION

"This is one reason why the opening of additional beds and new services such as the cardiac cath lab and nuclear medicine department are so critical. A significant percentage of our business remains cash and fee for service medicine. In this type of environment, utilization of services is what creates additional revenue. I do believe that in the not-too-distant future more and more of our major business will be on a pre-payment basis, such as ARAMCO, or negotiated per–diem or per-case payments. Such a major shift will require a complete re-focusing on utilization, but is probably a good thing for the patient population as a whole."

REDUCE VARIABLE COST

"I firmly believe this is the one area that we have the most control over. My evaluation of our ratio of employees to occupied beds is high when compared to other international hospitals that I am familiar with. We must do a better job in controlling our manpower, which means we really need to evaluate our staffing ratios. You may not be aware that our manpower total cost increased 13% in fiscal year 1997 compared to 1996. You may not be aware that for every riyal we spend on direct salary cost, we spend another riyal on employee benefits such as housing, visas, etc. You may not be aware that in 1997, overtime was approximately 7% of our entire salary cost even though it appears that our staffing ratios per occupied bed are high. One reason you probably are not aware of these issues is because you have not received needed departmental budgets verses actual cost information. This is another problem and another reason why we are converting to the new OASIS computer system as quickly as possible. Our cost of supplies in 1997 increased 17% over 1996. This is an important area where certain standardization of supplies will not only increase quality-of-care but reduce cost as well. We must become more proficient in the use of all supplies throughout the hospital. This beautiful magnificent facility is a two-edged sword. The fixed costs are very high and basically out of our control. This makes it that much more important to have tight control on the variable costs."

REDUCE ACCOUNT RECEIVABLES

"This is another area we can have a major impact upon. It does no good to increase revenue if we cannot collect that revenue. At the end of 1997 we had a 47% increase in accounts receivable owed to us by both companies and individuals when compared to 1996. Much of this is more than 180 days old. There are a lot of reasons behind these outstanding receivables that we have limited control over. We must, however, do a much better job in getting the invoices out to our customers in a timely fashion after patient discharge. The current delay in billing for services rendered is unacceptable."

ORGANIZATIONAL RESTRUCTURING

"During the past month a lot of effort has gone into reviewing the various functions of the hospital and trying to decide where best they fit. In developing an organizational structure, one does not look at the incumbent at all, rather where it makes best sense for the function to be located.

"After making a determination where the function should be located, we then looked at the various human resources that were available to head each of these functions. Effective immediately the new organizational structure will go into effect. Certain changes are already occurring. We will be creating a centralized Material Management department with a qualified Director of Material Management employed. We have merged the Human Resources Department and Personnel Department into one and we are currently recruiting for a Director of Human Resources and Personnel. Dr. Khalid is serving as the Acting Director of Human Resources and Personnel until such time that a final decision is made here. Dr. Mohsin Hussein desires to continue to contribute his majority of time to Neurosurgery, but also has agreed to continue to provide administrative support. We have created the position of Associate Medical Director so this can be accomplished. We are in the beginning process of recruiting a Medical Director who will be working exclusively in the area of Medical Staff Administration. We desire to recruit an individual who has excellent clinical credentials, but who has also a significant amount of medical administrative experience working in a hospital or health care delivery system. This individual will not have clinical responsibilities so he/she can focus exclusively on the administration affairs of the medical staff, with support from the Associate Medical Director.

"We have created the position of Director of Support Services and Special Projects so that significant more focus can be directed towards the critically important support services. Our Director of Nursing Service is in the process of recruiting additional western nursing supervisors who will be able to provide the necessary oversight to our nursing division. There are several other refinements that are planned in nursing, including a full time nursing educator and infection control coordinator.

"I have placed the quality management function directly under the CEO in an attempt to provide a hospital-wide quality management initiative, and to demonstrate the commitment that senior management has regarding this program. Several of the individual departments will be reporting directly to the CEO in those specific areas that touch directly upon the four major objectives previously discussed.

"There will be other changes that I can assure you. An organization is a living organism and it will be necessary to refine the organizational functions and reporting requirements as time goes on. It will not be static; changes and refinements will be made as necessary.

"It is very important that reporting takes place within the structure of the organization. Department heads, directors and chiefs of services must set the example for their specific areas. When problems occur, which they will, staff should work directly with their supervisors and keep their supervisors informed. Going around the managers rather than through the managers will create organizational breakdown and must be discouraged.

"I believe each of us in supervisory roles, including myself, has a responsibility to serve those that report to him or her. In serving, it is our job to provide the necessary resources, to resolve conflicts, and to develop the necessary team work that will allow those we serve to perform their work in the most effective and efficient manner possibly."

At this point in the presentation, I discussed twenty-seven specific action plans that needed to be accomplished to be able to achieve fully the four major objectives that had been introduced. I completed the presentation with the following closing remarks:

"Undoubtedly, as these action items are initiated, some of your employees or even colleagues may approach you complaining about the aggressiveness and insensitivity of the CEO and the changes that will be taking place. Your continued support, including making sure that such staff are referred directly back to senior management is absolutely essential to accomplish what we all desire to be accomplished. It will not be easy. It will take a major change initiative. Some current staff will have to be discharged. I truly believe that certain "tough minded" business decisions need to be made in the short term and such actions will have a positive outcome. Some of the complacency that I have noticed will be replaced by an urgency to provide an upgrade in our service and productivity levels. This I am sure of. Again, thank you for your time this evening."

Later that evening after a delicious dinner was served and the staff had left for the evening, I returned to my hotel room. The presentation had started at 8 p.m. and was completed an hour later, as planned. The dinner lasted until 11:30 p.m. As I lay in my bed thinking about the past couple of hours, I felt good about the presentation. I felt it was properly received by those who were present and that it had accomplished its purpose. I wished that Sheikh Sultan had attended. It seemed that he simply had no interest in the hospital, a critical missing ingredient for a hospital Board Chairman.

The kick off was now complete. It was now time to put on our helmets, fashion our chin straps, and get down to the business at hand.

Chapter Four

Taj Mahal

"Vanity, vanity, all is vanity."
King Solomon

During the next six weeks, I was determined to become more involved in the construction side of the new hospital. The general contractor was Saudi ABV, a subsidiary of a holding company named Saudi ABV Rock. The hospital project was a turnkey project with the general contractor responsible for all phases of the construction. This included constructing the building according to the specifications, selecting the equipment and furnishings, purchasing and placing all equipment into operation, and finally handing over the entire project to the Al-Salama Hospital's owner.

Saudi ABV Rock is a company partially owned by Prince Sultan Bin Abdul Aziz, Minister of Aviation and Defense. This company had been established to complete a multi-billion dollar project associated with oil storage facilities, similar to the underground oil storage facilities the US government has in California. The Saudi government stipulated, for security purposes, that Saudi ABV Rock could only be involved in this one project. The company got around this stipulation by creating subsidiary construction companies such as Saudi ABV. I have heard that Sheikh Khalid Bin Mahfouz was one of the owners of Saudi ABV Rock; however, that rumor is not substantiated.

The primary challenge of building the new facility was that its construction was precisely where the existing hospital was located and functioning. The owner, Sheikh Khalid Bin Mahfouz, insisted that the new hospital be built while simultaneously the old hospital continued to function with all services operational, all in the same location. It would have been so much easier to have built the building in another location or even adjacent to the existing building and then simply move into the new facility when it was finished.

Ulf Norehn was the on-site project manager for Saudi ABV. He was a Swedish chap as were most of the other key construction site personnel. Sheikh Mohammad Hussein Al Amoudi, a wealthy Saudi businessman, owned the Saudi ABV subsidiary. At one time, he worked for Sheikh Khalid at the National Commercial Bank; the two were very good friends and were in business together in other projects. I have heard that Sheikh Khalid was the individual behind the rapid rise of Sheikh Al Amoudi at the bank.

As I think back about all the problems that developed between the general contractor and the Al-Salama Hospital ownership, I remember what my first boss said to me about friends in business. This individual was a respected orthopedic surgeon who had brought into his clinic partnership one of his schoolmates. After about a year, the partnership ran into serious problems because of difference between the two of them.

"Gordon," Dr. Cotton pointed out, "always remember that friends in business together is one step below prostitution, and families in business together is one step below that."

Well, I am not totally convinced that Dr. Cotton was correct, but there have been many friendships destroyed and great divisions created among families because of business misunderstandings or differences.

The Saudi culture is such that the families play critical and important roles. Certain family names dominate in this society. Many of the businesses, even very large businesses like National Commercial Bank, are family owned. Some of these families like the Bin Ladins and Bin Mahfouzs are families who have immigrated from Yemen and other Gulf countries. Financial dominance by some families, especially those who have immigrated from outside the Kingdom, has become a source of concern to the Royal Family of Saudi Arabia.

I set up a meeting with project construction manager Norehn, to try to bring myself up to speed regarding the project. He was very happy to see that I was interested in trying to help him solve some of his problems. He spent considerable time telling me about the history of the project and about why the delays had occurred. He also didn't hesitate to directly inform me what was necessary to complete the "Monster."

I was very much interested in having a clear understanding of the problems surrounding the project. I did not realize that many of the delays were associated with political problems between the families, all of this happening since A.R. had gradually taken over from his father Sheikh Khalid Bin Mahfouz.

"Gordon," Ulf began, "do you realize that we do not even have a contract between Saudi ABV and the hospital owner Sheikh Khalid Bin Mahfouz? This whole project has been based upon verbal understandings and hand shakes between Sheikh Mohammad Al Amoudi and Sheikh Khalid probably over tea and a hubbly-bubbly (an exotic Arabic smoking apparatus; in Arabic, *hashish*). What started out as a reasonable new hospital expansion of about 50 additional beds costing perhaps 150 million riyals (approximately 40 million dollars) has mushroomed into this lavish, resource-demanding, 400-bed Taj Mahal, approaching 1.5 billion riyals (approximately 400 million dollars). Now that Sheikh Khalid has taken a back seat regarding this project, his son A.R. has assumed more and more responsibilities of not only this hospital project but of other key businesses as well. Unfortunately, Sheikh Mohammad Al Amoudi does not have the same close relationship with Sheikh Khalid's son A.R. There have been many disagreements between them regarding this project.

"There was a time, not so long ago, that Sheikh Khalid was taking an aggressive role in this project. He sanctioned the appointment of a physician's medical equipment committee to advise Saudi ABV what equipment to purchase. These physicians were told to go for the top quality brand names, that money was no issue."

I had heard from several physicians that Al-Salama Hospital was just a "drop in the ocean" for Sheikh Khalid, a mere "bleep on the radar screen." Of course, this was not true. Four hundred million US dollars is no drop in the bucket for even the wealthiest families.

"Gordon, I remember the day when Sheikh Khalid toured the hospital and instructed us to replace all the marble flooring because he noticed that it was not of good quality. This marble had been imported from Italy. Not only was the cost extremely high, but also the work involved in replacing all the marble floors was tremendous and certainly time consuming.

"Some of the physicians demanded that we make changes in the design after construction was already complete. Can you believe we were required to take out and then replace a major supporting wall and several doors in the new emergency room four different times? Every time a new physician joined the hospital, he would have a go at the design drawings; change orders were made by the hundreds.

"Let me tell you an interesting incidence. I remember once we had been requested to make several changes in one of the patient's rooms. We had decided that until we finished the changes, we would lock the room. One day Sheikh Khalid toured the facility and wanted access to that room so he could examine the changes. When we told him that we were not finished with the changes yet and preferred not to show him the room at that time, he became extremely angry. He picked up a chair from the corridor and threw it against the expensive door of that room to break it down. Of course, all that was accomplished was the destruction of the chair and marring of the door. Sheikh Khalid was known to be a determined and at times a very stong willed individual.

"One last example why this project has continued so long and why the cost has exploded is the construction of the new facility in the same space occupied by the existing facility without any discontinuations of services. Think about that. It is almost an engineering impossibility. The laws of physics state that two masses cannot occupy the same space simultaneously."

Ulf led me over to a window and pointed to a large two-story cylinder block building adjacent to the north side of the partially completed hospital. "That temporary building now contains the radiology and laboratory departments and a couple of other clinical services, including a couple of operating room. We have moved those services from their old locations to that building thus vacating the space in the old hospital. We are now able to go into that vacated space and rebuild according to the new design plan. The construction of that temporary building cost more than 40 million riyals. Once we are completed with the new space, these services will be relocated back, and that building will be demolished. As a matter of fact, precisely where that temporary building is located is where the main entrance to the new hospital will be.

"Gordon, these are just a couple of good examples of why we have had delays and cost over-runs. I could give you a hundred more."

This information from Ulf was not totally surprising to me. I had heard similar statements from others as to the way this major construction project was progressing. Along with these complaints, I had firsthand knowledge that several physician members of the medical capital equipment committee were taking advantage of free trip vacations and other incentives from several of the major equipment and pharmaceutical companies. There was absolutely no acknowledgement of the concept regarding conflict of interest. When I approached several of the committee physicians, they became outright angry that I was interfering in their right to accept anything offered to them by these companies. I'm not talking about a hundred-dollar pen set. Most of the incentives were elaborate trips via first class air tickets to great vacation locations with lodging at the best hotels for several days. Even luxury ocean liner trips were not unheard of. Although I have no solid proof, I strongly suspect that there were kickbacks that could have totaled several million riyals over the time this equipment purchasing was taking place to individuals serving on this important capital equipment committee and to certain other employees.

The problem of kickbacks (*baksheesh* in Arabic) is rampant and, unfortunately, as common as negotiating with the local vendors at the souqs. It is simply a way of doing business in this society. Any active business here should budget at least 10% towards administrative fees to cover baksheesh requirements. This is simply part of doing business in The Kingdom and Middle East in general.

I was able to partially control the suppliers' incentive trips by requiring all such invitations to be forwarded and approved by the administration first. This may have slowed the practice somewhat, but it certainly did not stop it.

The cost of the turnkey 400-bed hospital construction project, including medical and non- medical equipment, was projected to be approximately 1.5 billion riyals. A typical rule of the thumb used in Saudi Arabia was that cost per in-patient bed ran between one to 1.2 million riyals. This facility was costing approximately 3.5 million riyals per in-patient bed, more than three times average. Many of the necessary maintenance parts were simply not available in the Kingdom. One example was the new energy-saving fluorescence light bulbs used throughout the hospital. They all had to be imported from Sweden. The cost of these bulbs was 40 riyals per piece (more than $10). The material used throughout the building was highest quality. The Royal suites and Junior Royal suites on the fifth floor of the VIP bed tower had solid gold plated bathroom accessories and fixtures. In addition to these expenditures, I'm sure that Saudi ABV was making a substantial profit on this project.

Ulf was adamant. "Gordon, we must get some type of signed contract between our company and your owner. The cost of this project keeps on going up and up with all the changes being requested. I am sure that there is a limit to what your owner is willing to spend. We also need you to take possession of completed departments and other completed areas just as soon as Saudi ABV turns them over to you."

This was one of our hospital's major goals. We needed to take possession of the new space as soon as released by Saudi ABV. When I reported for duty in April, the sections of the hospital that were completed and being used were all the out-patient clinics; one bed tower that we referred to as the OPD Tower, for it was located above the out-patient department clinics; radiology services; and most of the support services such as kitchen, laundry, and mechanical areas. The emergency room, VIP bed tower, operating rooms, delivery rooms, ICU department, laboratory services, health club, main entrance, and lobby area were all still in some stage of planning or construction. Some of these were well on the way, but on others the construction had not even begun.

Human nature is such that change is more often than not seen as a threat to be avoided if possible. I experienced difficulty in persuading departments to relocate to their new areas even though these areas were larger and superior. Department heads tended to drag their feet, making every excuse why it was not safe for patient care to relocate. Eventually, I had to issue a memorandum to most of the departments, simply instructing them to relocate regardless of whether or not they deemed an area ready. Of course, this assumed that the patient's safety would not be jeopardized. Most of the snags were mere inconveniences and could be easily worked around. There was not a single relocation that, within a week after a department moved, was not regarded as the best thing that could have happened to that department. We assured the staff after they were in these new locations for about two weeks, they could produce a final punch list that the contractors would correct all at once. Thus, we finally convinced everyone that the relocation was good for all concerned.

Ulf again spoke up. "Gordon, one final thing has to be done immediately. You have to convince your owner to release additional funds to us. No additional money has been released since your arrival. There is a schedule of payments, and your side is not keeping to that schedule. If funds are not received soon, we will have to begin stopping the payment to the sub contractors and the project will come to a grinding halt."

"Is there some reason that payments have been stopped?" I asked.

"Recall that there is no formal contract, so in reality there is no written payment schedule. In the past when we required additional funds, we asked for them and they were received. I believe that since A.R. has taken over, he does not desire to pay what is required. He doesn't seem to understand that the many requested changes cost a lot of money."

"Ulf, I will get on this today and find out what is going on. Also, in the future please do not make any design changes or modifications without first bringing them to my attention. This will allow me to research why the change is required and who is requesting it."

The entire process or lack thereof, was totally baffling to me. But, after a couple of visits to the private office to discuss the situation with A.R. and Dr. Rayes, I began to understand why the delays in payments were occurring. Because all prior agreements regarding the project were basically done on a handshake with no formal signed contract between the hospital and Saudi ABV owners, the only means that A.R. had available to him was this drastic action.

Within a week, we had established a committee that I chaired to study the changes being requested; almost simultaneously the number of approved change orders dropped dramatically. Additional funds were released and the project continued.

Syed Mustafa, the hospital administrator, had by now been placed in charge of support services. While he was no longer involved in the construction project, he did have a fair understanding of the history of the project.

"Gordon," he cautioned, "let me tell you something. Don't be convinced that this payment episode has seemingly been resolved. It has occurred in the past, and I am sure it will occur again before this hospital is completed. The work has stopped and restarted at least three times in the past and is one reason why the project has taken so long. Frankly speaking, Saudi ABV is screwing our owner. They are charging exorbitant prices for the equipment being purchased and any design changes that have been requested. Sure, much of the problem has been the way the doctors have been given an unrestrained equipment budget with no system in place on our side to review change orders. Just look at what Saudi ABV charged to replace the marble floors."

This replacement of the marble floors that occurred before my arrival, I had already looked into. Before the marble was put in place, it should have been pre-soaked in a special solution that would seal it and make it stain-proof. Thus, when fluids such as coffee spilled on the floor, they could easily be cleaned rather than soaking into the marble. Saudi ABV had not done this. When Sheikh Khalid saw that the expensive marble floors had stains that could not be removed, he rightfully became furious and demanded their replacement. I am sure that we ended up paying for this one way or another.

"Syed, why have the doctors been mistakenly allowed to assume that there are no funding constraints or accountability? Why have there not previously been processes in place to review change orders before they are done? Wasn't that a specific area that you were at least partially responsible for?"

And so it went. I fully understood the magnitude of the changes that had to take place. Mindsets had to be rapidly changed. New personnel needed to be commissioned fast. Processes had to be put into place quickly and then refined later. When the ship is sinking, you really don't need to worry about a leaking faucet. When a fire is out of control, you don't need to be thinking about tomorrow's objectives.

I remembered something that I had read regarding Lou Gessner, who had assumed the CEO role of IBM when that company was going through its most difficult times. IBM recruited Gessner after the RJR/ Nabisco merger that was so brilliantly described in the book *Barbarians at the Gate.*

Shortly after he took over the reins at IBM, Gessner was at his first, or perhaps second, board meeting when one of the members asked him about his vision for IBM. He said something like this: "Hell, we don't need a vision; we need action today to change the direction of this company. Our competitors are eating our lunch. We don't have the luxury of time to think about vision at this moment."

Certainly Al-Salama Hospital was no IBM. But exactly the same imperative applied to the situation concerning this 1.5 billion-riyal Taj Mahal. Drastic action was required immediately. Refinement and vision would have to come later.

I did my best to plug the gaping holes that were obvious and it did help considerably. Unfortunately, there were too many conflicts of interest present amongst our physicians, and this thinking regarding unrestrained spending had been in place too long. The political issues between Sheikh Al Amoudi and the Bin Mahfouz sons were way beyond my control. Much had been lost that would not be able to be reclaimed. Even though many of the changes that took place were better than nothing, in reality, to play on an old saying, most were "a day late and many riyals short."

The project was unofficially completed in June 2000. But even then the Bin Mahfouz family continued to reject the claim by Saudi ABV that the project should be officially handed over and declared complete. There was still a legitimate claim by the owner that the cost charged for this project, even with its many changes and luxuries, was exorbitant. A critical mistake made by the owner was that all monies were paid in advance of the work as it progressed. Virtually no funds were placed into a withhold-pending-construction acceptance.

Despite all of the problems associated with the project, the final product was a lavish, ultra-modern 400-bed hospital. The unique architectural design, as well as the excellent quality of materials used in construction, makes this a remarkable building in Jeddah. The hospital is located in a prestigious location within the city and is highly visible from a distance.

The hospital has two distinct bed towers. The east bed tower has luxurious private and semi-private rooms on the 1st through the 5th floors. The ground floor houses virtually all outpatient clinics, and thus is known as the OPD tower. Each day an average of 1200 outpatients visit these various clinics. Al-Salama was the only hospital in Jeddah where outpatient services were grouped into specialty centers such as ob/gyn, cardiac, orthopedic, neurosurgery, internal medicine, etc.

The west bed tower is known as the VIP tower. There is very easy access to the entrance of a luxurious lobby where valet parking is available. The VIP parking lot is well landscaped with all types of plants, palms, and lavish grass. The different colored flowerbeds along the sidewalks make this area very pleasing to the eyes; gardenias fill the air with their fragrance.

The ground floor of this tower houses the executive suites and VIP clinics. Also, an ultra-modern female health club with all amenities is located on the ground floor. Floors one to four are designated for VIP suites. Each of these floors contains only nine suites. Each patient suite has an extra large room for families and friends, a kitchenette, and extra bathroom facilities. The Royal suites and Al-Salama suites (Junior Royal suites) are located on the fifth floor. All the suites on that floor have gold accessories and fixtures throughout, but especially in the bathrooms. The five Royal suites are each about 6,000 square feet.

The auditorium lies between the fourth and the fifth levels of the VIP tower. It accommodates 160 seats and is equipped with the latest audiovisual technology. This is one of the truly outstanding features of the hospital and resulted in our hosting several international seminars and conferences in this splendid auditorium.

In between and surrounded by the two bed towers is a three story renovated structure that was previously the old Al-Salama Hospital. This section of the hospital is home for many of the key ancillary services such as radiology, the ICU's, and operating rooms. There are seven state-of- the-art OR's with one of these having a special viewing dome for training purposes.

The radiology department also has state-of-the-art equipment including two M.R.I. units, (1.5 Tesla symphony and one open unit). There are two angioplasty suites, one for rotational arteriography. There is also a spiral sub-second scanner and bone densitometry, dual head gamma camera, and a full range of ultrasound machines with color Doppler. The PAC system for picture archiving and retrieval was the only one present within the Kingdom at the time.

There are no floors beyond the third level in the middle section. Thus, the hospital has the east and west patient bed towers and the north and south balcony corridors that connect both towers surrounding the lower middle section. From ground level, the facility appears completely symmetrical.

All nursing floors in both bed towers are designed in a U-shape. This outstanding feature allows for a near panoramic view from the patients' rooms. The Red Sea is clearly visible from the upper floors of the VIP bed tower. Those patients who are in the rooms facing south see the city center of Jeddah, while patients in the rooms facing north view upscale residential areas and the airport in the distance.

There are 28 designated elevators throughout the hospital that allow for easy flow of patients, visitors, staff, and materials. Ongoing maintenance of the elevators alone is quite an undertaking and very expensive.

The utility building is located immediately north of the main hospital entrance and lobby. A 150-foot glass bridge connects the utility building with the hospital's first floor and crosses over a city boulevard just in front of the main north hospital entrance.

The ground floor of the utility building accommodates most of the hospital support services. The hospital's kitchen is the largest kitchen in the region containing about 25,000 square feet. It is fitted with the most modern equipment available made by the world famous Electrolux company. The American Aladdin Tray system is used to serve in-patients meals. These trays keep food hot for up to 45 minutes, thus assuring that the meals reach the patient at the correct temperature. Because of the huge capacity of the kitchen, besides providing meals for patients and staff, the hospital can cater an additional 600 meals per day for outside functions. At the time, the Jeddah Sheraton Hotel had a contract with the hospital to manage its food service activities.

The cornerstone of the hospital's information management system is run by two state-of-the-art IBM RS-6000 main frames that run the Oracle-based software package. The two main frames run parallel to each other, thus assuring virtually no downtime. Each computer has the capacity to run several hospitals simultaneously. These are the same computers that IBM called "Deep Blue" when that company challenged a world famous chess player a few years ago (After three days of engagement, "Deep Blue" did checkmate its human opponent).

The floor space of the new hospital, including the utility building, has about 90,000 square meters (approximately 850,000 square feet) whereas the previous Al-Salama Hospital had about 20,000 square meters.

When Syed Mustafa mentioned to me that the utility cost had exploded over the past couple of years and that the overall employee number had more than doubled, I could easily understand why. The hospital had increased in size almost five-fold.

I asked Syed what we were doing to control those costs that are controllable and to find new sources of revenue to offset the increased expenses. He really didn't have too many answers to these questions.

In my heart, I knew many of these enormous cost increases, such as utilities, were, for the most part, not within our power to control. With the space of the new facility being almost five times that of the previous Al-Salama Hospital, there would be tremendous fixed cost increases.

I couldn't help but think about equipment maintenance costs that would begin to hit in about a year, once the warranty periods expired. On the elevators alone, Mitsubishi was asking for a yearly maintenance contract of two million riyals. The huge cooling systems and UPS power systems, not to mention sophisticated medical equipment in departments like radiology and laboratory services, would all require maintenance contracts within a year and half.

As Syed and I were casually walking back to our offices after one of the routine facility inspections, I remarked, "Syed, it is good thing that Sheikh Khalid Bin Mahfouz owns this hospital. It is clear to me why previous routine operational cash injections by the owner have been required. Let's hope that his benevolence doesn't change regarding this momentous hospital he is providing Jeddah. Pray that National Commercial Bank continues to prosper. It's evident that this hospital will take some time to reach profitability."

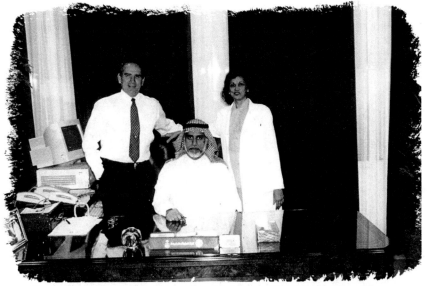

YR-2000/Myself / Dr. Rayes Bin Mahfouz / Dr. Pritina Kaushik

V.I.P. Entrance

"Taj Mahal"

Out Patient Clinics

Al-Salama Patient Suite

Chapter Five

Uphill Climb

"The achievement of your goal is assured the moment you commit yourself to it"

Mack R. Douglas
(June–November, 1998)

Now that the presentation was completed, all key staff knew that I had challenged each one of them to step up the pace and rise to a higher level. The goals and the timetables were clearly laid down. The challenge was now to execute the plan. It would definitely be an up-hill climb.

The phone rang. "Hello, Mr. Gordon. This is Dr. Pritima Kaushik. It was a very good and meaningful presentation. Most of the people got the message." I thanked her and we exchanged cordialities. She inquired when my family was to join me.

"They are supposed to come in a couple of weeks, at least by the end of June. As a matter of fact Mark, my son, will be arriving next week and Linda and Emily will come two weeks later."

Dr. Kaushik mentioned that she was looking forward to meeting Mark and the rest of the family and inquired if Mark liked Indian food. I mentioned that I couldn't speak for Mark, but as for me, what time is dinner. She was glad to hear my enthusiasm and invited both of us for dinner just as soon as he arrived.

"Mr. Gordon, the primary reason I called is to share something with you. We need many changes to make our hospital of highest quality, and this is one of the reasons the owner has appointed a real CEO. Sheikh Khalid has big plans for the new hospital. Any new CEO of a hospital needs the trust and cooperation of the physicians. I think you need to know this regarding Syed Mustafa. The physicians believe that Mr. Mustafa takes you in. He is not respected or liked by most of the physicians; they perceive that you are aligning closely with him, something that will not help you to achieve your goals with the doctors for this hospital. He is not an asset but a liability to you. I have nothing to gain by sharing this with you other than I would like our CEO to succeed for the good of our hospital. Our owner is exceptionally good with the employees, especially with the doctors, and this hospital has a special place in his heart. We really want this hospital to be the best in the Middle East. Take a good look at what Syed Mustafa has achieved in the last two years. You may wish to talk with other physicians regarding this matter to know more. One more important thing, he has managed to be supported and backed by Dr. Rayes, and most doctors are not happy with that situation."

"Dr. Kaushik, I am looking forward to that Indian dinner when Mark arrives. Thank you for sharing information regarding Syed. I will talk with some others."

I reflected upon what Dr. Kaushik had said. Syed Mustafa had been very attentive to me since my arrival. But I was not impressed with what had been accomplished in the areas under his control and authority.

Upon visiting with several of the key physicians, I quickly realized that Dr. Kaushik's assessment of' Syed's relationship with the doctors was correct. I also had a chance to visit with the nursing director regarding her perception of Syed's leadership skills.

The nursing director was a South African named Yvonne Bester. She was unusually tall and was an attractive individual. Ms Bester had previously been the nursing educator at Al-Salama hospital and had only assumed the director position just prior to my arrival. I was very much concerned about nursing man-hours and overtime, areas that required immediate attention. Those problems, however, were not the reason I was talking to Ms. Bester this particular day.

"Mr. Utgard, you have asked me to comment regarding how I perceive Mr. Mustafa's leadership abilities. In my view, he tries hard but sometimes he is his own worst enemy. Have you heard about the Irish nurses recruiting fiasco?"

I knew that our U.K. recruiting agency was upset with Al-Salama for going around them when they were supposed to have an exclusive nurses recruiting agreement with us in the UK. But I had really not had an opportunity to research their complaint.

Ms. Bester continued, "Mr. Mustafa took it upon himself to fly to Ireland and negotiate directly with another agency. We warned him that we should continue with the arrangement already in place. The personnel office also suggested that he back off the recruitment initiative since this was not his area of responsibility. I'm not sure why he so activity pursued the nurse recruiting initiative. Perhaps, Dr. Rayes had specifically asked him to get involved, I just do not know. I was serving as Nursing Education Director and knew that the Director of Nursing at that time and Syed were very good friends. Perhaps she had asked him to get involved. I just don't know.

"Gordon, the bottom line was that Mr. Mustafa recruited about twenty Irish nurses. Then, within two months after their arrival, all with the exception of one were asked to leave the country. Obviously, they had not been well screened. Several were deported for carousing too much in the open. Plus, they were just poor quality nurses. The word got around that instead of recruiting nurses, Mr. Mustafa had recruited prostitutes. Thus, what first seemed to be an aggressive approach by the administration to solve our nursing shortage, backfired into a full-blown fiasco."

After a few more inquiries, I decided that Mr. Syed Mustafa was too much of a liability for the senior management team. After much last minute maneuvering by Syed, then Dr. Rayes, trying to convince me that his services continued to be needed, I had to fire him quickly when he would not resign. Dr Rayes outwardly supported this action, but he continued to allow Syed to keep his sponsorship (*Igama*) with the hospital, which was a mistake.

Even after he was fired, he kept hanging around. This seemed to be a standard occurrence at the hospital. Once people were fired or resigned, they would not go away. Because of the close family relationships among many of the staff, aggressive action such as calling security and preventing these employees from entering the work place was perceived as being to harsh.

Eventually, they returned less and less frequently and finally disappeared for good.

Most employers immediately issued exit-only visas for expatriate employees who are fired, resign, or complete their contracts. That the Bin Mahfouz family did not was simply another example of why it was considered to be a kind and thoughtful employer. Many times employees and ex-employees took advantage of the family's kindness and generosity.

Dr. Abdul Raman Ashey was a very well known Saudi surgeon who worked as a part time physician, but was paid as though he were a full time employee.

In the private practice of medicine in Saudi Arabia, most of the physicians are employed by the hospitals or clinics. Some of the physicians also have part-time or full-time assignments with the teaching hospitals in Jeddah and Riyadh. Most of the Saudi physicians have private practices part-time and work part-time at the university hospital. We had twelve such part-time physicians who had offices at Al-Salama hospital that they used exclusively for their private patients.

In Dr. Ashey's situation, he had been a full-time physician working in the surgical department while he had his sabbatical leave from the university. He was very well known and brought good business to the hospital. He excelled in a specialized operative technique of gastric banding for which he was receiving excellent reviews. He was also well known for his laparoscopic procedures. When his sabbatical ended, he went back to his part-time job at the university but refused to have his Al-Salama salary reduced accordingly.

Dr. Mohsin Hussien, acting Medical Director, would not touch the problem.

"Gordon," he would say, "I will deal with any problems associated with the non-Saudi physicians. The Saudi physicians, especially a couple of them like Ashey, are very much politically connected. They have the power to get any one of us non-Saudi physicians in a lot of trouble and even deported."

This was one example of why I felt the hospital needed a full-time western Medical Director.

Dr. Rayes and I discussed how best to deal with Dr. Ashey. Basically, there were three options. He could return full time to the Al-Salama hospital, thus giving up his job at the university. He could continue as is (part-time) and take a fifty percent salary reduction. He could quit the hospital as an employee and become an independent physician. The last option would allow him to continue part-time at the university, see private patients as he desired, and continue to use the Al-Salama hospital for his patients. The hospital would then be relieved of any salary obligations, but would benefit directly when he used the hospital for out- patient and inpatient services.

When I approached Dr. Ashey about the options, he did not like them. "Gordon, I prefer to keep my situation as it is. I want to continue part-time practice at Al-Salama and part-time at the university hospital. Furthermore, I am not interested in having my salary reduced."

"Dr. Ashey," I explained, "I'm sorry but the current situation can't continue. It simply is not fair to the hospital. Why should we pay you a full-time consultant's salary when you are only working part-time?"

"Gordon, you know I can do twice as much work in the same time period as your other surgeons. Look at the amount of revenue that I am putting on the books and I believe you will agree with me."

At the end of the day, I had to terminate Dr. Ashey's contract. He never totally forgave me for taking this action. He ended up contracting with the hospital as a part-time private physician. As it turned out, it was probably the best thing that could have happened to him personally. It took a shove from our side to push him over to private practice. The monthly salary of an employed physician is somewhat risk free if the physician is a good producer. The private side has more risks, but it can be much more lucrative for those physicians with good reputations who are willing to work hard. Dr. Ashey discovered this fact after a dramatic departure from the hospital's direct employment.

By now, Linda and Emily had arrived in Jeddah for the summer. Mark had come about two weeks earlier. We had already experienced the excellent Indian food prepared by Dr. Pritima Kaushik. Soon my family and I became good friends with Dr. Pritima, calling her P.K. as some of her close colleagues did. In these early stages of our friendship, I became more aware of her outright straight- forwardness and her acute observation of the various personalities who worked at the hospital. These particular characteristics are not easy to find in this culture and, frankly, were refreshing.

The family enjoyed that first summer very much. Of course, I was elated to have them in the Kingdom. The villa at the Nueva Andalucia was a perfect setting for them. They all enjoyed the beautiful swimming pool and many amenities that were available in this small, upscale western compound.

Linda frequently accompanied several of the other women whose families lived in the compound on shopping outings. They visited a different souq each day. For those who enjoyed this type of adventure, Jeddah has much to offer.

Mark ended up with an assignment at Saudi ABV Construction Company at the hospital site. This assignment turned out to be an excellent opportunity for him. Before he had arrived, I had approached Ulf Norehn to inquire if Mark could be assigned, without pay, to the hospital project in some capacity where he could apply some of his mechanical engineering academic knowledge. Ulf had no problem with that, and Mark became one of the regular members of the engineering team.

I believe without this assignment he would have become bored over the course of the summer. The reference letter provided to Mark from Ulf proved most helpful in the future. I anticipated rightly that, in a couple of years, prospective employers back in the U.S. would be intrigued by a young man's experience working as a junior engineer for a foreign company overseas. This was exactly the case.

Mark also took advantage of the excellent diving opportunities in the Red Sea. He was able to secure a couple of advanced diving certificates. He became friends with the son of one of the Saudi physicians who worked at the hospital. This young Saudi had access to various ski boats and other water sporting equipment. Mark enjoyed his first summer in Jeddah very much. He had been only eight years old the first time he visited the Kingdom. The only thing he remembered of that experience was missing his grandma and grandpa.

This was Emily's first time to Saudi Arabia. She was in those early teenage years when she preferred to be with her friends back home instead of being in Jeddah. Fortunately, she also enjoys swimming and hiking, so we were able to keep her somewhat occupied. Unlike her mother, after one or two trips to the souq, she had seen enough. She enjoyed riding camels and four wheeler scooters at the Cornish during the evenings instead of traveling through the souqs of Jeddah.

I happened to see a letter that she was writing to one of her friends back home. I got a laugh when I read part of it, for it went something like this:

"Hi Elizabeth, I'm having an interesting time in Jeddah. I recently rode on some camels and have done some other neat stuff, but I am getting bored and ready to come home. You won't believe that all the men are dressed up like ghosts and the Saudi women all wear black dresses and hoods. It's like Halloween here every day."

While the family was here during those two months we took several excursions on my days off to various points of interest. Dr. P.K. usually came along with us.

One of the exciting excursions was a combination diving/ fishing boat expedition. We went with Eric Mason, the skipper for the Dessert Divers boat company. At 7:15am one Friday morning, the family and P.K. left the dock. To get out to the open sea, these boats have to travel through a long inlet that is referred to as the "creek."

At the mouth of the creek that opens up to the sea is a coast guard station where boats have to stop and provide various documentation and passports of those on board. Just before the station is a beautiful palace that faces the creek. Because of the close proximity of the palace to the creek, boaters have an outstanding view of the beautifully manicured grounds of the palace and of how it is built with its several uniquely designed minarets.

That particular day Mark and I dove two different locations, one being an outstanding reef dive and the other an old shipwreck referred to as the cable wreck. While we dove, Emily, Linda and P.K. were enjoying themselves snorkeling. The cable wreck was an old freighter that must have been carrying tons of cable when it went astray and struck a reef. A very large, friendly grouper lives within the wreck, and that particular day his curiosity brought him out face-to-face with Mark and me.

Later, we caught several jackfish and a large barracuda while trolling. The fishing gear used was top of the line and we had great fun in landing these fish. The entire afternoon while trolling we saw only one other boat; anywhere else in the world we would have had to contest with many others. Plus, the charter fee was very reasonable. We returned that afternoon about 5 pm, exhausted but happy.

I could not help but think about the huge potential for tourism that the Kingdom has to offer with such attractions as the Red Sea. The government has recognized this and is truly promoting the tourism segment within certain parameters they have established for such activities. The first step has been taken, and it is just a matter of time before the tourist industry really takes off. Unfortunately, 9/11 set this back many years.

Later that evening back at Nueva Andalucia, we barbecued our fresh catch-of-the day and enjoyed a scrumptious meal.

By mid-summer, some of my new, key staff members were coming on duty. A new Director of Material Manager and Human Resources had joined and several internal reassignments had been made. A number of western nurses had been recruited. A new Director of Quality Management had also joined the hospital. We had identified a potential Chief Financial Director from the states we were trying to recruit.

The Information Management Services continued to be a major source of concern. The department head was a Saudi physician named Dr. Salim Bin Mahfouz, Dr. Rayes's older brother. This gentleman was a primary care physician who had an interest in computers and found himself in a very difficult position. He had to depend upon the developmental software expertise of Software Data System (SDS), which was suspect as far as I could tell. He also lacked some basic knowledge and experience for such a massive implementation project.

Dr. Salim was, indeed, a very intelligent individual who could communicate well, but he was assigned to an area in which his expertise was limited. There were two political issues involved regarding his assignment to the implementation project: first, he was the brother of Dr. Rayes and second, he was being paid directly by the owner of the hospital. I felt a change would have to occur, but I didn't know how best to get around these two obstacles.

The second employee in charge of the Information Management Services was also a family member. Engineer Khalid Bin Mahfouz had good computer hardware experience but had little interest in the hospital's software conversion. He felt that he should not be working under Dr. Salim and had a major disregard for SDS.

I had come to the conclusion that there was a combination of reasons why this software implementation was not working. Not only did the senior staff in this area have limited knowledge, SDS seemed to lack the technical experience in actually implementing the type of programs we required. Dr. Hesham Mehriz, CEO of SDS blamed hospital information management staff for the lack of progress being made, and our staff blamed

SDS for lack of implementation knowledge. At that time, Dr. Hesham, a hospital board member and the ex-Hospital Director still had considerable clout at the hospital. When he presented to me the resume of a very well qualified American, I saw this as an opportunity to restructure the hospital's Information Management Services with his blessings.

Alex Haley was a high energy individual and one who had excellent technical software conversion skills. He was very detail-oriented and desired to see quick action. He came into the department and quickly ascertained that the implementation process was in serious need of reorganizing. Unfortunately, both Dr. Salim and Engineer Khalid saw Alex as a threat and simply would not give him their support. They also perceived him as an insensitive, boisterous American. Rightly so.

Alex's personality was too outspoken and too aggressive for this culture. After a couple of months on the job, I realized that, unfortunately, he was being severely undermined.

After seeing a couple of nasty e-mails between him and Engineer Khalid, I called a meeting with the Information Management Services personnel. I discussed the importance of teamwork and of how I expected that department personnel to support Alex and look at the objective of completing this implementation. I could sense the tension in the room and the distinct dislike that Engineer Khalid and, to a lesser degree, Dr. Salim had for Alex.

Alex visited with me after the meeting about taking aggressive action and firing both Dr. Salim and Engineer Khalid. He had a hard time understanding the political realities of such a maneuver with both of these individuals being members of the Bin Mahfouz family.

About a week later I was visiting with Dr. Rayes. "Gordon, we believe that Alex may be a member of the C.I.A. The Bin Mahfouz family has done some checking and we have reason to believe this is true. During the past six years he has been living in many suspect locations, including Iran and Afghanistan."

I was completely shocked. "Are you convinced that this is the case? I know Alex is different, but I never would have taken him as a spy."

"We have to be careful, Gordon. The Bin Mahfouz family is unique and there are governments, including your own, that try to gather intelligence regarding the various enterprises of the family. Please check this out thoroughly at your earliest convenience."

By now, the rumor was out that Alex was in trouble and was being investigated by the family; Alex, himself, thought it was quite humorous.

What made matters worse was that Alex was married to a woman who was a senior staff member at the Jeddah U.S. consulate. She was the primary breadwinner of the family, and they had decided long ago that Alex would follow her when she took new state department assignments. Typically, expatriate assignments for the state department are no more than two years at a particular location. When I checked out her assignments, they were, in fact, at locations such as Iran, Afghanistan, and Israel.

I informed Dr. Rayes that as far I was concerned Alex was in no way involved in clandestine activities involving the Bin Mahfouz family. Dr. Rayes was not totally convinced.

I understood full well what had happened to Alex. The Bin Mahfouz relatives in this department who did not like him were behind this. Such underhanded maneuvers are quite common and have to be dealt with sometimes with kid gloves. Unfortunately, Alex had to leave, not because of C.I.A. type of activities, but because the family relatives prevailed in his dismissal. The hospital lost a valuable resource with the departure of Alex, and the implementation process continued to flounder.

With the end of July came many requests from employees, primarily the medical staff, to take the month of August off for their vacations. August is typically a slow time in the Kingdom because so many of the Saudi population leave the country to go to cooler climates. It was a good time to have the physicians and other patient-care related employees take vacations because of the severely reduced patient census.

The problem was that all requested their vacation leave days paid in advance before they left. These advance leave payments were creating a major cash flow problem.

When I stopped the advances, most of the physicians felt I was robbing them. They seem to care less if this practice was placing the hospital's cash flow in serious jeopardy. Their complaint was that they would not have access to this money to use during their vacation if it was not received in advance and that it was a violation of Saudi labor law, which technically was true.

Primarily as a result of these problems, we established electronic funds transfer for payroll between the hospital and the National Commercial Bank. The bank provided to each employee a cash withdrawal card that could be used at virtually any A.T.M. throughout the world where such machines were located.

Thus, with few exceptions, the excuse of not being able to access funds while on vacation was solved. We stopped the leave cash advances, thereby helping to slow the negative cash flow problems, and received the informal blessing of the labor office.

This change resulted in several process changes that also uncovered another problem. Most of the employees had huge accumulations of leave balances. At the time, there was not a payroll time system or even time sheets. Employees got permission to go on leave with no documentation that they had left. Some employees who had been working at the hospital for six to eight years claimed that they had not taken one single day of vacation.

The accumulated vacation was a huge liability for the hospital as this bonus had to be paid out in cash when the employee contract eventually ended. Very little accrual provision for this liability had been made. Employees were claiming that we owed them anywhere between six to ten months cash in lieu of vacation days when they left.

Of course, we knew this was not what actually had happened. Most of these employees had used probably more than twice their due amount of leave. It simply had not been documented. This was another example of the lack of operational processes. It was also an example of employees again taking advantage of a generous owner who was not hands on.

By this time, we had numerous employees who were resigning or being terminated because they could not adapt to the changes. The departure of these non-conformers was positive except for the excessive bogus service awards they were claming.

We began to have a rash of labor office complaints and hearings. Believe me when I say that the labor office is ninety percent on the side of the employees. Employers tend to get shafted when employees complain. This is one area in which the Saudi government will need to revamp if it is serious about privatization and joint ventures with foreign company participation.

As we became more knowledgeable regarding the tactics of employees and the labor office, we began to review the passports of these individuals.

We discovered that most had their passports in their possession, an illegal practice. When we did review the passports, the exit/re-entry stamps in their passports provided excellent proof that these employees had, in fact, been out of the Kingdom for long periods of time.

The deeper I got into the personnel situation, the more corruption I uncovered. In fact, the previous head of the personnel department, Mr. Shabrawishy claimed never to have taken any leave in his entire employment period of several years and also claimed a huge sum of money. I could understand why the hospital was having financial problems without even taking into account the new hospital building program.

We had to terminate almost all of the employees in the personnel office and immediately put in place new processes designed to stop the huge leakage of cash that was occurring.

Despite my heavy workload, most Fridays, my family and friends had been able to explore different areas in the desert and mountains outside of Jeddah (many of these unique areas are thoroughly described in Chapter Eight, "The Day of Rest"). All were memory makers that none of the family will forget.

By now, though, the family had returned to Texas. I had scheduled a four-day layover for them in Zurich, Switzerland. They spent two days there and two in Lucerne enjoying the cool temperature compared to the scorching heat and humidity of Jeddah in the summer. Unfortunately, I was unable to accompany them to Switzerland.

By early fall, I had recruited a new finance director, Mr. Bill Dunn, from California. Dunn had previous experience in Saudi. It did not take him long to recognize what Arthur Anderson Company had already stated, but he felt the situation was even more negative than that reported. Bill Dunn was something of a fatalist but had a good hospital technical financial background. Nevertheless, certain Egyptians within his department took advantage of his naivety. This was probably due to his inexperience in managing Egyptians, who are generally known to be master manipulators. His technical expertise and hard work did offset some of these disadvantages. I quickly realized that it would be necessary to give him frequent pep talks to keep his optimism up regarding our financial situation and the hospital in general.

I remember one visit to my office that Dr. P.K. made pertaining to Dunn. "Mr. Gordon, I asked Bill about some financial billing problems that were uncovered by one of our quality management projects that I'm chairing: he just slumps his shoulders and says, 'That's just the way it is; it can't be changed.' Gordon, if he can't do anything about it then why is he here? He is supposed to at least try to solve such problems, isn't he?"

Likewise, if Bill told me once, he told me a hundred times that we were not going to be able to make payroll the next month (Incidentally, we never missed a payroll). He constantly mentioned that our expenses were more than our gross revenues, forget about the net revenues. We both understood the importance of receiving the additional cash injection from the owner and that we could not indefinitely put off paying our account payables to fund current operations. He became very nervous when we discussed having to start paying for maintenance contracts for all the new specialized equipment once the warranties on the new equipment had expired. He was a worrier, a characteristic I like to see in a finance officer, but unfortunately carried to a fault in his case.

My pep talks usually started out that I was aware of how critical our financial picture was and that was precisely why we both were here. I reminded him that this would not be able to be turned around over night and the owner understood this. As long as today's picture was better than yesterday's and tomorrow's was better than today's, we would end up doing fine. I found myself constantly encouraging him to keep his "dabber" up. We didn't need to give the impression to the employees that there was no hope.

The financial situation was bad, much worse than what I had initially thought and more than what Arthur Anderson had presented.

Between August and November 1998 we took the following aggressive actions to stem the flow of the red ink and to improve the cash position of the hospital: (1) implemented time sheets; (2) reduced overtime by 40%; (3) stopped all salary increases; (4) reduced vacation days; (5) eliminated cash advances for leaves; (6) sold unused old equipment; (7) reduced certain salaries that were excessive compared to market; (8) required the use of economy class ticketing with no cash in lieu of air ticket; (9) renegotiated sub-contracts; (10) reduced consultant education leave benefits; (11) restructured independent physician's contract to be more beneficial to the hospital; (12) refined hospital discount policies so that only authorized employees could give discounts; and (13) reduced employee-housing benefits.

All the changes were necessary, but significantly reduced employee benefits and salaries. We already knew that Al-Salama hospital paid the highest salaries and offered some of the best benefits when compared to other private hospitals. As we implemented these activities, I was not the most popular person around.

Many of the old timers, especially physician staff, simply could not understand why all these changes were necessary. The altering of mind-sets is the toughest job there is. They still had the impression that Sheikh Khalid would provide whatever funding would be required. After all, the hospital was only that "drop in the ocean" of the Bin Mahfouz resources, according to them.

Dr. Erfan Mamoon was head of the radiology department. He was American Board certified and was one of our more qualified and well-known physicians. He had been at Al-Salama hospital since it had opened. His salary was approximately fifty percent higher than salaries of other private radiologists in the Kingdom.

I contacted Dr. Mamoon's office.

"Dr. Mamoon, we need to discuss your current compensation package. You are aware that we are in the process of restructuring our salary scales. I noticed that your salary and service award benefits have grown significantly over the past nine years. Dr. Mamoon, I am willing to pay your service award benefits off now even though you continue to be under contract. In return, I must reduce your salary by thirty percent."

He replied, or should I say screamed, "You can't do that to me. Don't you understand who I am and how many referrals I get from all over the Kingdom? It is not fair. I am going straight to the owner about this issue."

I asked Dr. Mamoon to be reasonable. I reminded him that paying his service award early would allow him access to a large sum of money. I also reminded him that we both knew that his salary was some 30 percent out-of-line with what the market required. I reiterated that our financial situation required that we bring ourselves back towards the mean regarding our controllable expenses.

Soon, after much ado, Dr. Mamoon's salary was reduced. The mistake I made was offering him the early service award payout. I should have been tougher minded and simply offered him the new salary, take it or leave it. If he could not accept this, he could go elsewhere. That, I was sure, he would not opt to do.

A couple days later after this ordeal with Dr. Mamoon was resolved, I received a call from Dr. Rayes. "Good morning Gordon. How's it going? By the way, I was just informed that your U.S. president has just bombed our owner's pharmaceutical plant in Sudan."

"Oh boy," I thought. I had heard about the missile raid on Al Shafa pharmaceutical factory in Sudan while watching CNN that morning before breakfast. Supposedly, according to CNN, the plant was producing biological war chemicals and the CIA had advised President Clinton that it should be eliminated. I had no idea who owned the plant.

I started joking with Dr. Rayes and mentioned that the U.S. was probably just trying to hit some target in Iraq and the missile simply went off course. We both laughed. Then Dr. Rayes advised me seriously that Sheikh Khalid did in fact own a significant percentage of this plant.

I had enough difficulty in dealing with the problems at the hospital. I did not need this added political problem of being a citizen of the country that orchestrated this missile raid. I was only one of a handful of Americans working at the hospital. With the aggressive actions that I had recently sanctioned by reducing the number of employees and reducing salaries and benefits of those who remained, the Middle Eastern employees jumped on this with both feet.

For several weeks thereafter, I was reminded over and over again about this aggressive American behavior regarding the bombing of the plant. I received a couple of anonymous calls and letters that generally stated that perhaps this type of behavior is genetic in all Americans as demonstrated by the hospital's CEO.

As time would tell, the CIA reports did appear to be incorrect. Not until several years later did I learn that the plant was owned by another Saudi commercial family, not Sheikh Khalid. I am not sure why Dr. Rayes stated that it was at the time. Perhaps he had been told it was, or perhaps this was just a way to make me a little more apprehensive. I prefer to think the former. The U.S. government never admitted that there had been a mistake. The incident was quickly swept under the rug. Rumor had it that some retribution was eventually paid to the owners.

I was having difficulty recruiting a new medical director. We had interviewed several candidates, but with the exception of one American physician who was working with ARAMCO in Dhahran, we had not identified the candidate of choice. The individual in ARAMCO would have been excellent, but simply was demanding more than we could pay.

In late September, I received a call from Helen Ziegler & Associates in Toronto, Canada regarding a possible new candidate for the position. This was one of several professional search firms that we used. The individual identified was a pathologist who apparently had extensive medical administrative experience, including work as an assistant medical director. Helen stated that his references had checked out well, but the candidate was requesting an on-site visit before proceeding. Helen assured me that the individual was very outgoing, unlike the stereotyped pathologist.

Usually, we used Dr. Norm Berkman in Houston, Texas to conduct the initial interview with U.S. physicians that were considered candidates. These interviews were by phone or in person with Dr. Berkman if feasible. Thus, we were saved the considerable cost of flying the candidates over for interviews. Regarding the Medical Director's position, we had no problem in meeting the candidate's request for an onsite visit after the screening was completed. The interview was arranged for early November 1998.

Dr. Mohsin Hussien, acting Medical Director, seemed to dislike the Director of Nursing, Yvonne Bester. I felt that perhaps part of this problem was the fact that Ms. Bester was direct and quite businesslike, a female personality trait that ran against the grain for many Middle Eastern male physicians. These physicians, especially Egyptians, have had their training where the nurse to physician relationship is very subservient. The nurse is to carry out the physician's orders only and not to question the physician in any way.

Of course, this is totally opposite from the manner western nurses, including South African nurses, are trained. Generally, they are trained to be much more team-oriented, physician and nurse both responsible as team members for the patient's care. The physician is always the captain of the ship, but he should know that he needs a good first mate and engineer. We were experiencing some problems between the new western nursing staff and the predominantly Egyptian medical staff.

Dr. Mohsin asked that I invite Ms. Bester to the following evening's Medical Executive Committee (MEC) meeting. This committee consists of all heads of clinical departments and is chaired by the medical director. I knew that some of the physicians, including Dr. Mohsin, were not overly pleased with the in-patient nursing care on the wards although it was improving. Over the past six months we had been successful in recruiting several western nurses, including an operating room head nurse, to help manage the predominantly Philippine nursing staff.

I informed Ms. Bester that she should attend the MEC meeting and be in a position to respond to certain physician concerns relating to nursing care on the floors.

I will never forget that meeting. The physicians attacked Ms. Bester from both a professional and personal standpoint. One of the committee members who was a surgeon and also headed up our emergency room was a true orator. When he got on his pedestal, he was more like a used car salesman than a physician. He seemed to love to hear himself talk and did so with ridiculous exaggerations.

He led the attack on Ms. Bester that evening with most of the others chiming in. After about thirty minutes of this unrelenting abuse, I interrupted in defense of Ms. Bester. Dr. Mohsin Hussien, who was chairing the meeting, should have done the same much earlier, but I believe he was enjoying this roasting.

"Gentlemen, I am caught completely off guard about the extent of your negative feelings towards the nursing services and Ms. Bester in particular. I was under the impression that the nursing service was improving. If you recall, I have stated many times before that I do not like surprises.

"Dr. Mohsin, as acting Medical Director, why have you not informed me of the magnitude of this problem before this evening? As far as that goes, why have I not heard from any of you regarding this matter if, in fact, it is so bad?

"Dr. Omayer, I have listened to you blast Ms. Bester for the past half hour. May I ask you if you have once spoken to her regarding your feelings or tried to give her your support? Never in my experience have I ever witnessed such an aggressive personal attack by a group of respected physicians upon a director of nursing who is supposed to be considered as a colleague in providing care to your patients."

I continued, "I have noted the genuine complaints that have been registered in between the insults that have been cast. Ms. Bester and I will formulate a written plan in the next couple of days and distribute that plan to you. I pledge that I will work directly with Ms. Bester in addressing the legitimate concerns that have been raised here this evening. The report will first be presented to Dr. Mohsin for distribution. I am requesting that I receive your written responses back concerning the proposed action plans within four days after you receive the report. I am going to ask Ms. Bester to attend next month's MEC for your input as to how well the plan is working. If we really desire to make the nursing services better, let's provide Ms. Bester our support. Furthermore, Dr. Mohsin, if there are any other such major physician issues in the future that concern the medical staff to this degree, I am sure that you will communicate with me in advance. This goes for all heads of departments."

Then I added, "While I have the floor, I need to discuss a few items that have caused me concern. I have reviewed many of the patient charts. I am appalled by the poor quality of documentation and progress notes. Orders are either non-existent or illegible. Frankly, I don't see why there are not a lot more patient order errors than there are. Even the insurance companies are kicking back claims because of the poor documentation. One company has asked why the physician ordered an MRI on a patient with a primary diagnosis of pneumonia, as there is no documentation of indications. We obviously are going to have that claim denied by the company. This type of poor documentation will result in no, or very much reduced payments. These insurance claims represent the financial viability of the hospital. We will very soon be developing a screening mechanism that will quickly identify which physicians are having claims suspended because of such factors and will take appropriate actions."

After that meeting, Dr. Mohsin apologized to me for not communicating in advance the extent of the problem concerning Ms. Bester.

I could not help but notice the way Ms Bester had acted in such a professional manner during this experience. Outwardly, she had appeared very calm and collected. This restraint had probably further agitated the physicians in their not being able to shake her up. I'm sure on the inside she was torn to pieces. She had done a good job in controlling nursing overtime and man-hours worked. But she had been deficient in listening to the physicians' concerns. Also, the Filipino nursing staff looked upon the primarily South African nursing management team as racist.

I knew why many of the key doctors reacted as they had during the meeting. The nursing care was improving. The problem was that the majority of the Middle Eastern physicians did not feel comfortable with the new western nursing standards and the way these nurses desired to be a part of the patient care team. Indirectly, they were also upset about the many process changes that would soon be holding them much more accountable for their work. Most understood that the new western nurses would probably not be as willing to accept certain poor, yet common practices, such as the lack of written orders.

We developed a plan and presented it to Dr. Mohsin for the next month's meeting. Ms. Bester did her best to communicate with the key members of the medical staff. In the end, there had been too much water under the bridge with certain physicians. Also, right or wrong, the predominantly Filipino nursing staff, which was the backbone of the nursing service, felt that Ms. Bester did have a racist streak in her. Personally, I did not perceive this and felt it was very much exaggerated.

From my viewpoint Ms. Bester was one of the best of the employees that I had inherited. But no nursing director can survive without the support of certain key medical staff members and the general nursing personnel. She resigned a couple of months later.

By November, I had become good friends with Steve and Allison Martin. Steve worked for a large drug company in Jeddah, and Allison worked at the National Guard hospital as one of their key-nursing supervisors. Even before Ms. Bester's resignation, we had offered Allison the position of assistant Nursing Director. She was to start her new position in January after she and Steve returned from their holidays in the U.K.

With Ms. Bester's resignation, my plan was to have Allison serve as the acting Nursing Director until we could successfully recruit someone else. Perhaps, she would prove herself capable of the permanent position.

In late December, while I was on leave back in the U.S., I received a call from Steve Martin. "Hello, Gordon, this is Steve in the U.K. I am afraid I have some bad news. Allison has been diagnosed as having advanced breast cancer and she will immediately be undergoing treatment. Our plans to return to the Kingdom are now very indefinite."

I was shocked and caught completely off guard and really didn't know what to say to Steve. I finally said how sorry I was to hear about this and if there was anything I could do for them upon my return to Jeddah, not to hesitate to ask. Steve indicated that there was really nothing that needed done for them at the moment in Jeddah, but prayers to God for Allison's recovery and for him the strength to be her pillar during the coming days. Of course I indicated that I would do just that.

"Steve, please tell Allison that all of us will be praying for her. Please tell her that whatever we can do from here just let me know. Her new position at Al-Salama is secure unless she decides not to pursue it."

This news was really devastating for me and the Martins' other close Jeddah friends. Unfortunately, she did not recover, the cancer continuing to advance. With the exception of a quick trip back to Jeddah with Steve to take care of personal business, she did not return again. Allison was a fighter, but was finally overcome by the disease in the late summer of 2000.

This situation really caused me to have a different perspective. To me, Allison had always been an out-going, fun loving, energetic person and the picture of health. We all are very vulnerable and our situations can change over night. While we all grieved her loss, however, I still had the hospital's problems consuming my time.

Since May, I had been appealing to the private office to provide a large cash injection to cover the past deficits. The hospital's cash flow was simply not enough to sustain operations at this time.

I remembered well what Jerry McDuffy had recently told me.

"Gordon, the hospital's previous management was routinely coming each month to the owner requesting additional cash. If I were you, I would request a one-time large cash injection instead of nickel and diming them each month. They will be more receptive if you can convince them that the sum is what you really need and you won't have to come back for more."

Bill Dunn, CFO, and I had been diligently applying this strategy in convincing A.R. and Sultan that a large cash injection was critical. Our vendors' accounts payables had risen to the point that they were threatening to cut off our supplies. Basically, we had been funding operations by postponing the payments to vendors. One vendor suggested that if we couldn't pay him cash, could we at least provide him and his employee's free medical care, which is exactly what we did. Unfortunately, this particular approach to solving the payment problem was very uncommon. Most demanded cash.

In late August, we finally received a twenty-two million riyals (about six million dollars) cash injection. A very large percentage of this immediately went out in the form of payments to vendors.

I made a strategic decision regarding early payment of service-award benefits to certain high paid long-term physicians. In retrospect, this turned out to be a poor decision for the short term, albeit a good long-term strategy. The service award benefit increased from a two-week salary to a one-month salary after the fifth year of employment. By paying these individuals off early, we could have them sign new contracts and again be able to accumulate future service award benefits at two-weeks per employment year instead of one month, at least until they had worked for an additional five years. They were willing to do this for they would have the immediate use of a large sum of money instead of having to wait until they left the employment of Al-Salama Hospital sometime in the future.

The downside of this strategy was the immediate requirement for about two and a half million riyals, some twelve percent of the cash injection we had just received.

At the time, we had no idea that a long-term strategy would not be necessary and the need for additional short-term cash would again raise its ugly head. I reminded myself, long term planning is essential, but with a short-term future, it becomes irrelevant.

In late September, the construction project came to a screeching halt. Saudi ABV stated that our owner was delinquent by some eighty million riyals. We claimed that Saudi ABV had charged excessive amounts for the equipment being bought and that many costs, such as the marble floor replacement, should have been the contractor's expense, not the owner's.

I couldn't help but remember what Syed Mustafa had said about the project stopping and starting, how undoubtedly it would stop again as a result of some payment issue.

By November 15th, some two months later, the issue was still not resolved and the new hospital construction was at a complete standstill. I began to fear that perhaps it would never be reactivated. Maybe the Al-Salama Hospital would end up being an uncompleted monument and a huge source of embarrassment to Sheikh Khalid and the Bin Mahfouz family.

Finally, a compromise was reached and our owner released an additional fifty million riyals to Saudi ABV. We retained ten million of this as a security bond. It is hard to imagine that almost the entire project, some 1.5 billion riyals, was paid in advance to Saudi ABV with no monies retained pending final acceptance by the owner. We had to keep reminding ourselves that both Sheikh Khalid and Sheikh Al-Amoudi, major shareholder in Saudi ABV, were partners in several other much larger construction projects. Whatever deals had been worked out with them were way above our heads.

I was elated when the project finally resumed. Still, this issue had caused another significant delay in the final hospital completion date.

A couple of days later, Dr. Mohsin Hussein called me while I was leaving for the hospital.

"Gordon, have you seen yesterday's front-page editorial column in the Wall Street Journal? If you have not, I have a copy that I will provide you. I think that you will find the article interesting."

I replied that I had not seen the morning Wall Street yet and was in route to the hospital, but was curious as to what the article had to say.

Dr. Mohsin continued," According to this article, A.R., Sheikh Sultan and perhaps other Bin Mahfouz family members have been providing financial support to Osama Bin Ladin, the internationally known terrorist."

The article was extremely negative. It actually mentioned the first names of certain Bin Mahfouz family members and stated that there was evidence that some five to six million dollars had been diverted to this terrorist. Apparently, according to the article, the funds had come out of the National Commercial Bank (NCB) that was owned exclusively by Sheikh Khalid Bin Mahfouz. I half jokingly said to Dr. Mohsin, "Hell, we better head to the hospital's basement. The U.S. is probably getting ready to launch missiles at Al-Salama Hospital."

The article itself was certainly disturbing. Plus, only a couple of months had passed since the U.S. had conducted the missile raid on what we thought at the time was the Sheikh's pharmaceutical plant in Sudan.

Other than the fact that A.R. and Sheikh Sultan were about the same age as Osama Bin Ladin and both families had migrated to Saudi Arabia from Yemen, there was nothing else visible to substantiate this article.

Excluding this one article in the Wall Street Journal, I am unaware of any additional information that may have indicated that there was any type of link with Osama Bin Ladin. The Bin Ladin head office complex was only three blocks from the Al-Salama Hospital. It was known that Osama was not a welcomed member of that family and that he was prohibited from even coming into the Kingdom. As far as I'm concerned, the article was an unsubstantiated story that unfairly indicated that some Bin Mahfouz family members had clandestine dealings with this terrorist.

About this time rumors began to surface that the government (Royal Family) might be assuming part or all of NCB. At the time, these rumors were no more than just idle gossip or so most thought. Everyone at the hospital knew that NCB was the engine that ran the entire Bin Mahfouz dynasty.

The Wall Street Journal article, the missile raid on the pharmaceutical factory, rumors about NCB, and rumors that Sheikh Khalid was recovering from post-operative drug dependency and under house arrest was all very disturbing. There seemed to be a pattern developing. It appeared as though all these rumors were placing Sheikh Khalid and the Bin Mahfouz family in direct odds with the Royal Family's desire to appear squeaky clean in the eyes of the West.

I began to hear second hand information about how Sheikh Khalid and NCB had been associated with the downfall of the Bank of Credit and Commerce International (BCCI) headquartered in Islamabad, Pakistan. After some research on the matter, I discovered that Sheikh Khalid was a major investor in BCCI and a member of the BCCI Board Between 1986 and 1989. In the late 1980's, BCCI came under investigation regarding its banking practices. About the same time the Sheikh withdrew his investment from BCCI and also resigned from the BCCI Board in 1989. In early 1989, Sheikh Khalid suffered a life-threatening motor vehicle accident in Jeddah and spent almost a year in recovery. Whether the withdrawing of his investment and resignation from the BCCI Board was due to the accident or inside information about BCCI operations is unclear.

What is a matter of record is that BCCI collapsed and was seized in 1991. Following the seizure, Sheikh Khalid was indicted in New York State on grounds that he had misled depositors by failing to disclose withdrawal of his major investments in the bank. At the same time the U.S. Federal Reserve was investigating him for possible violation of bank regulatory rules.

All U.S. federal and state charges were evidentially dropped. Sheikh Khalid agreed to pay $225 million into a Federal Reserve settlement account.

Even though he had made a major withdrawal of his investment in BCCI in 1988, Sheikh Khalid continued to deposit family funds and NCB funds into the bank. Rumor had it that a senior Pakistani official at NCB had made rather large unauthorized NCB deposits into BCCI and Sheikh Khalid had to take the heat for this subordinate's actions. At any rate, the Bin Mahfouz family had approximately $230 million on deposit in BCCI in 1991 when BCCI was seized. NCB held about $330 million on loan notes when BCCI failed. The entire Bin Mahfouz family deposit was lost at this time. In addition to this substantial loss, the shareholders of NCB to whom this loss ultimately accrued were again Sheikh Khalid and other Bin Mahfouz family members along with the Kaki family. According to recent information, no Royal family members were at the time shareholders of NCB. There were strong rumors that certain members of the Royal family had lost substantial deposits that had been at NCB, but these rumors are not substantiated.

The financial losses that Sheikh Khalid and the Bin Mahfouz family sustained as a result of the U.S. federal and state indictments and the collapse of the BCCI were staggering, even for a family as wealthy as theirs.

At approximately the same time as the BCCI collapse, the U.S. was experiencing the Savings and Loan Association debacle. In America this scandal overshowed the BCCI seizure because of it's national interest. In terms of total assets lost, however, I have been told that the BCCI collapse was more devastating than the U.S. savings and loan disaster.

Sheikh Khalid was required to make many trips to America defending himself. It must have been a very difficult time in his life. In the end, he was completely vindicated by the U.S. and state court system, but it cost him $225 million. I am not so sure that the Royal family, as a result of everything that was happening at NCB and it's association with BCCI, was as forgiving as the U.S. government.

When it rains, it pours. During this difficult time period, the Sheikh was recovering from the automobile accident which almost took his life. It was common knowledge at Al-Salama Hospital that he had become addicted to the post-operative pain medications that were given to him. This is not an unusual situation, for many post-surgical patients and those that suffer severe pain problems do form addictions in this manner. Owning a hospital provided him easy access to pain medications at any time. Given this factor and his reported unbelievable work schedule, and perhaps with the aid of a couple unscrupulous physicians, it was strongly rumored that he became addicted.

Sheikh Khalid Bin Mahfouz was the second son born in 1949. Strangely enough, I never met the Sheikh. I had asked Dr. Rayes and A.R. several times to get me an introduction, but it never happened. In my mind he seemed much older than I, when in fact, he was two years younger. I had heard so many stories and rumors about Sheikh Khalid. When his name came up in various conversations, it was almost like talking about Moses. Even though most of the newer hospital staff, such as myself, never met him, his presence was felt in a sort of mystical way. Yet his physical appearance and mannerisms were reportedly quite unassuming and humble. Dr. P.K. had told me about an accidental encounter that she had with Sheikh Khalid – she was rushing, as usual, from one location to another in the hospital enroute to the delivery suites and was on one of the many hospital elevators. On the elevator with her was a rather ordinary looking Saudi gentleman wearing the traditional Arab male white thobe and checkered red and white head gutra. The quite unassuming Saudi standing next to her, whom she assumed was just another patient's family member, smiled a little and casually said "Salamwa Lekum" (universal greeting) "Dr. Kaushik." Not until she was off the elevator did she realize that this was the Sheikh. She felt badly that she had not recognized him and wished him well. He was known to be a modest and unassuming individual who did not flaunt his wealth. From my vantage point, he was and still is a very unique individual. He was a very generous, extremely intelligent, and a strong willed person who loved the hospital and gave it tremendous support.

At about this time, I was advised by reliable sources that Sheikh Khalid was under house arrest in Taif, Saudi Arabia, a mountainous city about two hours by automobile south of Jeddah, until late 2001. Recent information indicates that he was never under any form of house arrest by the Saudi officials. One thing was for certain and that was he virtually disappeared from the Jeddah scene during this time. Whether his disappearance from Jeddah was the result of the alleged house arrest, self imposed disappearance, or his immediate family's own doing for his sake is still not totally clear. Many rumors surround the reasons for his disappearance from Jeddah. Most likely it was the result of convalescing from the rumored addiction to pain medications brought on by the motor vehicle accident several years earlier.

I have recently heard that his health is now quite good and that he has completely overcome the health difficulties he was experiencing. I also hear that he is as strong willed as ever.

Sheikh Khalid's father, Salem Bin Mahfouz, was born in 1906 in the mountainous Hadhramout region of Yemen. Salem's family were proud mountain people but were extremely poor. The family migrated from Yemen and eventually settled in the Mecca region of Saudi Arabia. In 1951, Salem and his partners founded a company that primarily engaged in foreign company and banking transactions. This business, after receiving the enthusiastic endorsement of the ruling family and King Abdul Aziz himself, developed into the National Commercial Bank.

Over the ensuing years, Salem's five sons joined the growing stable of family businesses. When Salem died in 1994, his estate was divided between Sheikh Khalid who inherited his father's holdings in the NCB, while the other four sons consolidated their inheritance in a company called SEDOC (Saudi Economic and Development Company). Even though Sheikh Khalid was the only son who showed any interest in the banking industry, rumor has it that the other sons were not satisfied with the split. Over the years, Sheikh Khalid's sons, A.R. and Sultan, were significantly influenced by their uncles, perhaps more so than by their own father.

In 1997, Sheikh Khalid sold a 20% stake in NCB to a group of investors. In 1999, a further 50% of the family's NCB holdings were sold to the Saudi Public Fund (Royal family) who eventually in 2002 acquired the balance at NCB. At one time, the NCB was the largest asset private bank in the world and Sheikh Khalid had basically total control.

At approximately the same time that Sheikh Khalid sold 20% of the bank, he began to pass his various businesses and banking interest and control over to his two sons, Abdulraham (A.R.) and Sultan, both also having the title of Sheikh bestowed upon them. The business interests owned by Sheikh Khalid were basically split up between the two sons with the banking interest being passed on to A.R. and Nimir Petroleum and Al-Salama Hospital going under Sheikh Sultan's control. This was also about the same time that Sheikh Khalid's growing disappearance from Jeddah and continuing convalescing in Taif was becoming more and more noticed.

NCB consumed almost all of A.R.'s time. Sultan showed little interest in the Al-Salama Hospital apparently preferring the more glamorous petroleum business and scuba diving in many exotic locations around the world. Both A.R. and Sultan, the younger son, were well educated and bright young men, mature for their ages, but they certainly lacked the business and political experience of their father, Sheikh Khalid.

We will never know all the ins and outs of what really went on. Perhaps the loss of control of the bank and then later, the loss of the Al-Salama Hospital were very much interrelated, perhaps not. My perception was that they were very much interrelated.

By early November, we had recruited a new American medical director, Dr. Lee Buckler. He had impressed us during his interview process. I informed him that the key factors in his success would be helping to bridge the gap between the nursing services and medical staff. Also vital would be his taking responsibility for the many aspects of medical administration, ranging from activating various medical committees to identifying and approving department heads' leave requests. The acting Medical Director, Dr. Mohsin Hussein, simply did not have the time, interest, or desire to provide the type of staff leadership that was being required. I looked forward with great anticipation to Dr. Buckler's arrival in early December.

By now I had a good suspicion that Dr. Hesham Mehriz was not one of my supporters. He was upset that the OASIS software conversion was still having problems and felt that his company, SDS, was not receiving the support required from the hospital management team. Alex, whom we had hired based upon Dr. Hesham's recommendations, had already uncovered the fact that SDS did not have the technical knowledge required for such an implementation. We had come to the conclusion that we were the beta-site for SDS and that this implementation was going to continue to be a series of trial-and-error. It was not as though this software program was a canned product that we could take from the shelf and install. We were actually building the can.

In addition, Dr. Hesham still had significant influence with key Egyptian medical staff members and other key Egyptian administrative staff. As the first Al-Salama Hospital General Director, he had become a sort of godfather to the Egyptians. Even before my time, when Dr. Rayes was the general hospital director, he had experienced Dr. Hesham's subtle machinations among the hospital staff. Dr. Hesham had first employed many of the Egyptian staff and there was still considerable loyalty to him.

Sound management practice suggests that it is usually not a good idea for the previous CEO to remain in close operational contact with the organization he has left. It can lead to undermining the new CEO's authority and causes other problems, even in the best of situations.

Dr. Hesham was a hospital board member, he headed up two key sister companies that had significant business with the hospital, he had influence with the Bin Mahfouz family, and he had the ongoing dedication of many of the hospital staff members that he had initially hired. In addition, he was a likable individual who had a certain amount of charisma. He liked to talk on any topic or discussion, as he could charm anyone with his smile and, whether or not he knew anything about the subject, he had the gift of gab.

The many process changes and personnel changes had created a number of management problems for me. The last thing I needed was Dr. Hesham acting as a source of refuge where disgruntled employees could go to express how this tyrant CEO was mistreating them. Rather than refer these individuals to me or to their immediate supervisors, he generally supported them in his own way and provided them encouragement, a strategy that re-enforced their resistance to change. What he failed to realize was that such action was harming the interest of Al-Salama Hospital.

As a board member with the influence that he had, there was very little I could do about this management situation.

One afternoon, I received a call from the private office. "Gordon, A.R. is on his way to the hospital. He wants an immediate meeting with you, Dr. Rayes, and Dr. Hesham. We have already notified the other two. Please be available in about half an hour."

I really had no idea why A.R. called this meeting on such quick notice. I did have the uncomfortable feeling that a couple of long-term, influential employees were openly expressing their dissatisfaction about the many changes that were being made. I also knew for sure that Dr. Hesham was not helping at all in these matters.

Dr. Rayes, Dr. Hesham, and I met in Dr. Rayes's office before A.R. arrived. We conducted some small talk and expressed to each other that we were all unsure of why A.R. desired to meet on such a short notice.

When A.R. did arrive, he stated, "Gentlemen, thank you for meeting with me on such short notice. I will not take much of your time this afternoon. I want it to be clearly understood by all in this room that we have appointed Gordon as our Chief Executive Officer and that he has complete authority to make whatever changes he feels necessary. As far as I am concerned, he can fire half the staff if he believes that is what is required. I expect from both of you, your full support regarding Gordon's plan and action. Is this clear?

"Gordon, I want you to know that I am judging your performance by the number of complaints I receive. As long as I receive complaints, I know that you are taking the necessary action to shake this place up. That is why we have hired you. Keep the tempo up."

At that point, A.R. left the room. For a moment, you could hear a pin drop. My suspicion had been correct. A.R. had heard that I was being undermined by Dr. Hesham and only partially supported by Dr. Rayes concerning the many changes taking place.

This quick meeting completely reset the stage for me to continue to move forward aggressively. Dr. Hesham could not have misinterpreted the direct comments A.R. had made regarding his expectations for my support. The brief encounter was a very significant event in the continued turn around phase we had embarked upon.

I never fully trusted Dr. Hesham, even after this episode. It did have the desired effect of his being much less encouraging to his old cronies who still came to visit with him at his home concerning happenings at the hospital.

I believed that Dr. Rayes was glad that this encounter with A.R. had occurred. Even though A.R. had directed his comments to both Dr. Hesham and Dr. Rayes, we all understood who had been the primary problem in these matters. Dr. Rayes was fully aware of the importance of A.R.'s bringing this matter to the attention of Dr. Hesham. I am sure Rayes knew that he would have benefited greatly if the same type of meeting had been held a couple of years previously when he was facing the similar interference from Dr. Hesham.

A short time after the meeting, Dr. P.K. came to my office.

I knew that she was very sincere regarding Al-Salama's progress and she would appreciate hearing about the meeting. I mentioned to her that I had just completed a meeting with A.R., Dr. Rayes, and Dr. Hesham and that she would not believe what the meeting had been about. She stated that she was not completely sure what was discussed but stated she had called A.R. in his office earlier in the day because she was distressed about what was going on. She apparently had given A.R. her opinion that he had to decide either to fire me or to support me so that I could overcome the politics and undermining going on at present. She stated that A.R. had reassured her not to worry, that he fully understood what she meant. She was surprised that he had taken action so quickly.

I knew that Dr. Rayes, Dr. Mohsin, and many of her colleagues respected Dr. P.K.'s sincerity, honesty, and forth rightness. I had not known that A.R. and his family had also felt this way regarding her opinions and insight.

Since May, the last several months had truly been an up-hill climb. I had discovered so much that required repairing. We had made many changes and the effects of the changes were beginning to pay off.

The last ten days of November, I had taken leave to work with one of my other clients, Blue Cross and Blue Shield Association (BCBSA). They had contacted me regarding the necessity to establish BCBSA network hospitals in Islamabad, Pakistan and Bangalore, India. My contract with Al-Salama Hospital allowed me up to two weeks off-site each year to work with my other clients, if necessary. The business trip to Islamabad and Banglore was a much-needed diversion from my intense work at Al- Salama over the past eight months.

"Mustafa, when I return from Pakistan and India, I believe we need to have another all-staff meeting. It's time we discuss our progress over the past eight months and establish our goals and priorities for 1999. I would like to conduct this general staff meeting before I leave in early December for holidays in the States."

We scheduled the meeting for the first of December, immediately after my planned return from the Far East and about one week prior to my Christmas holidays back home.

Chapter Six

Reflections

"There is no sudden leap into the stratosphere.... There is only advancing step by step, slowly and tortuously, up the Pyramid towards your goals."

Ben Stein
(December 1998)

The business trip to Bangalore, India and Islamabad, Pakistan had been a success. Both hospitals displayed a keen interest in being part of the BCBSA worldwide hospital network. Both institutions had passed the stringent credentialing criteria. Contracts had been negotiated and accepted by the Blue Cross and Blue Shield Association in Chicago.

The trip had also proven to be a diversion that I needed from my everyday duties at Al-Salama Hospital.

As usual, I was able to have enough free time in both locations to take at least half a day and explore my surroundings. This had been one of the primary benefits of developing the hospital worldwide network for BCBSA. I was usually able to explore the area and experience the various cultures, climates, and landscapes before I left the area.

On my last day in Islamabad, I hired a hotel driver to take me to the hilly town of Murree, some hundred twenty kilometers outside Islamabad. This quaint old town had all the hills, narrow streets, and various sidewalk open shops and markets imaginable. It serves as a pleasant weekend holiday resort for many of the Pakistanis who live and work in the large cities such as Islamabad. Being there was like stepping back almost into the biblical days where men pushed their vegetable carts to their markets and women carried their belongings on their heads as they went to and fro from their houses. In the markets, the pleasant aromas of the various spices filled the air. Often, the people had wide smiles that would reveal some missing teeth. All seemed quite content living and working in this peaceful small town. I really enjoyed my day tour of this enchanted spot away from the hustle and bustle of Islamabad.

Bangalore was a very efficient city. I was impressed with the several high tech firms such as Microsoft and IBM who had company offices there. Bangalore was beginning to be known as the silicon valley of the Far East. Although one of the less populated cities in India, it appeared to me to be densely populated and very busy with literally hundreds of small motor bikes scooting here and there. It was easy to understand why such large multinational companies were establishing themselves here in a location where there was such an abundance of population, many being fairly well educated and willing to work for a fraction of what was required by home.

My personal secretary Mustafa greeted me at the Jeddah airport when I returned.

I mentioned to him that I thoroughly enjoyed my visit to Murree and time spent in Pakistan. He was quite happy that the trip was productive and that I had taken his suggestion regarding the side trip to Murree. I agreed with him that Islamabad is an exiting bustling city and Murree is the exact opposite in a refreshing way. I can understand why the city folks like to visit the place over a long weekend.

"Mr. Gordon, Dr. Lee Buckler will be arriving tomorrow evening at about 8 pm. We have his vehicle purchased and his temporary flat at Saudia City reserved. Wendy, his wife, will arrive in about two weeks. We were also finally able to arrange for their dog to be able to come with her."

"Thanks Mustafa, I will pick Dr. Buckler up at the airport tomorrow evening. I'm glad to hear that we were finally able to make the arrangements for the dog. You know, Dr. Buckler had informed me that unless the dog came, the deal was off. Apparently it's a large dog and a real member of the family."

Bringing a pet dog into the Kingdom is more difficult than getting visas for a true dependent. The government relation staff in the personnel department had spent the last two weeks working through the paper detail that was required by the Saudi officials to bring the Bucklers' dog into the Kingdom. Because of its size and breed we were able to classify it as a guard dog, which helped considerably.

Mustafa continued, "The all staff-presentation is scheduled for the day after tomorrow at 9:30 pm after clinic hours. As you had suggested, we invited all key personnel. We will be able to use our new auditorium this time instead of the hotel conference room. Our dietary services have planned for a large dinner following your presentation. Mr. Gordon, I think all the details regarding your presentation have been taken care of."

"Thanks Mustafa. It's a shame that Dr. Buckler won't have more time to rest before having to attend the presentation. By the time dinner is through, it will probably be about 1 am. I hope he can stay awake that long because of jet lag. He'll not have much of an opportunity for me to introduce him around before I leave for the states over Christmas."

At the time, I did not realize the consequences of not having the opportunity to properly introduce the new Medical Director to his new environment. In retrospect, I would not have gone on this scheduled holiday if I had known in advance the consequences of not being closely aligned with and available for him during his critical first month on duty.

The following evening I drove to the airport to meet Dr Buckler.

As Dr. Buckler was exiting the customs area, he spotted me. We shook hands; I gave him a hardy welcome to Jeddah and helped him gather his luggage. He was genuinely happy that I had been there to receive him. His long flight was routine but tiring, as usual. We walked to the car park with his overseas suitcases on a trolley being pushed by a Bangladeshi porter.

"Lee, here is your new vehicle. I hope you like it. It has four-wheel drive, which should allow you to experience the many unique places this area has to offer."

During the drive back from the airport, Dr. Buckler remarked, "Gordon, I see that the vehicle has large Al-Salama Hospital logo decals on each of the doors. I would like to remove them. By the way, I thought I would be authorized a Land Rover or other up-scale vehicle such as yours."

At first, I thought he was joking. Quickly, I realized he was not. "Lee, I believe you will find this Cherokee Jeep satisfactory. If not, we will see what can be done. I believe we need to leave the decals on, for this is our standard policy for all the hospital vehicles."

I detected what I thought to be an irritation from Dr. Buckler, which caught me by surprise. At the time, I simply wrote it off as I knew he was quite exhausted and perhaps somewhat irritable having just gotten off a twelve hour flight, likely twenty-four hours from his point of origin.

"By the way, Lee, it is my understanding that your wife will be joining you soon. Both of you are welcome to use my villa during my upcoming holiday. The only restriction is that the compound does not allow dogs. I believe you and your wife would enjoy my villa much better than your temporary quarters in the Saudia City compound. At any rate, let me know if you desire this so I can make the necessary arrangements for you. I will be leaving in a couple of days and will be gone for about five weeks."

He quickly took me up on the offer and stated that they could make necessary kennel arrangements for the dog. I was glad he accepted my offer; I knew that he and Wendy would be much happier at my villa than at the temporary one we had secured.

"Lee, that's great; I think that will be best for you. I know Wendy will enjoy it very much. Just don't get too used to it. I will want it back when I return," I joked.

I mentioned to Lee that tomorrow evening was the all-staff presentation. This would give me an opportunity to introduce him to all key staff members. I also mentioned that my upcoming absence would be a good opportunity for him to get to know the medical staff members and their perceptions of the opportunities for improvement.

"Lee, I wish I could be here during your initial period on the job, but I am sure you will be fine. This particular respite back in the USA has been planned for the past six months. Dr. Rayes will be available for you if you need anything at all. Plus, you will be able to reach me if needed."

The following day, I prepared for the evening's presentation. This was only the second time since my arrival that I would be presenting to all staff members. I knew that it was very important to praise the hard work that had taken place during the past six months. It was also critical that I show proof that the changes that had been made and the hard work of the up-hill climb were beginning to pay off. I also had to lay forth the new challenges and opportunities for the next fiscal year, which would begin on the first day of January 1999.

While the various staff members were casually strolling into the new hospital auditorium finding their seats, I reflected on how much had changed since the first all-staff presentation some six months previous. I was sure that every single individual entering the auditorium had in some way or another been affected by the many changes that had taken place. I also could not help but notice the numerous new faces of employees who had recently joined Al-Salama Hospital, as well as the absence of many others, previous employees who, for one reason or another, had not been willing or able to step up a notch and adapt to the changes that had taken place. Once again, I could not help but wonder why the hospital's Chairman, Sheik Sultan Bin Maufouz, had elected not to be present after being extended a personnel invitation. Perhaps he was on some exotic diving excursion or perhaps he had more pressing business.

I opened the meeting by thanking all for their presence and reminding them of the fine dinner that had been prepared for all immediately following the meeting. I then took a moment to introduce Dr. Buckler, and to mention how glad we were in his choosing to join the Al-Salama team as Medical Director. I thought to myself that Lee appeared somewhat tired and was undoubtedly still recovering from jet lag. I introduced a couple of other new key staff members and provided regrets from Sheik Sultan for not being able to attend.

I reminded all that it had only been six months since we had the first of such key all-staff meetings, the last having been held at the Intercontinental Hotel. Now we had this beautiful and spacious state-of-the-art auditorium to conduct such meetings and the most up-scale kitchen in all of Jeddah to prepare the dinner that would be served afterwards. I invited them to think back over the last six months and to be proud of the many positive developments they had helped create. The hospital was much further along, new processes were being put into place in virtually as departments, patient and family satisfaction survey results were improving, and the hospital's financial picture was looking up, to name a few of the positive changes.

Even though we had made significant strides in focusing upon our customers and the "hotel" aspects of care, focus sessions with a fair sampling of previous patients and families indicated that we still had three major delinquencies in this area: (1) Patients who had scheduled out-patient visits were experiencing long waits before seeing the physician; (2) Logistic problems occurred with patients and family trying to navigate from one location to another within the hospital without becoming totally disoriented; (3) Inpatient nursing staff was still perceived as needing to be more compassionate and quicker to respond to nurse call lights.

I discussed the significant progress that had been made in the implementation of the OASIS computer system conversion and the manner in which the new centrally automated outpatient clinic scheduling module was going to reduce patient waiting time. The new OASIS system would also provide much improved information in most all areas that would allow us to manage the hospital much more efficiently.

Time was given to describe the progress we had recently experienced regarding our financial situation. Expenses were a little lower than budget, bills were being produced sooner and out the door faster than before, and collections were improving. I mentioned that we had seen much improvement in all of these areas, but much more had to be done.

Of course, the excellent progress regarding the new hospital construction was discussed in detail. I was extremely happy to be able to report to the attendees that I had just been informed that very day that our owner and Saudi ABV Construction Company had apparently resolved their differences over the payment issues. Thus, within a couple of days construction activities should be back to full force. I mention with luck, we could see the hospital finished by the end of 1999, *Inshalla*.

All present understood the importance of this announcement. Many of the employees had begun to believe that the issues between the two parties would never be resolved and the Al-Salama Hospital would simply stand as a half-completed monument. I must confess there were times when I had the same thought.

I took time going over in detail the hospital's recently approved mission statement and major goals for 1999 and how important it was to think about these each day to keep us focused on what was really important.

AL-SALAMA HOSPITAL MISSION STATEMENT

"Al-Salama Hospital is a privately owned, tertiary health care center dedicated to providing compassionate, superior healthcare services in a financially viable manner to all age groups in the Kingdom of Saudi Arabia and, more specifically, to Jeddah and its surrounding communities.

The employees of Al-Salama Hospital are its most valuable asset. An environment that enhances employee excellence through continuous improvement, education, and services will be provided ensuring both internal and external customer satisfaction through a teamwork approach."

After this I discussed the six major goals that had been established and approved by the Board for 1999:

(1) To improve the financial condition of the hospital by cutting costs, finding revenue enhancements, reducing account receivables, and restructuring departments and services where necessary;

(2) To complete the implementation of the OASIS software system regarding all major modules;

(3) To complete the move into the new hospital with these facilities opening as designed and as turned over to us by Saudi ABV;

(4) To improve the quality of service to our customers by identifying areas needing improvement through focus groups and patient and family satisfaction survey results and by taking action to address these so as to score at least 92% on follow-up surveys;

(5) To market the hospital's services much more aggressively;

(6) To use external organizations to help raise the quality of care through on-site education sessions and the surveying and testing of our processes and procedures.

I spent considerable time discussing the first goal, for unless we were successful here, we would not have the necessary resources to achieve the other five goals. I talked about the reality of seeing fewer cash paying patients as more and more of our business was insurance- and employer direct arrangements. The impact of this change would be reduced margins because of the price concessions these third party payers would demand. It would be essential that we control utilization of services in this new type of environment. Our thought patterns would almost have to change 180 degrees regarding utilization of services when we receive fixed predetermined payments for patients in advance under programs such as what ARAMCO had (a type of HMO program) versus fee for service patients. I mentioned how operating expenses were anticipated to be 14% more than net revenues due to the huge depreciation expenses for the new facility. Fortunately, the owner understood that our financial performance should be evaluated only after removing a significant percentage of the depreciation expenses. It wasn't our doing to build such an elaborate and expensive hospital with gold fixtures in the seldom-used Royal suites. I drilled the importance of doing everything possible to save expenses, even small things such as turning off light switches to save utility costs and controlling supply costs by standardizing where possible. At the same time, I mentioned that we must be creative in identifying new sources of revenues such as the female Health Club that would soon be coming online and Bernie's Coffee Shop located in the large outpatient clinic lobby.

The primary issue regarding the hospital's financial operations, as far as the owner was concerned, was his disinterest in our approaching him about another cash infusion for our operational needs. The owner had helped us out of a difficult cash flow situation earlier in August, and we now had to manage accordingly.

As the meeting was approaching forty-five minutes, I shifted gears into identifying specific action items required if we were to accomplish our six main hospital 1999 goals laid out by our Board of Directors. There were some thirty-one specific action items with most being measurable. A few of the more significant ones included establishing a unit dose system in pharmacy; establishing an open-heart surgery department; bringing operational the Excimer eye laser, cardiac catherization lab, nuclear medicine department, and audiology department; becoming a pilot hospital for the USA based Joint Commission of Accreditation of Heath Care Organizations (JCAHO) to test their new international hospital standards; complying with all ARAMCO quality criteria and surveys; and developing an affiliation with the King Faisal Specialty Hospital and Research Center (KRSHRC) in Riyadh for educational and training programs and potential sharing of scarce medical resources.

At the time, there was no way to understand that accomplishing this last action item would be so disastrous and would reinforce the old saying, "Be careful of what you wish for. You might actually get it."

After presenting the action items to be accomplished in 1999, I spent the last ten minutes of the meeting going over the three-year business plan. In reality, it's almost impossible to plan for what is going to happen next week in Saudi Arabia; much less what may happen three years down the road. Regardless, it was a useful exercise at the time. But, as with so many longer-term ideas, the best laid plans often go astray.

I answered a few questions from the audience, the meeting was adjourned, and we all proceeded to the hospital's luxurious restaurant facilities where we received a very nicely prepared and delicious dinner. The meeting had taken about one and a half hours.

After it was over, I felt good about the presentation. The following day several staff members stated that it was an upbeat presentation for it served as an excellent reminder of the progress that had been made.

I knew in my heart that we had much more to accomplish when compared to what had been done. Step by step, little by little, we would climb the mountain. As long as Al-Salama Hospital was a little better today than yesterday and would be a little better tomorrow than today, we were on the right track.

I had purchased a round-the-world trip airline ticket, having decided to fly from Jeddah to Singapore, conduct two days of business there for BCBSA, and then visit one of the small islands located in the South China Sea. From there I would head on eastwardly to Dallas.

Business in Singapore concluded as I expected, and then I went to Binyan Tree Island by hydrofoil. This was a beautiful small island, and the three days spent there were very relaxing. It is amazing how much beauty there is to see in the world.

From the island, I returned to Singapore and flew direct to San Francisco and then on to Dallas.

The family would be leaving for Vail, Colorado about one week after I returned home. We planned to spend Christmas in Vail and have a ski holiday for a Christmas present. Then, we would be back home in time to use our tickets to the New Year's Day Cotton Bowl Classic football game, *Inshalla*.

During the long flight over the Pacific, I reflected upon what had taken place during the past nine months. There was no way in my wildest dreams when I started that I could have imagined or anticipated in advance the events I would experience or places I would see. Overall, it had been an exhausting but exhilarating and adventerous nine months.

I was really looking forward to the five weeks back home with my family. It would be refreshing not to think about Al-Salama Hospital for a while.

Chapter Seven

Metamorphosis

"The first step towards getting somewhere is to decide that you are not going to stay where you are."
John J.B. Morgan & Ewing T. Webb
(January—July, 1999)

I had been on holidays about three weeks when I called my assistant, Mustafa, to know if everything was okay back in Jeddah. This was the second day after Christmas. When Mustafa answered the phone, as usual, he was upbeat and seemed genuinely happy to hear from me. When he asked how I was enjoying my holidays and if I had had a nice Christmas, my response was that we were all having a wonderful time. I then inquired if all was going smoothly at the hospital.

"Well sir, as you know it is the middle of Ramadan and is quite slow. As I expected, as soon as you left, several managers put in salary increase requests, and certain staff are trying to slip things through while you are gone. All of these issues I have given to Mr. Safar and suggested that he hold until your return."

"Thanks, Mustafa, for taking these steps. By the way, how is Dr. Buckler adjusting to his new environment?"

"Mr. Gordon, he has been active. He seems to be right at home here. But Dr. Kaushik has asked me your telephone number. She looked concerned to me."

I knew that Mustafa was a very loyal individual. I also knew that if there were some serious problems, he would tell me so.

At that time, we only had one more ski day left before we would be leaving and making the seventeen hour drive back to Grapevine. Mark, Emily, Linda, and I had really enjoyed this particular ski holiday at Vail. Mark and Emily had become quite good skiers. They had no trouble on the steep blues and had even mastered some of the less difficult blacks. I usually tried to stay with them until they went down a black diamond. Linda was quite content to retake, for the third or fourth time, her beginner's lessons and stay on the moderate greens, while she was not enjoying the comforts of reading a good book and drinking hot chocolate in front of a large open fireplace back at the lodge. By now we all had several routine aches and pains, but fortunately, after five days of intense skiing, nothing out of the ordinary.

Since Mustafa had mentioned a concern, I decided to give Pritima a call to see if everything was okay. When I finally got through, she asked how we were all doing and asked me to give Linda, Mark, and Emily her best wishes and love. We conducted some small talk about the holidays and then I mentioned to her that I was calling to hear what she had done over Christmas and just checking up with her.

After confirming that she had celebrated Christmas with some western friends in Jeddah and was doing fine, she confided, "The reason I asked Mustafa for your number was that I wanted to share with you my concern. If it were a hospital in America or England I would not bother, but since this is Al-Salama Hospital in Jeddah, I think it is important that you are aware of some things. This Dr. Buckler is not acting in the best interest of our hospital. He is acting as though he is the CEO and the president all wrapped up together. Dr. Mohsin, however, believes this guy is the best thing since sliced bread. In my opinion, he is a phony. The way he explains the management policies gives the impression that he does not agree, but has been told to implement them! He has recognized that some key people here resent you for making the required changes and is exploiting that situation during your absence. He doesn't know his job as a medical director; he only talks a lot. Dr. Mohsin is a nice, but naïve man. It will take him some time before he sees the reality."

I was surprised by Dr. Kaushik's comments and the sound of her voice.

"I really don't trust this guy, Mr. Gordon. I think his intentions are not good. Personally, I did not think he is what we needed for a medical director when I first met him during the interview process. I have already given my opinion to Dr. Rayes. The way he is dealing with people is neither professional nor good for the hospital."

"P.K., I believe you are overreacting to the situation. Before I left, I mentioned to Dr. Buckler that he should take this opportunity to become acquainted with the medical staff."

She added that she had an uncanny feeling that he was going to be bad for the hospital, that he did not know his job, especially what was required for Al-Salama. I told her that she should stop worrying about it. Even if there were some type of problem, which I doubted, there was nothing that I could currently do until I returned to Jeddah in about two weeks. Surely, any such problem could wait until then to be dealt with.

"Gordon, it is my opinion that you should have not gone on holidays for so long. Why do we need you if you can be gone at length, especially now when a new medical director is prancing around here like he owns the place? This is Al-Salama Hospital, not America, you know."

I again cautioned her to stop worrying; I really thought she was overreacting. Understanding very well her sincere commitment to Al-Salama Hospital, I mentioned that I would again contact the office, including Dr. Rayes, and asked her to give me another call immediately if anything more unusual developed. I truly appreciated her concern, even though I felt it was very much exaggerated.

Still, P.K.'s conversation disturbed me. I had placed Mr. Safar Abu Milha, a senior Saudi national administrator, as acting CEO during my absence. I knew that Dr. Kaushik did not have a high opinion of Mr. Safar's performance and also felt he was not one of my supporters. Still, I was quite comfortable with his acting on my behalf while I was away. I was glad that he and Dr. Buckler had seemed to hit it off. I was also pleased that Dr. Buckler had apparently developed a positive relationship with Dr. Mohsin Hussein, who had been appointed Associate Medical Director. It would be important that these two work well together.

I was curious why P.K. felt that Dr. Buckler was undermining me. Although I had come to appreciate what I considered almost a sixth sense she had regarding such matters, I wondered now how she could draw such a conclusion in such a short time period. Surely, her feelings would not be correct this time.

I spent the next two weeks back at my home in Grapevine, Texas. We took in the New Year's football game at the Cotton Bowl in Dallas as planned. Then, I spent a couple of very pleasant days with my parents in central Texas at Lake Whitney. The days passed rapidly and before long it was time to board the flight to Jeddah. It was always hard to leave home and go back to the Middle East.

This was the continuation of the second half of my round-the world trip ticket. Delta Airlines took me as far as Zurich, where I had my usual stopover and jaunt to old central Zurich for a couple of hours. Swiss Air then took me on to Jeddah.

When I arrived in Jeddah, Ramadan was in full swing. Ramadan is a four-week period each year that Muslims recognize as their holy month. It's typically a slow time for business. Fasting occurs during the day, so most business is conducted upon its completion during the evening.

The entire population's working and sleeping routine flip-flops from the normal routine. People generally sleep in the day and work during the evenings. Each evening, when the sun sets and the day's fast end, there is a rush of activity. The Saudis are not the safest automobile drivers in the world, and during Ramadan their driving habits deteriorate even more. It is not a safe time to be out driving.

Like all service organizations within the Kingdom, the hospital must adopt the standard Ramadan schedule. All outpatient clinics are opened most of the night and are closed during the day. A complete reversal of most of life's normal routines occurs during Ramadan.

Even when Ramadan is not occurring, the Saudis are notorious for being much more active during the evening than in the morning, a lifestyle which may be attributed to the extreme temperatures this country experiences in most locations. But with Ramadan, almost the entire population stays up all night and sleeps during the day.

When I reached my villa at the Nueva Andalucia, I was happy to see that Dr. Buckler had already vacated that same day. I was anticipating that he and his wife might still be in the villa although he was aware of my return date. The villa was clean and looked exactly as I had left it, a good sign.

I went to the office first thing in the morning and was immediately met by Mustafa. He welcomed me back and asked about my vacation. He then inquired if everything was in order at the villa when I arrived.

As usual, Mustafa had checked the villa and had made the necessary arrangements to pick me up at the airport upon my arrival the previous evening.

During the next half hour, Mustafa gave me a quick briefing. I signed some papers for him and that was it. He was glad that I was back. Fortunately, there seemed to be no out-of-the-ordinary problems such as those Dr. P.K. had alluded to a couple weeks earlier.

Later that morning, I visited with Dr. Rayes and conducted a brief staff meeting with my direct reports. According to the information I was receiving, nothing unusual had taken place during my absence. Actually, since Ramadan was in process, activity was even more abbreviated than normal, proving this a good time to have been away. As far as I could tell, Mr. Safar had done a fine job in covering for me during my absence.

I wanted to have some time with Dr. Buckler to see what his initial impressions were and to see how he had fared during the past five weeks. He and I went to a small restaurant close by the hospital for a late lunch. Lee drove his car.

"Lee," I commented, "what happened to the Al-Salama logo decals on your car?"

"Gordon, those decals would not allow Wendy and me any privacy. Plus, it made the vehicle unattractive. I really did not want the decals on my Jeep any more than you would want them on your Land Rover or Dr. Rayes would on his Mercedes."

I made no comment. We had our lunch and Lee gave me a good briefing on his activities while I was gone. Most of his time had been spent visiting one-on-one with physicians and getting to know them. This is exactly what I had hoped he would do. As I listened to him, I could see that he really liked to talk. There was something in his personality that seemed to border on arrogance. I couldn't put my finger right on it, but at the time I felt that whatever it was might cause him some problems.

Dr. P.K. had been working at Al-Salama Hospital for several years. Before my arrival, she had been the hospital's top revenue producer for a number of those years. Having forty to fifty deliveries per month was fairly common for her during those high producing years. She was well known in Jeddah; her patients were primarily the upper middle class clients and paid cash for her services. She had several VIP patients.

Anything P.K. was assigned; she would vigorously take on and do whatever was necessary to see the task or project completed. As a result, she found herself chairing various committees and participating as a member on several others. She possessed a unique character. She was decidedly professional and quite decisive. But, she had one serious shortcoming. She was absolutely apolitical and extremely outspoken, qualities which made her unpopular with some of her colleagues.

Before I arrived, all of the hospital's medical records were in shambles and, due to the construction of the hospital, were stored in no particular order in outside portals. This was creating lots of delays and problems in day-to-day management of the patients. Having practiced in the U.K. for several years and being board certified by the Royal College of Obstetricians& Gynecologists in Britain, P.K. understood the importance of documentation and of having proper medical records at all times. She served as chairperson of the medical records committee and apparently had complained repeatedly about the situation to the administration. As a result, Dr. Rayes appointed her acting head of the medical records department while she continued to keep her heavy clinic schedule.

She and her small staff reorganized the medical records department so the files could be retrieved. A proper medical records committee was formed with members from the various medical departments. New policies were approved, and Dr. P.K. appointed qualified staff for the department.

The new facilities with their modern equipment were outstanding. But physically reorganizing and relocating the records from the old portals to this new space was a Herculean task. P.K. handled it efficiently. She also chaired the medical records committee and remained very active in various other committees like quality management and credentialing for as long as she was associated with Al-Salama Hospital.

Her straightforwardness and "get things done yesterday" approach was not always appreciated, especially in this culture. Mediocre staff members found it uncomfortable to be in her presence. Even the best physicians knew they had to be on their toes when doing a case with her. Her intolerance for mediocre performance and her frankness and honesty did put some of her colleagues on edge. In the end, however, this type of tenacity and the way she cared for and treated her patients won her the respect of almost all of her colleagues and the administration. She was eventually assigned as head of the ob/gyn department.

I remember one of my first encounters with Dr. Kaushik, before I had gotten to know her. Dr Rayes and I were visiting regarding some items when Dr. P.K. came storming into his office.

"Dr. Rayes," P.K. started, "I don't know how many times the outpatient director has to be reminded that my new clinic is located on the 1st floor. Today, three pregnant patients wandered around the hospital for a long time trying to find my clinic. I have gone personally to the outpatient receptionists and provided them with maps to give to my patients. This is not good publicity for our hospital; Dr. Rayes. What our employees lack here is the commitment to their jobs."

Dr. Rayes mentioned to her that he and I would immediately look into this matter, that it couldn't be that difficult a problem to solve.

"Dr. Rayes, this is not the first time the problem has occurred. These receptionists just don't care. I think you and Mr. Gordon have to take some action. They do take advantage of your kindness, but if we can't provide what our patients need then this kindness is no good for our hospital's success. These are pregnant patients walking around in circles."

She then stormed out of the office, obviously not satisfied with the response provided by Dr. Rayes.

Dr. Rayes looked at me with his large, sheepish eyes and great smile reflecting his perfect while teeth and said, "Tornado. I believe that is what you Texans call a real tornado." I found this a perfect description of Dr. Pritima Kaushik when she was frustrated with a lack of professionalism in the hospital.

It had not taken me long to recognize that she had an excellent knowledge of the hospital and of who was doing what. Her ideas and thoughts were usually right on target with no bias. I could see why Dr. Rayes took her counsel seriously when discussing certain hospital issues, even those unrelated to the ob/gyn department.

Dr. Kaushik truly had a sixth sense when it came to issues involving work relationships and their outcomes. I really don't believe in E.S.P., but she did have some extra perception that was out of the ordinary. Throughout my time as CEO at Al-Salama, I came to respect her points of view and perceptions very much.

Because of her dedication, hard work, and sincerity regarding the hospital, the Bin Mahfouz family had provided her a large, beautiful clinic just outside the labor and delivery suite on the first floor. All other outpatient clinics, with the exception of her arch-rival's, Dr. Magdi El Sheikh, head of the artificial reproduction technology department, were located on the ground floor of the outpatient bed tower. Unfortunately, this was another source of irritation that some of her colleagues held against her. "Why should she be provided with such fancy, spacious facilities?" they complained.

I thought the answer was easy. "That's what the owner desires," I responded.

By the time I arrived as CEO in April 1998, Dr. Kaushik had resigned from her position as head of ob/gyn and had become an independent physician practicing at Al-Salama Hospital. Even in her new position, she continued her active participation in various medical committees and continued to have direct access and influence with the hospital's senior management. By this time, she had delivered some 5,000 babies. This fact alone is remarkable, not even taking into consideration that she was a single, non-Muslim, Indian female with only moderate knowledge of the Arabic language.

Later that first day back from my holidays, I bumped into Dr. P.K. She seemed happy to see me back. I mentioned that the family had a wonderful time on the ski trip and had returned home without injury. They had told me to say hello for them. I then took a moment to explain to P.K. that I thought that she had overreacted when she had contacted me in Vail.

"Mr. Gordon, mark my words, Dr. Buckler is going to be a problem for you in the very near future. I am not suggesting any particular action. Just don't trust him. As far as Mr. Safar is concerned, he is lazy and has few brains, which are mostly used in dreaming of becoming the CEO of Al-Salama Hospital without doing any work. Dr. Buckler, on the other hand, can be dangerous for you especially if some of the unprofessional employees join with him."

About two weeks later in early February, I was having one of my routine daily sessions with Dr. Rayes. Most of the time, during these sessions, I shared with him what was going on and actions that we were taking. I knew that certain staff continued to discuss hospital business with Dr. Hesham, who would then relay it directly to the owners. I knew that these physicians had better access to A.R. and Sultan than I did, unfortunately. Thus, I didn't want Dr. Rayes to get caught off guard if A.R. or Sultan asked him about a particular action being taken that someone had complained to them about.

By now Sheikh Khalid Bin Mahfouz was completely out of the picture. It was common knowledge with the hospital staff that Sheikh Khalid was spending almost all of his time in Taif recovering from an illness that was some how related to his injuries substained several years earlier in a vehicle accident. The family businesses, including the hospital, had been turned over to his sons to run. Even though Sheikh Sultan had the responsibility for the hospital and served as hospital chairman, it was A.R. who took the necessary interest in it. Sheikh Sultan seemed to have little interest in Al-Salama. He was much happier enjoying the ability to jet here and there to various scuba-diving locations throughout the world. Rumor had it that his interest lay in the more glamorous businesses, owned by the family.

This morning with Dr. Rayes was a little different than most. "Gordon, I am afraid you have to talk to Dr. Buckler about his mannerisms. I'm getting feedback that he is coming across to the physicians in a condescending manner. They are complaining that his body language is offensive, and they do not feel comfortable talking with him."

After the session with Dr. Rayes, I went back to my office to contemplate how best to approach Dr. Buckler regarding this sensitive issue. I had also learned that during the time he had used my villa, he had kept his large dog there after I had indicated that the dog would have to be kept elsewhere. He had also had several staff parties at the villa, which I did not appreciate.

The following day, I again met with Dr Rayes to discuss specifically the new project equipment budget.

"Gordon, the private office has been informed by Saudi ABV that completing the project as planned will cost an additional sixty million riyals (sixteen million US dollars). The family is not going to put any additional money into the new project. Thus, what we have to do is to reduce the amount of new equipment purchases by this amount."

The original new equipment budget was some two hundred eighty million riyals. Approximately one hundred and sixty million had already been spent towards equipment with the majority of those items already delivered and installed. For example, the entire radiology and nuclear medicine departments, featuring the latest Siemens equipment, were already completed. Of the balance to be purchased, somehow we had to cut that amount by some sixty million riyals.

"Lee, we obviously have a major task ahead of us that must be completed within a very short time period. We will instruct Saudi ABV to postpone any additional equipment purchases until we can review the bill of quantity (BOQ) and determine what can be cut. Of the one hundred and twenty million for the medical equipment requested and not yet purchased and delivered, we have to cut out sixty million riyals worth. I am going to assign you and Tom Wallace to this high priority project and ask you to be the lead person."

I had employed Mr. Wallace when I first arrived at Al-Salama Hospital to head up the material management and logistic support department. Tom was a fellow American and had considerable experience in materials management. He had not been involved in the new project equipment purchasing because it was a turn key project with Saudi ABV. A major aspect of their responsibility was medical equipment purchasing.

I immediately meet with Dr. Buckler to discuss this matter. "Lee, it will be necessary to visit with each of the physician department heads and go over their approved equipment listing. Together, you and the key medical staff members will need to identify those items that need to be deleted. We must complete this task within six weeks, maximum two months. Saudi ABV has agreed to hold upon any additional medical equipment purchases until we get back to them with the revised list. The longer this initiative takes provides Saudi ABV with a legitimate excuse for additional project completion delays.

"We are currently holding only ten million riyals (approximately 2.6 million dollars) until the completion of the hospital. The release of these funds is partially dependent on Saudi ABV's meeting their completion schedule. Knowing them, I am sure they will be looking for any excuse why they cannot meet the deadline. I suggest that you start by reviewing the twenty six million riyals order for Siemens patient monitors. I believe the number that has been requested is excessive. This order has to be placed through Al Hikma; I am sure Dr. Hesham will complain bitterly if we reduce his company's order. But that's tough. If it can be reduced, we must do so. I would also suggest that you request Dr. Mohsin Hussein to be present during your meetings with each medical department head. He has been around here for a long time, and the physicians know him well. Since you are still the new kid on the block, they may be more receptive if he is part of this equipment review process.

"Lee, remember we do not have a choice. We must cut out sixty million riyals. I believe this approach will be much better than arbitrarily cutting items out without the medical staff input. We will do that if we have to. I believe, however, that there is enough excess to be able to reach the savings required without cutting into the muscle."

I could see that Dr. Buckler was not overly excited about this assignment. But I felt that as medical director, he had to play a major part in these decisions. Between Tom Wallace and him, and with support from Dr. Mohsin Hussein, the task could be accomplished quickly.

Even with the new equipment-financing problem and the beginning of some second thoughts regarding my new medical director, I could see good things beginning to happen. We were finally starting to recognize some of the fruits of our labor.

I was able to convince A.R. that a new hospital Board of Directors, with appropriate bylaws and routine meetings, had to be set up. The Board needed at least some community representatives. Sheikh Sultan Bin Mahfouz became the Chairman. Vice Chairman was Dr. Rayes, and the Secretary/ Treasurer was Jamal Salim, the CFO from the private office. We had also selected a Saudi who was the CEO of Red Sea Insurance Company, a sister company; he was also a family relative. We had one of the senior banking officers from NCB as well. I was selected as a non-voting member.

This six-member hospital Board began meeting each month. The agenda always included a report from the hospital's finance director. We arranged Board education sessions and really attempted to have the Board function in a traditional manner.

Unfortunately, the Chairman Sultan never came to a single meeting. In normal situations, the Chairman's responsibility in chairing meetings then fell to the Vice Chairman. Of course, these were not normal circumstances.

Vice Chairman Rayes was shy and most uncomfortable in chairing any such meetings. I always had to take up the agenda and ended up directing the meetings.

Of course, that was not all bad. It allowed me to lead these meetings and generally move the members in the direction I desired them to go. Their being first time Board members made keeping the focus on hospital policy and the bigger picture verses bogging down in trivia a difficult task.

The Al-Salama Hospital had been selected by Joint Commission International (JCI) a subsidiary of Joint Commission of Accreditation of Health Care Organizations (JCAHO) to be one of four pilot international hospitals. This pilot program was designed to test the international quality standards that had recently been developed by JCI. Having JCI as a previous client developing the BCBSA's worldwide hospital network, I am sure had given us an advantage in the selection process.

With JCI we developed a three-phase approach with the ultimate goal of receiving accreditation. Being selected as only one of four hospitals outside the USA to test these standards was a significant honor.

The first on-site JCI survey was performed in early June, 1999. It was a three-day affair and turned out to be one of the most positive things that happened to the hospital. The surveyors pointed out our shortcomings in areas like medical records documentation and patient-and-family education. They also advised us of our strengths in such areas as Board of Directors' development and physician credentialing.

We had called a special Board meeting while the surveyors were on site. They provided the Board with an education program regarding their responsibilities and protocol. All of the physicians, nurses, and other patient-care providers were very much motivated by JCI education process. Because of the pilot testing, it was less an actual survey and much more directed at various quality education issues. Phase one of the JCI pilot survey process had been a true success.

There were other significant developments. Several new patient care services had been activated. Our patient care satisfaction surveys showed excellent improvement. With the exception of the director of nursing and a few other exceptions, all key positions were now filled. Our centralized purchasing effect was beginning to pay off. The inventory levels were falling to much more acceptable levels.

Even though we still had many difficulties ahead, most of the staff, including the active Board members, felt things were moving in the right direction within the appropriate time frames.

The one major goal that continued to prove elusive was improving our cash flow situation. Our controllable expenses had stabilized. The non-controllable expenses, however, such as utilities and equipment maintenance were on the increase. The government owned Saudi Arabian Airlines owed us about eighteen million riyals. This one account represented more than thirty percent of the account receivables. We simply could not get the airline to pay us even after allowing them huge discounts. The government services and Royal Family members, such as various prince and princes and their staffs, were notorious for being very poor payers. Our net revenues were not meeting budget because of the increased discounts demanded by the increasingly insured population. The number of full paying cash patients was decreasing as we had projected, only faster, as they converted into some of the new insurance schemes.

In addition we had received a notice, along with other private hospitals in the Kingdom, that the electricity cost would increase from 12 halala (about 3 cents) to 38 halala (10 cents) per kilo volt per hour. This was more than a tripling of the cost.

Such notices seemed to be the normal modus operandi of how the Saudi government responds to changes. Things stay the same for a long period and then, boom, overnight it tries to make up for the shortcomings. At this particular time the price of crude oil had fallen to ten dollars per barrel, and the government coffers were feeling the pinch.

Our electric bill for the hospital was running an average of three hundred ten thousand riyals per month (eighty two thousand dollars). With this increase, it could jump to about a million riyals per month.

This pending problem was solved in a unique manner. A representative from the electricity company contacted our finance department with an offer. We could continue to receive monthly-computerized legitimate statements that would be no more than three hundred thousand riyals per month. Based on the new rates this would represent a savings of more than six hundred thousand riyals. Of course, the "representative" demanded fifty percent of these savings to change the meter readings. We finally negotiated it down to twenty percent of the savings.

Because of the lack of sophisticated systems in most Saudi ventures, this was a normal way of doing business and occurred on a regular basis. We always had to pay someone something in order to get things done. It might range from giving someone in the immigration office money to expedite a visa or giving cash to some officer at Saudi Arabian Airline to release payments that were due to the hospital. Unfortunately, this type of corruption is rampant.

One other ridiculous example had to do with the ARAMCO retention payments.

We had a capitation (payment in advance of services provided on a per member per month basis) arrangement with ARAMCO, one of our major clients. The company was required by the Saudi government to withhold ten percent of the capitation due until the end of the hospital's fiscal year, until such time the hospital had payed due taxes (Zakat) to the government. Then the funds would be released. In Al-Salama's case, this represented about 1.5 million riyals.

Compared to that of other countries, Saudi taxes are very minimal and are figured on a small percentage of asset value. Each year after a company's year-end audit financials are completed, this information, along with any tax money due, is provided to the government. Once these monies are received, the tax office issues a certificate that can be provided to organizations such as ARAMCO, who then release the withheld payments.

The problem is that a company must have the certificate, or at least a letter of no objection, from the tax office to receive the funds due that are being held.

Typically, we paid about two hundred thousand riyals (fifty four thousand dollars) to some official at the tax office so the certificate would be released. It didn't matter if we had paid the due taxes or not. If a company requires the Zakat certificate to get the funds released, it has to pay the baksheesh to someone.

One way to look at it is that paying two hundred thousand riyals to be able to receive 1.5 million from ARAMCO is not that bad a deal. The alternative was to do what we initially tried and turn the whole issue of the Zakat certificate to Arthur Anderson Company. After two years of red tape and failure to receive our final certificate, we decided the best thing to do was to pay the bribe and just consider it a cost of doing business.

About this time Ulf Norehn, Project Manager from Saudi ABV contacted me. "Hello, Gordon, I need to advise you of two items. One, we need to receive the revised equipment bill of quantity (BOQ) listing from you as soon as possible. Any additional delays in receiving this will cause us to miss the planned construction completion date. Second, I will soon be leaving Saudi ABV and moving to Malta where a new hospital project is under way."

I really was disappointed to hear that Ulf was leaving. I knew that he had become very frustrated regarding the on and off nature of this project, now entering its fifth year. I knew his assistant, David Lane, who would be taking his place. David was a very capable construction manager and we worked well together, but I was still sad to hear that Ulf was leaving.

I had anticipated the comments about the project completion delays because of the delayed completion of the revised BOQ. Dr. Buckler, Tom Wallace, and Dr. Mohsin had been focusing on this task for about four weeks; and I knew it was going slowly and with difficulty. The various medical staff department heads were extremely reluctant to give up any of their equipment that had originally been approved.

At the same time I started receiving new complaints from the physician department heads regarding Dr. Buckler. I had to weigh their complaints against the very difficult task that Lee had regarding the equipment reduction. The complaints, however, were not regarding the reduction, but rather his mannerism and condescending nature in dealing with them.

I called Dr. Hussien. "Mohsin, please confide in me how the medical staff is relating to Dr. Buckler. I need to know the straight and skinny regarding Lee."

"I have been reluctant to talk to you regarding this subject, Gordon. I felt perhaps it would appear that I am trying to strike back at him for taking my place as the Medical Director. Frankly, I am disappointed in Dr. Buckler. As Associate Medical Director, I had hoped that he would use my past experience and established relationships to his advantage. This has not occurred. On the contrary, he keeps me at a distance and doesn't involve me in medical staff matters, such as this medical equipment project. I have accommodated what I perceive he desires our relationship to be. Unfortunately, he has managed to upset every single medical staff department head in the way he is dealing with them on many issues. There is no negotiation. He simply tells them what is going to be cut or cancelled. And the way he goes about it is not acceptable. He comes across as arrogant and his body language is disturbing.

"Well, Gordon, you asked for my true opinion. I have given it to you. Instead of a bridge that brings the administration and medical staff together, he is perceived as a wedge that is driving the two apart. I am sorry that I have been so direct. But you need to know what is happening here."

"I really appreciate your frankness, Dr. Mohsin. Remember a strong point I made to you at one time regarding problems with the previous director of nursing. I told you that I do not like surprises and want to be informed about potential problems in advance so they can be corrected before they become too big to solve. I will deal with this problem."

I knew that while talking one on one, Lee had a way of slouching down in a chair with his legs crossed almost as if he were lying down that projected a very casual nonchalant attitude. This slouched position caused the soles of his shoes to be pointing almost directly toward the person with whom he was speaking. In the Arab culture such exposure is a sign of disrespect and, thus, is extremely impolite. I had reminded Lee a couple of times previously to no avail. Having experienced his somewhat arrogant nature, I knew that he could become quickly defensive if challenged. He was coming across as the stereotypical insensitive, boisterous American with the know-it-all attitude. This was getting him into "deep shit" with the medical staff.

I met with Dr. Rayes regarding the problem and told him that after some discussions with several physicians, including Dr. Mohsin, I had concluded that I had a major problem with Buckler that must be dealt with quickly and aggressively.

"Gordon, I was wondering how long you were going to let it go on. I have been getting complaints from all the doctors on a daily basis. I decided not to interfere and let you make the call when enough is enough."

I thought to myself, "Hell, this is a typical Rayes approach to things." If he had been informed about these problems, he should have advised me and not waited until I brought it up.

"I know that Lee has certain offensive mannerisms and has shown what appears to be an arrogant approach to things. I'm sure part of the complaints registered are the result of his having to identify some sixty million riyals of previously approved medical equipment that now has to be cut. But, I agree he has apparently succeeded in building a gap between himself and the doctors."

"Gordon, I believe that he is perceived as just another administrator instead of a medical director who has the best interest of the medical staff in mind. I also know that he has failed to use Dr. Mohsin in the manner we had hoped."

"You're absolutely right, but I am not ready to pull the plug yet. I want to have a heart-to-heart talk with him to see what he believes can be done to salvage the situation. Plus, Dr. Rayes, I'm counting on Tom and him to produce this revised BOQ listing in the next couple of weeks."

Before I could confront Lee, I received a call from P.K. "Gordon; do you know what is going on? I'd like to tell you about Dr. Buckler. There are two aspects that are important. One is that he does not know how to deal with the doctors about this equipment listing. Are you sure he is a doctor? The anesthesia department head told me that he has no knowledge about the medical equipment. He told them to cut out the most important machine and keep the others that are relatively less important. He comes out with ideas that suggest that he has not practiced clinical medicine for a long time. Second, he has been undermining you by putting the official point of view in such a manner that he does not agree with your policies but he has to implement them. He has also managed to create some problems between you and your few American employees. Lee says he wants to live in better housing like yours, and you are not helping the American employees as you should. Apparently, he invited hospital staff to your villa while you were away. This has created feelings, because your villa is so much nicer then the others.

"I told you before that he was bad news. Really, if you want to achieve good results from the doctors, Lee needs to leave. He is not good for our hospital."

"O.K., Pritima, I will have a meeting with Dr. Mohsin and find out what is going on; meanwhile I would like you not to talk with the doctors regarding this matter."

We had used a highly reputable Canadian search firm to recruit Dr. Buckler. He had come to us with high recommendation. I was aware that he had resigned from his previous position because of what had been stated as a problem with the owner of a private hospital. The incident was pertaining to his treating a patient who had no money and had come to the hospital's E.R. for treatment. Quitting his position under these circumstances gave no reason for alarm. In fact, under the circumstances, his resignation was actually perceived as a positive characteristic.

I called a meeting with Lee that I anticipated would be quite difficult.

"Gordon, I'm sorry but I simply do not agree with what you are saying. This business of my mannerism and my being perceived as arrogant is ridiculous. These doctors are just pissed off because I'm reducing their equipment budget, nothing else. Frankly, Gordon, I am up to my ears with this crap. I am doing my best and if that's not good enough, then I will just leave."

The meeting with Lee was about what I expected. In the end, we agreed that he soften his approach and strive to rebuild his relationships. I made it very clear that this was a serious matter and his continuation as the Medical Director depended upon his ability to turn the current situation around. In my heart I knew he had a blind spot regarding how the physicians and I perceived him. I knew a lot of water had gone under the bridge, and it would be extremely difficult for him to turn the situation around.

Four weeks later, we still had not completed the revised equipment list. The team had shaved about forty-five million riyals, but still had another fifteen million to go.

By now, Saudi ABV had advised us in writing that each day of delay in receiving the revised list would result in three days of delay in completing the project.

The largest potential savings was in the area of the patient monitors. The task force team had done a good job in working with the medical staff to reduce the number of monitors by half and also to switch to Hewlett Packard equipment. The revised monitor package would cost a maximum ten million verses the original twenty four million riyals that had been initially approved. There was one major problem in realizing these savings, and it came with our sister company, Al Hikma.

As mentioned, Dr. Hesham's self interest as CEO of Al Hikma had played a major role in the initial Siemens patient monitor order. Before my arrival, the project coordinator and Dr. Rayes had apparently instructed Saudi ABV to use Al Hikma as the single dealer in securing the order. I am convinced that it had been grossly inflated to benefit Al Hikma. We had already instructed Saudi ABV to cancel the Siemens order. Dr. Hesham, representing Al Hikma, continued to say that the order had already been previously placed with Siemens. According to him, Siemens had specially manufactured the monitors, and they were ready for delivery to Al Hikma and then on to Al-Salama Hospital. Dr. Hesham stated that any cancellation of the order by Saudi ABV would result in a one hundred percent penalty being accessed against Al Hikma, who had placed the order on behalf of Saudi ABV upon the original instructions of the hospital.

Dr. Hesham stated that any penalty accessed against AL Hikma by Siemens would automatically be passed on to Saudi ABV for reimbursement. Saudi ABV stated that they would require the hospital to reimburse to them any penalty they might have to pay Al Hikma for the order cancellation. And so it went.

We bogged down in the situation to the point that nothing was getting done about the monitors. After some six weeks of continued run-around between Al Hikma and Saudi ABV, we were about to throw our hands up in despair.

In conjunction with the private office, we developed a strategy whereby we would reduce the number of monitors and eliminate certain monitor accessories. We would stay with the Siemens brand, but the new order would be for approximately half of the original order. We provided a letter of guarantee to Saudi ABV. If Siemens sued Al Hikma for the approximately twelve million riyals worth of cancelled equipment, and if Al Hikma subsequently sued Saudi ABV for reimbursement, we would reimburse Saudi ABV.

Actually, we believed this whole issue of one hundred percent cancellation fee was a smoke screen being generated by Dr. Hesham. In my opinion, he simply did not want to see the order reduced. Al Hikma was having a very difficult time and was already on the verge of bankruptcy; any additional loss of revenue would certainly not help their situation.

Should we have to reimburse Saudi ABV if Al Hikma successfully sued them, we would use the ten million riyal construction contract withhold monies to honor our guarantee. There was no way we were going to pay any additional money, outside of the withhold money, to Saudi ABV.

In the end, this strategy worked. There was no cancellation penalty accessed by Siemens. They were happy to get verification that half of the original order would now be required and funds would be forthcoming. Saudi ABV did not lose anything. Al-Salama Hospital requested and eventually received a much more realistic order and saved twelve million riyals. Al Hikima ended up with half of their anticipated previous order and descended into bankruptcy a couple of months later.

It had taken about two months longer than what we had anticipated to come up with the sixty million riyals saving in the medical equipment orders. Most of the delays could be attributed to the monitor problem. I felt the task team had done a very good job, and, for the most part, the medical equipment cuts were across all departments and were done in as fair a way as possible.

During this time we had recruited a new Director of Nursing, Rose Stephens, a British nurse with previous experience in Saudi Arabia. Her arrival date continued to have to be delayed due to her failure to receive a letter of no objection from her previous Saudi employer. Some Saudi employers have strict policy that regardless, they will not issue a letter of no objection. Without such a letter, technically an ex-pat has to wait for two years before he can reenter the Kingdom and work for a new employer. This is an extremely unfair labor practice, but works in tremendous favor for the employer. It keeps ex-pat personnel from jumping from one employer to another for an increase in salary. This policy does help control labor cost but at the expense of the ex-pat employees.

An employer's way around this problem is to have the individual secure a new passport. Usually, the previous employer/sponsor will not know this has occurred and that the individual is back in Kingdom. It can become a little risky if the individual is in a high profile position and returns to the same city for employment.

In Rose's situation, she would be coming to a completely new location; plus, her position was not that much in the limelight. In the worse case, if a previous employer discovered that an individual were back in the Kingdom working for another employer, the previous employer could register a complaint to the labor office. The new employer would be liable for a small fine, and the employee would have to be deported.

We moved forward with Rose by suggesting she obtain a new passport. She joined our staff in late June and quickly established herself as a very able nursing director. The hospital had been without one for almost six months.

In the meantime, the situation with Dr Buckler had gone from bad to worse. He looked at me as the individual who was against him and began to show outward signs of resistance and outright insubordination. Simultaneously, I continued to receive feedback from the medical staff that things were not improving. I was still reluctant to give up on Lee. I knew how hard it was to recruit a qualified American medical director.

Two events occurred one after another that made my mind up. At an MEC meeting that Lee chaired, I could sense the tension in the room with the heads of departments and could see they were working against him. That same day I happen to walk into Bill Dunn's (CFO) office unannounced. Lee had his back to me and did not realize my presence. Bill tried to give him a sign with his eyes, but Lee failed to pick it up. I overheard Lee criticizing several things I was doing and, obviously, trying to persuade Bill to support his position against me.

I immediately met with Dr. Rayes to advise him that I was going to ask for Lee's resignation. The nonconfrontational Rayes had become somewhat soft headed, however, and requested that I give Lee more time.

"Dr. Rayes, I usually go along with your recommendations. But this time, I believe we must move forward rapidly in dismissing Dr. Buckler. He is now trying to gather support against me and, more importantly, his relationship with the medical staff is non-existent. I will visit with him tomorrow regarding his resignation."

A couple of days prior to this, I had received a call from one of my American colleagues who was CEO of a new hospital in Dubai, UAE. He was seeking a medical director. I told him about Dr. Buckler and that perhaps he would do well in a new environment.

When I visited with Dr. Buckler the following morning, he asked for additional time. I could see that he was not surprised that he was being asked to leave. I told him about the opportunity in Dubai and that I had arranged for him to visit with the CEO there if he desired. This softened the blow considerably. We worked out a severance package, shook hands, and went our separate ways.

When I look back on what I could have done differently to change the outcome of Lee's appointment, I saw one major thing. Perhaps if I had been present during his initial five weeks instead of off on holidays, I could have provided him the necessary coaching to avoid the pitfalls he encountered.

I also could not help but reflect upon what Dr. P.K. had predicted. I was beginning to believe that she must posses some ancient Indian magic that gave her this uncanny sixth sense. She had been right again!

Immediately, I asked Dr. Mohsin to meet me.

"Dr. Mohsin, I am going to ask you to consider assuming the permanent part-time Medical Director's position with certain provisos. You must be willing to contribute at least half of your time performing the duties of Medical Director. You must be willing to be strong when you need to and not be swayed from making tough decisions. After further thoughts, I think you have the necessary talents and experience working with these physicians to be that bridge between administration and the medical staff. You have had the opportunity to observe Dr. Buckler's strong points, and you should capitalize on those observations. I already know that you can avoid his shortcomings."

I knew that Dr. Mohsin had the respect of the medical staff, and with proper coaching he could carry the ball if he wanted to do so. I also knew that the additional high cost of a full time western Medical Director who was not practicing in the clinical areas was an overhead cost that we simply could not afford at this time.

He accepted the part-time position and performed his medical administrative duties in an excellent manner while simultaneously continuing his neurosurgery practice for the remainder of his time at Al-Salama Hospital.

Other things were changing as well. We again heard rumors that the government was taking over a big part of National Commercial Bank Though only rumor, we understood the implication if it turned out to be true. The NCB was the financial engine behind the Bin Mahfouz enterprises. Unfortunately, during the coming months the rumors turned out to be true.

Early April 1999, I received an important call from A.R. in the private office.

"Hello Gordon, how are you doing? I have already spoken with Dr. Rayes about this matter and I want to bring you on board as well. We have decided that it will be in our best interest if we can find a joint venture partner for the hospital. We might even consider selling it outright or leasing the facility. I want you to make some discreet inquires with your contacts in

America. We need to keep it very low profile and certainly need to keep it from becoming known to the employees. Perhaps we can locate an American hospital company that would be interested in managing the hospital along with having some type of equity position. See what you can find out."

This was not what I wanted to hear. Normally, such actions would come through a hospital's Board of Directors. This was no normal situation. This Board, in reality, played a very secondary role.

I could sense that the philosophy governing the creation of Al-Salama Hospital was drastically changing. The Bin Mahfouz sons simply did not have the same feeling for the hospital as did Sheikh Khalid. They looked at it as just one of the family businesses, one which would probably continue to be a cash drain for the foreseeable future.

Things do change. But even with this altered philosophy, I was thinking that the action A.R. contemplated seemed premature. The new facility was still six months from being completed. We were on the right track, and the operation of the hospital was being refined with new processes being put to work. We had just started to market the hospital in a more aggressive manner. On the other hand, it was still going to be a long road before profitability would be reached. The facility was huge and had very high fixed cost. The non-controllable cost such as utilities, equipment maintenance contracts, and depreciation would continue to be huge.

As requested, I started to make inquiries in the U.S.A. and put together a package of materials to mail out to potential interested parties.

One morning Dr. P.K. called. "Gordon, Dr. Mohsin Hussein's father is seriously ill and has been admitted to the Al Hada Military hospital near Taif."

I had met Dr. Mohsin's parents before, and I wanted to visit him. It was her suggestion that I join her to visit Dr. Mohsin's father. We decided to go early one April morning.

P.K. and I left Jeddah about 6:15 am that morning and arrived still early in Al Hada, a suburb of Taif some two hours south of Jeddah. Mecca was about half way between the two cities. P.K. had never seen that mountainous area before, so we decided to drive around for about an hour before going to the hospital where Mohsin's father was hospitalized.

We were on a two-lane road known as the Al Baha highway about twenty-five kilometers outside of Taif. This particular road was one of the

Kingdom's older asphalt highways. The shoulders were quite steep with many large boulders just off the narrow, steep inclines.

I was following a Toyota station wagon that was full of kids in the back. Both vehicles were traveling about one hundred and ten kilometers per hour. I glanced across at the map P.K. had in her hands for just one moment. When I looked up, the station wagon had locked its brakes. I could see a goat had narrowly escaped being hit. I slammed on my brakes, but could tell I was not going to be able to stop in time before ramming in to the back of that station wagon with all those kids aboard.

In a blink of an eye, I had to decide whether to continue to slide and ram the station wagon, to let up on the brakes and try to maneuver around the right steep narrow shoulder, or to take my chances and go high to the left side into the other lane. I decided to go to the left. To this day, I still believe it was the right decision. If I had slid into that station wagon full of kids, perhaps real tragedy would have occurred. Going to the right I believe would have resulted in going off the narrow shoulder down the incline and perhaps slamming into one or several of the huge boulders that were everywhere.

Suddenly, I saw a Chevy Suburban traveling at a high speed from the opposite direction. It did not give an inch. If only it had given a couple of feet, we could have avoided the accident.

There was a grinding explosion. I could feel myself being thrown forward with my seat belt slamming me backwards. I felt pain in my ribs and left shoulder. My sunglasses flew off my face. I felt the vehicle turning sideways after the head-on collision. Then it stopped. I heard P.K. say, "There is a lot of blood here. Who got hurt?"

I looked over at P.K. and could see that her air bag on the passenger side had inflated. For a split second, it seemed that both of us were uninjured. Then I saw her hands and mouth. I also glanced up to see that the Toyota station wagon, which had slammed its brakes ahead of us, was quickly accelerating and leaving the scene of the accident. The Suburban I had hit was sideways half on the pavement and half off with substantial damage. I quickly had the sinking feeling that the only ones who did not get hurt were the goat, now nonchalantly walking off through the maze of boulders on the opposite side of the road, and the Toyota station wagon that sped off into the horizon.

P.K. had unconsciously tried to protect herself by bracing her hands against the dashboard, which contained the air bag. When the air bag exploded out, it had torn her fingers. Her left thumb and right index finger lay dangling on her forearms, almost 180 degrees opposite her other fingers. Blood was coming from both hands where her thumb and finger had ripped backwards. Her mouth was bleeding.

I tried to open my door, but it was jammed. The engine was still idling roughly, and I could smell gasoline and smoke. The ignition key would not turn the engine off. I quickly disengaged my seat belt and climbed over to the back seat. Those doors were also jammed. I feared the vehicle might burst into flames any moment, and we both would be trapped inside. Knowing I was not hurt except for the bruises caused by the seat belts, I kicked the rear door of the Land Rover open and quickly went to the side of P.K.'s door and forced it open.

By now P.K. was just sitting bent over with both her hands tucked under her breasts. Her mouth looked as though she had taken a right punch from Mike Tyson. I helped her out of the car; somehow, she had put the thumb and the finger back into place and was tightly holding them to stem the blood flow. She stood at a safe distance from the vehicle. I quickly ran to the other vehicle, praying that no one was injured, and was relieved to see that the Saudi family inside the Suburban all seemed O.K. The vehicle was carrying three or four adults and about four children. It was a miracle that none of them appeared hurt even though the left front of the Suburban was demolished. I took a quick glance at the front of the Land Rover and quickly surmised that it was totaled. The way the front of the vehicle had been caved in, I wondered why the engine was not in the front seat. I was also surprised that the vehicle did not catch fire, for the smell of gasoline and smoke was still very strong.

By now other vehicles had stopped and several Saudi men had rushed over to us. One Saudi man in particular took charge and flagged down a passing vehicle. I told this Saudi gentleman that P.K. needed to go to the Al Hada Military Hospital E.R. quickly. A local Bedouin drove the vehicle that was stopped. He and his young son were probably on their way to Taif that morning to buy supplies. The Saudi gentleman who had taken charge instructed the driver where to take us. Also, using his cellular phone he contacted the Taif police and gave them instructions on how to reach the accident scene. He advised me that the wrecked vehicle would be seen to and the police would catch up with me later at the military hospital.

I never saw this Saudi gentleman again, but I was extremely impressed in the way he took charge of the situation and got us headed to the hospital.

Before we got into the Bedouin's car, P.K. reminded me to get our Igamas and travel papers out of the Land Rover's glove compartment.

By now, P.K., although extremely brave, was becoming faint. I was really scared for her as I remembered her dangling thumb and finger. I knew that her bones must be broken for them to dangle like that and was concerned that she might have to have them amputated. They appeared to be hanging on by torn strings of muscle and fiber. Her profession depended on the dexterity of her hands.

We were in the back seat of the Bedouin's car while the son was sitting in the front with his father. I continued to give him the directions the best I could to the military hospital in Al Hada, which was just outside Taif. We hoped that we would not have difficulty in having her cared for at the military hospital; typically it is reserved for the eligible Saudi military personnel. P.K. had worked at the military hospital in Jeddah, however, and Dr. Mohsin's brother was a consultant nephrologists at Al Hada Military Hospital; Dr. Mohsin, himself, had worked here as a neurosurgeon prior to joining Al-Salama Hospital.

We went directly into one of the E.R. examination rooms without any hassle. I was escorted to a waiting area and provided a phone. I was easily able to locate Dr. Mohsin, who was present in the I.C.U. with his father. He immediately came down, and I informed him of the entire ordeal. Very much concerned about P.K., whom he had known for many years, Mohsin went to see her in the E.R. and examined her for any neurological injuries. He established that apart from her hand injuries and missing tooth, no other injuries had occurred. He also inquired about the availability of the surgeon, as it was Friday (equivalent to a Sunday in the west).

We were very lucky that Friday. Dr. Felemban, head of the orthopedic department, was actually in the hospital. He quickly arrived, x-rayed, and assessed the injury; and in short time P.K. was having her hands operated on by this surgeon. I could do nothing but wait for the operation's completion to know the prognosis of her hands.

Dr. Mohsin and I both had waited about two hours in the E.R. waiting area when the Taif police arrived to interview me. Thank goodness, Dr. Mohsin was present, for these policemen knew no English. After about ten minutes of Arabic conversation between the police and Dr. Mohsin, he turned to me to explain what was being said.

"Gordon, they have stated that both your Land Rover and the Chevy Suburban have been taken to a local garage in Taif. Your vehicle is totaled as you had expected. The Suburban has sustained major damage. Fortunately, the passengers in the Suburban had no injuries. Gordon, the police are saying that the cause of the accident is your fault because when you attempted to dodge the vehicle in front of you, you went into the oncoming lane."

Technically, this was correct. At that stage it did not matter that had I plowed into the back of the Toyota station wagon with all those kids, the outcome would have probably been disastrous.

I asked Dr. Mohsin to tell the police that I accept the responsibility of the wreck but to make sure they understand all of the circumstances involved.

Dr. Mohsin continued to speak in Arabic with the police. He turned to me an said that the Saudi family involved in the wreck was asking for forty thousand riyals (approximately eleven thousand dollars) for the damage sustained to their vehicle and they wanted me to pay it now. I asked Dr. Mohsin to tell the police that I just don't normally carry that much money when I go to visit someone in the hospital. He responded that most likely they would place me in jail until I was able to provide the money.

Dr. Mohsin again turned to the police and continued the discussion for about ten more minutes.

He turned to me and said, "You are lucky because of my brother working here at Al Hada; they are going to allow him to put up a promissory note that you will pay the funds. Can you have the funds delivered to the police tomorrow?"

I quickly responded that absolutely I would have the money by the next morning. I would have someone bring the money back to the police tomorrow from Jeddah, or I would come myself if needed.

This seemed to satisfy the police, I was asked to sign several forms, which were all in Arabic. I had no idea what I was signing. Dr. Mohsin told me that basically they stated that I accepted the responsibility for the accident and agreed to pay the amount requested by the other party.

I thought to myself, no insurance forms; no second or third estimates; best of all, no attorneys. It was settled very quickly. Perhaps this approach was better than what ordinarily takes place in America.

If a Saudi had been seriously injured or killed in the other vehicle, blood money ranging from thirty thousand to one hundred thousand riyals could have been required for each victim. Had they been non-Saudis, the legal due would be about one-fourth that amount.

I felt relieved when the police finally left.

Dr. Mohsin stated I was lucky on two accounts. They did not make me go to jail pending receipt of the funds, and they did not ask any questions as why I was driving alone with a female who was not my wife. No matter whether or not a couple works together or has traveling papers from their employer, it is against the rules of the country to travel alone with a woman who is not a spouse. Normally there is no problem until something like this occurs; then all hell breaks out.

It took four hours for P.K.'s operation to be completed. We learned that she was very lucky. Amazingly, she suffered no broken bones. Her thumb and finger joints must be extremely flexible to have survived the injury without severe permanent damage. Dr. Felemban stated to us that he had repaired the torn muscles and nerves the best he could. With luck she would be able to work, but it would take at least three months before she could go back to her surgical duties. He went on to state that he preferred to keep her there in the hospital for three or four days.

Well, at least the news from Dr. Felemban was encouraging. I thought he would be reporting something much worse. I couldn't believe that she had not suffered any broken bones.

While the surgery was in progress, Dr. Mohsin's father passed away in the ICU. This was not unexpected but had occurred quicker than anticipated. It was a very hard day for all concerned.

I had been at the hospital since 10:30 am, and since Dr. Mohsin was to stay in Al Hada overnight to help prepare the arrangements for his father, the hospital arranged for a taxi to take me back to Jeddah.

That evening after I was safely back at my villa, I thought about how extremely lucky we had been. This head-on collision could have taken several lives. Having the expert surgeon available to manage P.K.'s hands had also been a blessing. God was looking after us that day, Al Hamdullilah (thanks be to God).

I called Linda and told her about the wreck. She was relieved that I was okay, but worried about what had happened to P.K. She took all the information and, being genuinely concerned about her, said she would call Pritima at the hospital in Taif.

For the next couple of days, Al-Salama was buzzing. "What was Dr. Kaushik doing with Mr. Gordon" was the common line. There were two reasons for this gossip. First, they were not aware that P.K. had become our family friend. Hospital staff was not comfortable with the close relationship she had with the Bin Maufouz family and now also the hospital's CEO. Second, it seemed that some of the staff still not on board with the many changes taking place saw this mishap as an opportunity to exploit. Most were concerned about P.K., but the incident did provide an opportunity for idle gossip, even though we were only going to visit a colleague's father and have a picnic in the area.

Dr. P.K. was discharged from the Al Hada Military Hospital four days later and was escorted back to Jeddah. During the next couple of weeks, her friends and ex-patients provided her assistance with meals and housekeeping.

About ten days post-surgery, she started physiotherapy and modified the cast, and in three weeks, rather than three months, resumed work. The surgery had been performed perfectly, and her hands healed quickly. She was fortunate, for she had lost none of the dexterity in her hands that is so important for her profession as an ob/gyn surgeon. Today, one can't even see the surgery scars.

She was really lucky. All involved in the accident were truly lucky.

By now, it was late June. Things at the hospital were going fairly smoothly. The Joint Commission International (JCI) had completed their phase one survey with good success. All key staff had been hired. I had sent out several discreet packages of information to U.S. companies regarding Al-Salama Hospital. Very little interest had been shown, however. The cash flow problems continued as anticipated with at least no further deterioration. On a personal note, Linda, Emily, and Mark would soon be en-route for their summer vacation, which I was looking forward to.

Other than having to deport one male chief lab technician for continuing to stalk one of the nurses and dealing with one serious medical liability case at the Ministry of Health, things were continuing to improve at a steady pace.

A British lab supervisor had met one of our South African nurses; the two had developed an emotional and physical relationship that is so common in this type of environment, although considered taboo by the authorities. Single young men and women working closely together away from their families and support groups many times find themselves in these situations. This nurse had found a new boyfriend, and the ex-boy friend, our employee, would not accept it. He continued, despite several warnings, to stalk her for a couple of weeks, even in the hospital. He was an excellent lab technician, but when he tried to break into her flat, we took immediate action and escorted him on board a plane back to his point of origin.

The chief of orthopedics at Al-Salama Hospital was a Saudi physician who excelled in knee arthroscopy techniques. Although a very good revenue producer, he had the personality of a stereotypical orthopedic surgeon. He was direct, blunt, and sometimes rough talking around the nurses.

He used to kid with me and say, "Gordon, hell, how do you expect me to behave around the O.R. staff? After all, we orthopedic surgeons are just fancy carpenters. We all have our standard saws, hammers, and nails. No wonder I raise hell every now and then in the O.R. You ever see a carpenter not get upset and say a few curse words when his nail goes crooked or the wood unexpectedly splits?"

This Dr. Khalid Hassan was a character. He was a red-haired Saudi, which is quite unusual. He seemed to enjoy intimidating people around him, even his own department colleagues. I saw through this façade when he and I got into heated discussions. Actually, we both liked and respected each other.

Unfortunately, his shortcoming was that he was overly aggressive and would not take advice from others.

One of his cases involved an elderly lady who was also suffering from a touch of pneumonia. The pre-operative clinic physician had advised against surgery until the elderly lady's health improved. Dr. Hassan, however, charged forward, basically ignoring the recommendation, and performed a bi-lateral knee operation. Unfortunately, the lady died in the operating room.

I had no doubt that in this particular case, the MOH would find us liable, and we would be required to pay the maximum one hundred thousand riyals (about twenty seven thousand dollars) as blood money. Because of these relatively low liability amounts paid, even in the most liable situations, private hospitals, including Al-Salama, did not carry malpractice insurance on its physicians. We were totally self-insured.

The weakest major department in the hospital was the pharmacy. Time and time again we had problems distributing the pharmaceuticals to the wards. Processes were poor and pharmacy supervision was nonexistent. Even the JCI survey team had commented about the pharmacy's deficiencies, as would King Faisal Specialist Hospital at a later date.

The problem that Dr. Mohsin and I again faced regarding the pharmacy was political. There were actually two individuals in charge at the time. One was an Egyptian professor of pharmacy, Dr. Samir Bayoumi. He was interested in the technical aspect of the pharmacy, but could not manage his way out of a paper bag. He was like the typical absent-minded professor.

The other person in charge was Dr. Siraj Bin Mahfouz, one of the brothers of Dr. Rayes. Dr. Siraj had actually been a student in Egypt under Dr. Bayoumi and had been instrumental in recruiting Dr. Bayoumi to Al-Salama Hospital. Most of the time, the two fought regarding who was in charge. Dr Bayoumi felt the best way to prove who had the better leadership skills was to move to an office on the fifth floor so he could study his pharmacy books. This was about as far away from the pharmacy as he could get. Dr. Siraj felt the best form of pharmacy management was usually simply not to come to work. He could manage from his home.

About the only time these two really worked together as a team was when the pharmacy came under fire by the medical staff or administration. When such occurred, which was really quite often, Dr. Bayoumi and Dr. Siraj teamed up to defend the pharmacy from what they deemed to be preposterous accusations made by the doctors and the CEO. Several times I mentioned to Dr. Mohsin that we needed a new pharmacy manager. He was in favor of Dr. Bayoumi, but sensed that removing Siraj was going to be a political problem.

I also approached Dr. Rayes about the pharmacy problems. He always stated that it was going to be very difficult and expensive to employ a new Saudi chief pharmacist. Dr. Rayes overly protected his younger brother and the professor. Even though the situation was not ideal, I elected to let it ride for the time being until one day Tom Wallace, the American material manager, came to my office for a requested meeting.

"Gordon, we have proof that Siraj is selling our Al-Salama pharmacy items to an independent wholesale pharmacy in Taif. I have been provided pharmaceutical items from that pharmacy that are still in Al-Salama boxes. One of the pharmacists who manages a pharmacy in Taif has indicated that he will testify regarding this matter."

This was a shocker. We knew our pharmaceutical cost was high, but we never expected that our stocks might be partially being depleted through such illegal actions.

"Tom, you know the serious nature of this allegation. You must be absolutely certain that you have necessary proof and that your source of information in Taif won't back down. Before we bring this matter up to anyone else, you must make sure you have hard proof. This implication could have grave consequences if proven correct."

During the next couple of days, Tom gathered additional proof. I had instructed him to go to Taif himself to talk with the informer. Instead, however, he sent his Saudi purchasing manager, Saleh Al-Zahem. This proved to be a major mistake. Dr. Siraj got wind that an investigation involving himself was underway.

Dr. Rayes asked that a meeting be set up with Tom to discuss the investigation. I did not realize that Dr. Rayes would also have Dr. Siraj present. I had decided not to get Dr. Mohsin involved until such time as the investigation was completed. The fewer who knew, the better.

During the meeting, Dr. Siraj accused Tom of slandering his good name and trying to destroy his reputation. Tom and I simply listened as Dr. Siraj angrily continued his assault on Tom. He demanded to know what was going on and what proof Tom had against him.

I interrupted, "Gentlemen, Mr. Wallace is conducting a confidential inquiry that has resulted from information provided by an apparently reliable source. Due to the nature of the investigation, it is very premature that anything be said at this time."

It was obvious that someone had informed Dr. Siraj of what was coming down.

After Tom and Dr. Siraj left the meeting, Dr. Rayes and I discussed the situation in detail. Dr. Rayes knew how I felt about the mediocre performance of the pharmacy. This, however, was a much more serious matter with potential embarrassment to the Bin Mahfouz name.

"Gordon, please wrap this investigation up quickly. Mr. Wallace better have good proof regarding this matter. I personally do not believe that Siraj would get himself involved in such an activity."

"I understand how you feel, Dr. Rayes, especially since he is your brother. With the information Tom was given, the only way to check it out was to pursue it in as confidential manner as he could. Obviously, someone has leaked the information regarding the investigation."

I was upset with Tom that he had not gone to Taif to investigate this matter personally instead of sending his purchasing manager about whom we had second thoughts anyway.

Within a couple of days, everything died down. The informer disappeared and no Al-Salama boxes appeared. Tom was left with absolutely no proof at all that Siraj had been involved in any such activity.

Dr. Siraj demanded a written apology from Tom and threatened to bring suit against him for slandering his name. Dr. Rayes was highly upset with Tom for the way it appeared that he had jumped to conclusions. I was upset that Tom had not taken the matter seriously enough and had really done a lousy job in performing such a confidential investigation when such high potential stakes were involved.

The eventual outcome was a letter of reprimand from me to Tom regarding the manner in which this investigation had been conducted. Tom felt that he had been set up, that I had not supported him. Actually, he did not understand how far I went to keep him from losing his job at that time.

A couple of months later, we were going through a reduction in staff. There was some redundancy in the job description of Tom and of an Egyptian named Adel Farrag. Adel had been with the hospital for many years and was a friend of Dr. Hesham. Adel's primary job was the project liaison officer with the construction company, Saudi ABV. We were going to have to combine Tom's and Adel's job functions into one position. I was somewhat neutral regarding who we should keep and who should be let go.

I really leaned towards Tom for he had been one of my first appointments, and I did not fully trust Mr. Adel. Dr. Rayes, on the other hand, strongly preferred that we keep Adel. Tom was cut loose before he completed his two years contract.

As it turned out, the reduction in force involved the elimination of some sixty-five positions, approximately 6% of the work force. When such reduction occurs, choices have to be made between who stays and who goes. Tom's departure, instead of Adel's, was the direct result of the incident Tom had involving Dr. Siraj Bin Mahfouz.

During this time, my family had been in Jeddah for about four weeks. That summer Mark had decided not to work and spent most of his time relaxing and having a good time. We had taken several excursions outside Jeddah on my one-day off each week. Dr. P.K. usually joined us and was very grateful for our showing her the places in the Kingdom that she had not seen in spite of being here for many years.

Linda, Mark, Emily, and I were planning a great trip to Italy when they were to leave the Kingdom going back to Texas. We planned to see Rome, Florence, and Venice over a period of ten days. Afterwards, I would fly back to Jeddah and they would fly back to Texas.

About a week before the trip, Mr. Safar asked to meet with me regarding a very confidential matter. He showed me a letter in Arabic relating to my vehicle accident in Taif. He had already translated it into English. It was addressed to Dr. Rayes Bin Mahfouz, President, Al-Salama Hospital, from Ali Bin Mohammed Bin Ali Al Hayyan, Head of General Presidency of the Promotion of Virtues and the Prevention of Vices.

The letter stated:

> *"For prolonging piety and devoutness for the benefit of human beings and country and the general interest conceding to God's law we would like to inform you that we were furnished with information that the so called Gordon Utgard -Christian Religion- who works in your Hospital Administration had made prohibited friendship with a female Hindu physician named Pritima Kaushik, an ob/gyn physician who also works at the same hospital. He accompanied her alone in his car to Taif, only God knows what they were up to. They had an accident, which resulted with some fractures etc. for*

your information, inquiry, and response regarding what action will be taken from your side regarding what occurred. May God help and assist you."

I found the letter very amusing and so did Linda. Dr. P.K., who had received a copy, found it quite disturbing. She felt someone from inside the hospital had been responsible for bringing the incident to the attention of the religious authorities. She was furious and called Dr. Rayes, upset with him for sending the copy to her. Dr. Rayes was surprised, as he knew nothing of this letter. That made her unhappier.

"Dr. Rayes, how come this letter is addressed to you and without your knowledge has been translated by Mr. Safar's secretary and distributed to me? I think Mr. Safar has found something to get at me at last. I will prove this to you. I want to go to this office of the Promotion of Virtues and demand on what basis they sent such a letter." She later went to Mr. Safar's office and asked him to take her to the place. He was a little concerned and said they didn't allow women there, a statement which really set her off.

After reading the letter, Dr. Rayes agreed with P.K. that the information and the description showed it was provided from inside the hospital. The office in Mecca would not have these details, especially regarding the religion, unless provided by someone else.

P.K. said, "Dr. Rayes, I have always told you that my enemies cannot get me on my profession, but they will try on my religion and my being a single woman."

Dr. Rayes and I simply constructed a return letter that informed the religious office that Dr. Kaushik and I had gone to Taif with a travel permission letter from the hospital to visit the sick father of one of our esteemed physicians. We never heard another peep.

I was sure that the religious office had been informed by one or more disgruntled hospital employees (current or ex), who were hoping, as it were, to kill two birds with one stone.

Dr. P. K. and I had a fairly good idea who the culprit was. But the best thing to do in this matter was to ignore it. The incident does demonstrate, however, the length that some people will go when they feel insecure or threatened.

As a matter of precaution, I did start changing my routine, such as the route I drove to and from the hospital. I also routinely checked under the vehicle for anything that might appear suspicious.

In mid July, the family left for the two weeks in Italy. We had a great time exploring Rome and the romantic city of Venice. We enjoyed Florence the most with its beautiful cathedrals and countryside. We traveled from city to city by train, which was much more fun than taking an airplane or having to negotiate directions with a rented automobile.

After a truly splendid holiday in Italy, Linda, Mark, and Emily returned to Texas, and I returned to Jeddah.

Chapter Eight

Day of Rest (Fridays)

"All work and no play makes one dull and gray."
Unknown

The work week of most private business in the Kingdom is six days. Al-Salama Hospital was no exception. Government offices and the ministries work five days a week, but almost all other businesses work six.

Fridays in Saudi Arabia correspond to Sundays in the West. The mosques have sermons from the Quran on Fridays just as our churches have services from the Bible on Sundays.

With the exception of my last couple of months of work, I took only Fridays off during the week. Being a Christian, I did not attend the Friday services held in the mosque. Since churches are not allowed, I did not attend religious services. I guess I was kind of like the kid who was always going fishing on Sundays back home. I thought I had a good excuse to play hooky on Fridays, so I used them to explore the Arabian natural landscape.

The Kingdom of Saudi Arabia has tremendous natural beauty and plenty of raw adventures for those who seek it. Areas within 250 kilometers from Jeddah offer varied experiences. Most of the areas require only a day trip. Some require longer.

One of my best early decisions involved selecting a company vehicle, one that would be available for both my business and personal use. I debated over several different types of vehicles, but ended up selecting a Land Rover Discovery. This four-wheel drive vehicle could go almost anywhere.

Another good fortune was being introduced to a paperback book, *Desert Treks from Jeddah*, written by British expatriate Patricia Barbor. I used this inexpensive guide on many Fridays while living in Jeddah and highly recommend it to anyone living in Jeddah who enjoys discovering new things and has some sense of adventure. There is a similar guide regarding treks from Riyadh, which is located about 1200 kilometers east of Jeddah in the interior of the Kingdom.

Most of the adventure excursions mentioned in Barbor's book, I have taken. Some of my favorites I have done several times. When my family was in the Kingdom, they would usually accompany me; and, of course, my friend and colleague Dr. P.K. joined us. Ordinarily, we also had at least one other vehicle traveling with us, but there were times when we didn't. From a safety standpoint, it's always good to have more than one vehicle on such adventure excursions. Besides, it allowed friends to accompany us. Some of the trips described here were fun and more adventurous than we bargained for!

Besides the vehicle excursions into the desert and mountains, there was always the Red Sea with its fantastic diving, snorkeling, and fishing.

Without question, I took maximum advantage of all the great natural beauty within Jeddah's surrounding areas on both land and sea. Considering I had only one day off per week, there is no way that I could have experienced more of the great outdoors of the Kingdom. Being able to get away to these natural resources on my day of rest allowed me to recharge my batteries and face the next week of work with a refreshed spirit. Those particular Fridays when I simply relaxed around the pool with the neighbors were nice, as long as they didn't occur too often. If I didn't get out and about on Fridays, the following week I never felt as refreshed as when I had elected to take some type of adventure excursion into the Kingdom or to the Red Sea. My family, including my parents, all enjoyed it tremendously. Our friends who joined us were also quite keen on these trips.

One of the closest locations and one of my favorites is Moon Mountain, Al Maqar. It's only about one hour and fifteen minutes from North Jeddah. I did not even need a four-wheel vehicle for this getaway.

Moon Mountain is a huge rock surrounded by a rocky landscape that gives it a lunar appearance. The climb up to the top of Moon Mountain takes about twenty minutes. It is somewhat steep in places, but for those in decent health, the climb to the top is no problem. Once on the top, there is a nice flat area for picnics or overnight camping. The view is spectacular in all four directions from the top of the mountain, a good two hundred and fifty meters high. I enjoyed several absolutely beautiful sunsets from the top of Moon Mountain. We regularly carried our Kentucky fried chicken and cold drinks up with us and enjoyed an evening picnic watching the sun go down into the desert far away. Several of my friends have been there with me. Once we went in a big group and had an excellent barbecue dinner under the full moonlit sky.

Another one of my favorites is Harithi Mountain located near Al Hada on the way to Taif. This excursion is an all-day affair with travel to the top of an escarpment and then on to Harithi. This area is about two and half hours south of Jeddah. The drive is outstanding with the climb up the escarpment an adventure in itself. I marveled at the engineering required to build this road. From the bottom of the steep escarpment to the top represents about 2,200 meters. Harithi is, indeed, one of the outstanding excursions, especially during the summer as its altitude makes it fairly cool.

We usually left Jeddah about 7 am and returned home shortly before dark. Once at Harithi, we always spent at least a couple of hours exploring the area and climbing the mountains that overlooked the escarpment below.

My first trip to Harithi has a very special meaning to me. I had gone with Linda and Steve and Allison Martin, who died about eighteen months later from breast cancer.

The Harithi trip always put a severe test to the Land Rover. Once the driver leaves the asphalt highway outside of Al Hada, there are about eighteen kilometers of the roughest and steepest road imaginable in Saudi Arabia. I never failed to be surprised at the way the much lighter Toyota four-wheel drive pick-ups negotiated these roads, even better than my Land Rover.

When we finally did reach Harithi, we parked the vehicle and headed to the top of the Camel Trail. Although less than one kilometer, the walk was quite rough. Supposedly, this was the area where the camel caravans of long ago traversed the escarpment carrying their goods to and fro. The view from this area is always magnificent. If there is any location left on earth where dinosaurs would still roam, it has to be in this area. It looked just like a scene out of the movie *The Lost World*. We saw no dinosaurs, but it is home of the fairly large and quite strikingly beautiful blue lizard. We also usually saw baboons scampering up the mountains ahead of us.

From the top of the Camel Trail, we could reverse our tracks over to one of the large, steep mountains. This area was already the top of the escarpment; thus, these mountains represented the backside peaks. Once we negotiated the thirty-minute climb to the top, the other side provided a view of the desert and wadis (river bottoms) some 2,200 meters below. Some of the vertical cliffs on the other side were literally thousands of feet straight down. We invariably saw several eagles soaring high above against a dark blue, cloudless sky. Harithi represented my favorite day-trip out of Jeddah.

On one such excursion, my son Mark and I were driving back to Harithi on that treacherous stretch of bad road. I had let Mark drive, or I should say inch, the Land Rover along to get to where we had to go. We only had about one more kilometer remaining when the vehicle's engine just quit and would not restart. At the time we happened to be down in a gorge.

There was no choice but simply to hike out. After about three hours, we came across one of those Toyota pickups. The Bedouins generously drove us to the highway and from there about another eight kilometers to the Sheraton Al Hada Hotel.

I knew the general manager at the Sheraton, who assisted us every way he could. He sent the hotel's maintenance engineer to fetch a wrecker to pull the Land Rover out. I knew that was not going to work. The only thing we managed to do was get the wrecker marooned as well. The only way to ever get the Land Rover out was to fix it on the spot and drive it out. Otherwise, the vehicle would simply become another landmark in Mrs. Barbor's treks book.

The GM at the Sheraton secured us a cab; Mark and I arrived back at my villa in Jeddah about 9 pm. I was really concerned about how we would ever retrieve the vehicle. The next day Mark, a couple of mechanics from the hospital, and one from the Land Rover dealership went back. I was glad that I had several appointments that Saturday and thus a good excuse why I could not go along.

They finally diagnosed the problem as a faulty fuel pump. After a couple of trips back and forth into Taif to secure the necessary parts, they fixed the vehicle. The Land Rover and Mark got back to Jeddah at 10 pm that evening, *Al Hamdullilah.*

We visited several wadis, most being about two and half hours from Jeddah in all three directions. There was Wadi Khulais, Wadi Mur, Wadi Milh, Wadi Rhyssan, Wadi Turbah, and Wadi Liyab. Each of these, which are essentially dried riverbeds between mountains, has its unique characteristics. Some have running water most of the year. Some have orchards of palm trees and fig trees and other various fruits. Some have old Turkish fort ruins waiting to be explored. Most have lots of camels; all, plenty of hiking. A couple of the wadis are known as natural bird sanctuaries where a set of binoculars and a little patience yield great results for those inclined to watch birds.

One of my favorites is Wadi Khulais located only about one and one half hours from Jeddah. As visitors approach the wadi, to the left, perched high upon the string of mountains completely covered with lava stones, is a large old Turkish fort. From the vantage point of the fort, one can see up and down the entire wadi. It must have been easy to defend against invaders who, in days gone by, might be trying to scale the mountain to overtake the fort.

There was one particular part of Wadi Khulais we enjoyed the most and where we frequently ended up for picnics after exploring other parts of the wadi. This particular campsite has nice palm trees that mark the beginning of a dry creek bed that runs between steep cliffs perpendicular to the main wadi. At some time or another, a roaring river must have gushed through these narrow ravines to carve out the canyon where the riverbed is. We could almost imagine the cool waters tumbling over the boulders in the fast moving stream; an image that was nice to contemplate during a hot day. Once, during the rainy season, the water was flowing so deep that it was not possible to cross the river. We were astonished to see the sight and had to turn back. It was also a splendid place to search for rocks of all shapes and colors. I made a very nice rock collection of small stones from the dry riverbed.

My parents liked their visit to this wadi a lot. To start with, we went for a walk to look at multi-colored rocks in the riverbed; then we collected the wood for our open campfire, which we enjoyed very much, and had our barbecue under the starlit night. Both parents were glad they made this trip to Saudi Arabia to see the variety of landscapes in this desert country.

Looking up the steep cliffs from the bottom of the riverbed, we could see different layers of stone from pink marble to dark granite. It was a spectacular location. P.K. and I had gone with my son Mark to this location previously and had done a more extensive hike over these same mountains.

One Friday morning, P.K. and I decided to travel to Rabigh Beach, about one and half hours north of Jeddah. I had secured a scuba tank the night before and was going to do a shallow shore dive off Rabigh beach. Another couple from our compound joined us.

While I was diving the coral reefs, the others were searching for shells along the beach. This particular beach was quite nice for it was secluded, clean, and easy to negotiate through the swallow waters out to the edge of the reef where the deep blue started and where the best snorkeling and diving was located. It was just far enough away from Jeddah that it was never crowded, yet was not too time consuming to reach.

After I had completed my dive, we were looking at our *Treks from Jeddah* book and decided to go to Wadi Mur, only about forty kilometers away. The four of us set out.

Wadi Mur was about seventeen kilometers off the main road and was a little difficult to find the first time. I mistakenly turned into the wrong riverbed and proceeded about 2 kilometers. I could see that the sand was soft, but the Land Rover's four-wheel drive was pulling well. Suddenly, the track disappeared, and before I knew it, we were bogged down. The Land Rover had sunk in the sand to the point that the bottom of the vehicle was resting upon the surface of the sand. All four wheels of the car continued to turn without our going anywhere. We were badly stuck.

This was a very hot day, and on Friday there would be no one around to help.

After we dug the wheels out of the sand, we gathered all the branches and dry twigs that we could find. I also used my towels and picnic rugs to place under the wheels to try to get better traction. All of these things were not getting us unstuck. As a last resort, I let most of the air out of all four tires so they had no more than about twelve pounds of pressure. We tried to dig the tires out once again, then placed the branches, towels, rugs and just about whatever else we could find under the tires. This time I was successful in breaking the Land Rover loose. Here is where having another vehicle along could have been a great help. We had been lucky. We had plenty of water, but to have to walk out of there in the middle of a hot day in the desert would not have been fun. It was adventurous, all right!

We slowly drove back to Rabigh where I aired the tires back up and bought petrol. We looked in our book trying to see where we had gone wrong and decided to try again. This time we went further down the highway about half a kilometer and then turned off on a well-traveled track that was described. We continued to follow this about seventeen kilometers, and suddenly we saw the running water of Wadi Mur. It was a delightful sight. I had a swim in the cool waters of Wadi Mur on that hot day.

This particular wadi has large farms of date trees. The river that runs through that wadi always has water. There are also some interesting old ruins where perhaps some of the early Bedouins once lived. Fortunately, the day's outing turned out to be a delightful success. Interestingly, after a major storm the same small river was some seven meters deep and a hundred meters wide in November 2000 when I went to see it for the last time. At that time, the amazing roaring waters reminded me of the Colorado River.

The trip to Wahba Crater is about five and an half hours from Jeddah and is definitely a two-day excursion. We went there two times, the first with Linda and the second time with my parents and P.K. We were all amazed to see the size of it. It is a remarkable site and a must trip for those living in Jeddah who enjoy such outings.

My excursion with Linda turned out to be most adventurous; we got lost on our way to the crater some thirty kilometers into the desert. It was getting hot. There were lots of tracks in different directions and no one in sight. Suddenly we saw a shepherd. We stopped to ask the Bedouin, but he did not seem to know about the crater which meant we were probably far away from our destination. Linda was noticeably worried. It was now extremely hot. At times the sand was blowing, and we could not decide whether to go ahead or to return. We looked at our book again and decided to explore another site in the same area, the ruins of old Muwayh. These ruins are actually of an old Turkish fort built towards the end of the last century. It once garrisoned those who manned the numerous watchtowers seen on the hills around the fort. Lying in the desert, this dark gray, forbidding ruin is surrounded by remains of old mud houses.

Two generations ago King Abdul Aziz Bin Saud refurbished it for his own use, adding a majlis (a long row of marble seats around his throne in the center where followers could set and partition the King directly). He used the place after he went to Mecca for the Hajj as a hunting lodge, inviting parties to hunt gazelle and other game, and falconers to pursue birds such as partridge and houbara (buzzards).

A four-wheel drive is a must for this trek as is navigation by a reliable compass reading. Tourists attempt to stay on the most traveled track, but as usual there are several tracks that fork off in one direction or another.

En route there were a couple places where the white desert sand met the base of hills several kilometers in the distance. There appeared to be a large lake of blue water in the horizon. Of course, as we got closer it disappeared before our eyes. The mirages were so realistic; I can easily understand how stranded desert travelers might crawl in vain towards the elusive, cool blue waters ahead.

I had decided that after just a few more kilometers if we could not find the palace, I would turn around and simply backtrack out to the main highway. Even that would have been a little difficult.

We came upon a Bedouin camp at precisely forty kilometers into the desert. There was an old Bedouin woman covered with the traditional black abaya standing outside one of the tents. She really stood out against the white sandy background and monotonous colors of a bright day in the desert.

We were able to ascertain from the old woman that the fort was only about one kilometer straight ahead.

Once we reached the old fort, we explored for a while. Linda and I sat on the old throne and took pictures. We then settled down in the shade of the ruins and enjoyed our picnic lunch; we were starving. When we left the fort, we decided to travel to Wahba Crater by way of an old salt marsh. Opposite the main entrance of the fort is a large flat area of crusted salt. We left the fort and traveled in a westerly direction on a track that led us through a huge lava bed and an amazingly large, dried up salt lake. Natives say that after a rainfall (very unusual) when the water dries up, it leaves the salt deposit that is quite crusty. If the ground is wet beneath the salty crust, it can be treacherous for vehicles.

We continued to travel along the track for another forty kilometers before we could see the town of Al-Hofr. The Wahba Crater is located nearby.

By the time we reached the crater, we only had about half an hour before dark to explore.

The Wahba Crater, said to be the largest of its kind in western Arabia, is a spectacular and impressive sight. Bumping along the sandy plain from the southwest offers no view of any crater for miles. Suddenly, the ground rises ahead, necessitating a sharp turn or resulting in a plummet into the heart of the crater. The rising ground is the encircling lip of the crater and no harmless small hill as it first appears.

The crater is 2 kilometers wide, and the cliffs drop steeply some 260 meters to a flat base, in the center of which is a huge saltpan half a kilometer across. The cliffs are broken on the northeast edge by a few more gentle gorges, the only area where one can safely descend to the bottom of the crater. This part of the crater has tall palm trees and long, luscious green grass, an extraordinary surprise in such a harsh landscape.

There has been much speculation as to the origin of the crater. One theory is that it was caused by the impact of a meteorite. The more shared theory is that it was probably a volcanic eruption. The crater lies in an area where there was intense volcanic activity in the past. The surrounding sandy plain is, in fact, a bed of volcanic ash.

The vast eruption that must have occurred, according to geologists, was probably caused by water seeping down into the underground chambers of hot molten rock with the subsequent steam causing a huge subterranean explosion. The cooling and contracting thereafter left this immense hole. It was an astonishing sight.

By the time we got back to Jeddah, it was past 1am in the morning, and we both were exhausted but satisfied to have had a memorable day.

P.K. and I had been planning a trip to a place called Marble Mountain in search of what is known as "the last birqat," the Arabic word for water hole. We asked our group of friends to join us.

Marble Mountain itself is a good place to visit and is about two and a half hours from Jeddah. The mountain is composed entirely of pink and white marble and protrudes by itself out of the desert. On a moonlit evening the White Mountain appears quite eerie. About one-fourth of the mountain has been excavated with the remaining left untouched. I had been to Marble Mountain twice before.

A famous, ancient pilgrim road, known as Darb Zubaida, runs from Baghdad to Mecca. Parts of this road may have been in use in pre-Islamic time, but it was future wealthy philanthropists who firmly established the road and provided necessary facilities for the caravans of pilgrims traveling to Mecca. The best known of these benefactors was Queen Zubaida from whom the road took its name.

Queen Zubaida was the favorite wife of the fifth Abbasid Caliph, Harun ar-Rashid (786–899 AD), reputed to have presided over a sumptuous court at Baghdad. We know him from "The Arabian Nights."

Queen Zubaida was renowned for her piety and generosity. At her instructions wells were dug and water cisterns and shelters built on the Zubaida Road. These served the many pilgrims traveling the road to Mecca with hundreds of camels or simply on foot.

Queen Zubaida gave orders that each birqat should be no further apart than one day's march, probably about 20 to 30 kilometers.

Several weeks before, Linda, P.K., and I had gone on an expedition in search of the last birqat at Al-Madiq. This birqat is on the famous Zubaida road and only twenty-five kilometers from Mecca. It was quite easy to find for it was only half a kilometer off the winding two-lane highway between Jamoum and Taif.

On this particular trip we had decided to attempt to find the next birqat at Al Aqiq and then the third at Al Khuraba. According to the map there was a short cut if we went to Marble Mountain and then continued on the gravel road on to Al-Aqiq. We estimated that the distance between Marble Mountain and Al-Aqiq would be about eighty kilometers. If we took the highway first to Taif and then on to Al-Aqiq, it was more than twice as far. We estimated that the time would be about the same, but the back road should prove more adventurous.

This particular Friday morning, we were four people in the Land Rover. We left Jeddah at about 6:30 am and arrived at Marble Mountain about 9 am. After a brief stop at Marble Mountain, we started down the gravel road in search of the birqat at Al-Aqiq.

The road continued to deteriorate and was mostly composed of lava rocks about the size of hen eggs. We could only travel at about ten, maximum fifteen, kilometers an hour. It was going to take much longer than we had originally estimated.

At precisely forty kilometers from Marble Mountain my left rear tire went flat. In the two hours it had taken us to get this far, we had not seen another vehicle, not even a white Toyota pickup.

This was the first time that I had changed a tire on the Land Rover, and I discovered that there was some problem with the jack. After an hour and a half, I finally managed to get the flat tire off and the spare on. There still had been no vehicle pass us on this road during the entire time I was wrestling with the tire and jack. Fortunately, on this day in late November, the weather was not that hot.

By now it was 1 pm. The best we could tell we were right at half way. We could either continue on or turn around and go back. If we had another flat we would be in serious trouble. Still, we decided to push onwards.

The road continued to get bumpier with larger rocks, thus causing us to go even slower. After about twenty kilometers more, we came to a fork in the track. It was impossible to say which way we should go. Both tracks were equally traveled in appearance. The map we had showed no fork. We gambled and stayed to our right.

The landscape was extremely rugged with lava rocks spread in all directions. There were small hills and ravines and larger mountains appearing in the horizon probably sixty kilometer away. The only vegetation was thorny bushes and occasional sagebrush. The day itself was striking with an absolutely gorgeous blue sky.

Suddenly, I heard that sickening sound of thump, thump, thump. The spare tire had been punctured.

We were now in a bad way. We would simply have to wait for a passing vehicle, which might be some time, as we had not seen one vehicle in over four hours since we had left Marble Mountain. My best judgment was that we were about fifteen kilometers from Al-Aqiq, assuming we were on the right track. Looking in all four directions, I surmised the nearest town could be a hundred kilometers away. We were truly in the middle of nowhere.

I jacked up the Land Rover and took off the punctured spare tire, swearing that if I ever saw civilization again, I would replace all tires with the best and most expensive ones there were.

By now we had been waiting for about an hour; the time was approaching four pm.

In the far distance, a small cloud of dust appeared to rise from the desert. The cloud continued to get closer and closer. It had to be a vehicle and this had to be the only track around—I hoped.

In the desert on a clear day, one can see forever. Perhaps the vehicle had not yet reached the fork in the road. It could very well bear to the left away from us. We were lucky though, for it turned to the right.

After about another ten minutes a white Toyota pickup was visible heading towards us. When it stopped, the two young Saudis inside quickly saw our dilemma. We realized that they were local Bedouins and they were going to help us.

We took the tire and all got into the back bed of the pickup; then, off we went. I had no idea of where we were going. After about two kilometers, the pick up turned off the main track and proceeded for about half kilometer to the location of the Bedouin camp.

There was a small tribe here, probably five main tents altogether. Several goats and camels were nearby, and a couple of children were playing outside the tents. No doubt we were the first outsiders that had been to their camp in some time. Two other Toyota pickups were parked near- by.

Of course, living in the wilderness as they were doing, tribe members had to improvise when it came to things like flat tires.

They had a very crude but effective method of breaking the tubeless tire off the wheel rim. Taking a spare inner tube, of which they had several, they inserted it inside the tire. They then managed to force the old tire with the new inner tube back onto the wheel rim. A gas generator provided the power to air up the tire.

I suspect that most flats in this area are the direct result of a sharp rock puncturing a tire. Now, this aired-up expanded inner tube covered the puncture hole in the tire. We threw our fully inflated tire into the back of the pickup. Before we left the camp, they insisted that we have a glass of hot tea and some camel's milk.

The two young Saudi males then drove us back to the Land Rover and helped us get the tire back on. They also assured us that the town of Al-Aqiq was only about fifteen kilometers straight ahead. That news in itself was a relief to know.

The whole episode from the time they picked us up until we were back in our Land Rover traveling again took only about one hour. I really don't know what we would have done without the help of these gentle desert people. The Bedouins have a reputation for hospitality and assistance to those in need. I had experienced it not only in this particular situation but a couple of other times that had been a little less dramatic.

As we progressed towards Al-Aqiq, I hoped that the tire would hold up. It would not take much to puncture the inner tube inside the tire. We could see the town of Al-Aqiq ahead. About two kilometers from the town the same tire went flat again. This time we did not have to wait long before another Toyota pick-up came by and took us, plus the flat tire, into Al-Aqiq.

I planned simply to purchase another tire regardless of the cost. We would be taking the highway back through Taif and then on to Jeddah. No way would I have transversed back the way we had come.

Al-Aqiq is a very small town with only two service stations available. They did not have the tire size necessary for my Land Rover. Thus, they performed the same ritual that was done by the Bedouins by placing a new inner tube inside the tire. As long as I kept my speed down going back to Jeddah, it should be okay since the road was asphalt all the way.

While waiting, we found out that the birqat at Al-Aqiq we had hoped to reach was only about three kilometers up the highway in the direction we would be traveling. We had come this far and were determined at least to find one of the two birqats that we had originally set out to find early that morning.

The birqat at Al-Aqiq turned out to be an extremely pleasant stop with large trees and pools of cool water. Green grass covered the slopes of the birqat. We only had about half an hour before sunset, but felt a sense of accomplishment in having finally reached our intended destination. Our picnic tasted especially good after all that hard work.

At just about midnight, we were back on the main Mecca super highway some thirty kilometers from Jeddah. I had only been traveling about seventy kilometers per hour because of the way the tire had been fixed.

Suddenly, boom! The repaired tire blew out. God was with us again that evening for the blowout occurred only about two hundred meters from a large service station. I limped the Land Rover to the service station and purchased a new tire.

The following day, I had four top of the line Goodyear Eagles placed on the vehicle and one as a spare.

Fortunately, most other Friday adventure excursions did not turn out to be major ordeals. But this experience illustrated why it is always a good idea to do such excursions with one or more other vehicles along.

I would not recommend trying to visit both the palace at old Muwayh and the Wahba Crater on the same day as we did. The maps show that they are fairly close to each other, but the distance is very deceiving. We ended up not being able to spend enough time at either location to explore thoroughly.

One of my last desert excursions, and one of best, was planned with the intention of going back to Marble Mountain to see it under a full moon.

P.K. and I left for Marble Mountain at 3:15 pm with an expected arrival at about 5:30 pm. About halfway there we noticed large clouds building up over the mountains in the direction we were heading. At this particular location we were traveling through a large flat desert area with mountains on all four sides separated by probably fifteen kilometers of desert.

The approaching storm whipped up the winds, and we found ourselves in a blinding sand storm. I had to pull off the highway, for we literally could not see the front of the Land Rover. I turned the emergency blinkers on, and we waited for the winds to subside. Just as quickly as it had developed, the sand storm went away; we proceeded towards Marble Mountain.

As we got into the mountains heading towards the town of Madrakah, the sky ahead of us now turned dark blue. Suddenly, the sky opened and we found ourselves in a torrential rainstorm. A few minutes previous to this, I had stopped along the road to attempt to take photographs of the magnificent lightning display. The sun shining brightly to our back and the dark blue storm clouds hanging over the mountains in front of us produced a beautiful sight, with a full rainbow to boot.

Because of the rapid runoff of water, flash floods are common in the lower wadis. Roaring rivers quickly develop in what only ten minutes previous is a dry sandy riverbed. Each year in the so-called rainy season (November through January), inexperienced campers find themselves in danger, trapped by the rapidly rising waters. It really does not rain that often, even in this time of the year. When it does, however, flash floods are common and can be quite dangerous.

Because of the rising water in the lower wadis, we did not make it to Marble Mountain. We pulled over along the side of a roaring river rushing through the desert valley. By now the rain had stopped, and it was almost dark. We watched the lightning bolts dancing across the sky and listened to the booming thunder. In two hours we had experienced a blinding stand storm, torrential rainfall, and raging rivers, complete with a magnificent lightning display followed by the thunder's sound effects and a full rainbow against the mountains in the background. It was a fantastic experience. My photographs have captured some of these wonders of nature.

This was a unique adventure that I am sure few expats have experienced. Even the Bedouins don't get to witness the magnificence of nature's display of power that often.

The following day we decided to travel to Wadi Khulais to see if it had rained there. As we were traveling to the wadi, there appeared to have been no rain. The track was as dusty and dry as ever. We were disappointed at not seeing any water, but as we got further into the wadi, suddenly we could see that water was roaring through the old riverbed. It must have run off this side of the mountain range as a result of the previous night's storm some eighty kilometers away.

We went through a small tributary as we advanced into the wadi until we came to the main riverbed. At that point the water was about one hundred fifty meters wide and flowing at a high speed.

We pulled off the main track and enjoyed our customary picnic lunch. I had never seen this wadi with this amount of water gushing through it. Almost the entire valley was filled with flowing water where only a few days ago it had been completely dry.

When we finished the picnic and our limited hiking, we turned the Land Rover around and started back out the way we had come in. Unknown to us, the water had been on the rise. What had been a small flow of water crossing the road coming was now flowing quite rapidly about fifty meters wide. I took a chance and plowed forward. The trustworthy Land Rover went through moving water about one meter deep. Fortunately, it did not stall and made it to the other side of the river. If we had been another fifteen minutes, I am afraid we would have been marooned until the water subsided.

Again, we did not reach our planned destination, this time the far end of Wadi Khulais. Like so many of the excursions, however, it was not necessarily the destination that mattered so much as the adventure along the way. What we saw was beautiful.

All these places were true adventures and became a big part of my life in the Kingdom.

Just as exciting as the desert treks, but a completely different natural environment was the Red Sea with all it had to offer, from simple sunsets while parked at the Cornish after a busy day at the hospital to boat excursions some forty-kilometers out where we dove the reefs.

The Red Sea is a remarkable area for diving and snorkeling. Many say that, excluding the Great Barrier Reef off the coast of Australia, the Red Sea is the best in the world.

There are many old shipwrecks waiting to be explored. The offshore reefs (referred to as the five-mile reef) have huge canyons of colorful coral with great numbers of fish. For those not certified to scuba dive, simple snorkeling can offer almost as much pleasure.

Fishing is also quite good. Most of the occasions when I hired a boat, I did a combination diving/fishing trip. When Mark was in the Kingdom, he always went with me on these Red Sea excursions. Diving excursions with my son will always be very special to me.

For those not interested in an all-day sea trip, snorkeling and scuba diving can be done right off the shore up and down the Kingdom's western Red Sea coastline. Divers wade out into knee-deep water some 50 to 75 meters to the edge of the reef. From here, the reef drops vertically from 30 to as much as 120 feet straight down. Plenty of fish and beautifully colored coral are easily visible on these simple shore dives and snorkeling excursions. From time to time sea turtles and large Moray eels appear right next to shore, and occasionally a reef shark swims by. It is very easy, and dangerous, to go too deep too fast in the amazingly clear, blue waters of the Red Sea. The deepest I went, by accident, was close to 200 feet and that because I had not monitored my depth gauge adequately.

During my time in the Kingdom, I took full advantage of my one day off each week. I'm sure some day in the distant future the maze of photographs that I have taken will bring back waves of nostalgia concerning my adventurous jaunts to the natural resources offered by the Kingdom. Unfortunately, most expats never take advantage of the opportunities there in the desert and at the Red Sea. Of course, these adventures occurred before 9/11 and other recent world events. Many of these excursions might very well be too risky in today's Saudi environment.

Long after I have forgotten about my experiences as CEO of Al-Salama Hospital, what I will remember most about my Arabian experience will be what my five senses provided to me during these adventures taken on the "day of rest."

Adventure to Wadi Liyab

Valley Beneath Harithi Mountains, near Al Hada, on way to Taif.

"Day of Rest"

Ruins of Old Turkish Fort—Wadi Mur

Caravan of Camels, Wadi Mur

Chapter Nine

Chosen Few

"Pride goes before destruction, a haughty spirit before a fall"
King Solomon

September 23, 2000 was the 70th anniversary marking Saudi Arabia's unification by King Abdul Aziz Al-Saad. Present day Saudi ancestors came from the Qatif region and settled in the historic community of Diriya, located in the middle of Wadi Hanifa in the Northwest corner of Riyadh. The founding of Saudi Arabia was the culmination of the fusion of powerful tribes that championed the course for religious correction.

From the beginning, the Arabian Peninsula was the heartbeat for the flourishing civilization between Egypt and Mesopotamia. Its history goes back as far as 7000 B.C. Arabia was known as the Cradle of Civilization. This region was the focal point for the trade in silk, ivory, spices, and other goods to and from the Mediterranean countries. Merchandise from the Indian Ocean was brought to Arabia where ships unloaded at Aden. From there, camel trains transported goods to markets in the western Mediterranean, Egypt, and Mesopotamia.

By 1792, the Saudi Puritan Islamic call had extended its domain to cover most of the Arabian Peninsula. Such vast expansion of the Islam became worrisome to the Ottoman Empire in Constantinople, the modern Istanbul. The loss of the holy cities of Mecca and Medina meant a loss of prestige and income to the Ottoman government, a decisive factor in their desire to undermine the progress of the Saudi state.

In 1901, Abdul Aziz Al-Saad captured Riyadh in a fascinating way by tricking authorities into allowing Abdul Aziz followers into the heavily guarded city. The demise of the Turkish ruler Ajlan, who was ruling Riyadh at the time, was the beginning of a new era under the formidable unifying power of Abdul Aziz. By all accounts, Abdul Aziz was a unique and great man. In 1945, Franklin D. Roosevelt, after meeting the ruler, who at that time was 65 years of age, had this to say about the man. "Abdul Aziz is a true servant of the Almighty, strong as a lion, straight as a scepter, beyond cavil, the greatest of living Arab rulers."

The Turks continued to lose their grip on Arabia under the dynamic rising star Abdul Aziz. Following World War I, Britain was a dominant force in the area. The King, known in the West as Ibn Saud, used his wisdom and political genius to obtain necessary help for liberating those parts of Arabia that were still under Turkish rule.

The movie *Lawrence of Arabia* provides excellent scenes of the region and a good description of how help from abroad was employed in the many battles with the Turks.

Britain and France, however, seemed determined to limit the new unified Arab state of Saudi Arabia to self-rule. The United States declared its support for self-determination. King Abdul Aziz admired President Roosevelt as a leader who represented a powerful and rich country that cherished democracy, justice, freedom, and dynamism. An atmosphere of understanding and rapport quickly developed between King Abdul Aziz and President Roosevelt.

Abdul Aziz foresaw the awakening of a new American giant on the horizon of world affairs even as British power and influence on Arab matters were in decline.

American oil interests gained momentum with the knowledge that vast oil wealth lay beneath the barren desert of Saudi Arabia. Because of mutual interests, in 1943, President Roosevelt declared that defending Saudi Arabia was of vital interest to the United States. The British looked upon the developing relationship between Saudi Arabia and the United States with suspicion and disapproval.

Abdul Aziz was always careful not to antagonize the mighty power of the British. He was a wise man, a man of principles. At the same time, he was smart and shrewd in his dealings with the British. He knew how to handle them despite their sometime problematic policies.

For those who desire a more detailed account of King Abdul Aziz and the unifications of the country, the book *Saudi Arabia—All You Need To Know* by Dr. Nasser Ibrahim Rashid and Dr. Esber Ibrahim Shaheen offers a wealth of information to anyone truly interested in learning about the history of the Kingdom and its modern day advances.

Saudi Arabia is a monarchy. Its official name is the Kingdom of Saudi Arabia, in Arabic, "Al Mamlaka Al-Arabia Al Saudia." The Holy Koran is the constitution of the land and Sharia is the Moslem law. At the conclusion of year 1999, the Kingdom celebrated its one hundred year anniversary.

The King of Saudi Arabia is known as the custodian of the two holy mosques. The Crown Prince, or Deputy Prime Minister, assists the King. The cornerstone in Saudi governmental policies is the majlis, an institution whereby anyone can petition the Saudi leaders. In theory, the leaders are all accessible to the populace. The application of Sharia sees that action is swift and strict. This approach makes the Kingdom one of the safest countries in the world.

At least weekly in the Arab News or Saudi Gazette run headlines such as "Rapist Beheaded in Riyadh"; "Drug Runner Executed in Hafr Al-Baten"; "Egyptian Loses Eye for Blinding Co-patriot"; and so forth. Perhaps the West could learn a lesson from the Kingdom on how to administer quick and effective punishment to offenders. Their system does make for a major deterrent to crime or to those that might be pondering an illegal action. It also cuts through the minutia that has bogged the legal system down in the West. The overabundance of American lawyers would not tolerate such a system in America, however. The downside of such a system is that due process and point of law is sometimes overlooked or even non-existent within the Kingdom.

Government actions in Saudi Arabia are the decrees of the Royal Family. There are no citizens of Saudi Arabia, but instead, followers of the Royal Family who rule the Kingdom. Upon the death of King Abdul Aziz Al-Saud in 1953, his successor was his son King Saud. King Saud's brother Faisal then became King in 1964 upon Saud's abdication. King Faisal did not live long enough to see the fruits of his labor. He was assassinated in March 1975. His successor was his brother King Khaled, a straightforward man who loved the desert and treasured Saudi traditions. When King Khaled died in 1982, the Kingdom's industrial revolution and educational transformation were well underway. King Khaled's brother, Crown Prince Fahad, became the new King. Fahad has been the ruler since that time.

King Fahad is the current head of the Royal Family, which numbers about 5,000 persons. Like any other group of people, they have their goals, aspirations and problems. The Crown Prince under King Fahad is his brother Abdullah with the third in charge Deputy Crown Prince Sultan, who is also Minister of Aviation and Defense. Fahad is known to be in poor health. Tradition dictates that Crown Prince Abdullah will be the next King—probably before too long.

Modern Saudi Arabia reflects the tremendous wealth that has come to the country so quickly. In just a period of about thirty years, the Kingdom has been transformed from basically a poor desert country to one of the richest in the world.

The government understands the importance of diversifying the economy. Oil accounts for over 70% of all revenues. Because of recent strong oil prices, the gross domestic product for year 2000 was estimated at 169 billion dollars. Government revenues were anticipated to be about 70 billion dollars. In 2001, the government ran its first budget surplus since 1982. The overall gross domestic product growth during 2001, a healthy 8%, was largely attributable to the high growth in the oil sector. As of the publishing date of this book, $60 plus oil is providing the Kingdom great wealth, even though maybe only for a relative short period of time.

A major problem facing the Kingdom is the high unemployment rate of Saudi males which has reached over 20 % for those in the 20–29 year old age group. Some 110,000 Saudis are coming into the work force each year with only about 40,000 finding jobs. Per capita income of typical Saudis, once on a par with that of the U.S., has fallen to about 7,000 dollars, less than a quarter of America's. The saudization of positions traditionally held by expats must and will accelerate.

The need for diversification is well understood by the Kingdom's rulers. With oil representing such a high percentage of all the Kingdom's revenues, an economic bust may well occur the next time oil prices head south. Only five years ago the price per barrel was about 10 dollars. In mid 2005, it reached 60 dollars per barrel. These types of gyrations must be offset by diversification into other industries.

Wealth or no, the aging of the Saudi leadership is not good for the future. Since the death of the Kingdom's founder, King Abdul Aziz Al-Saud in 1953, all four subsequent rulers have been chosen from among his sons. Twenty-four of these sons survive, but most are in their 60s and 70s.

Crown Prince Abdullah is undoubtedly thinking about the eventual need to pass the leadership to a third generation of princes more in tune with modern times. There has been a lot of talk about the need for privatization of government run enterprises such as Saudi Arabian Airlines. Discussion about joining the World Trade Organization, building the tourist industry, and taking steps to entice foreign investments are under way. The rulers want to lure back the hundreds of billions of dollars that Saudis have stashed off shore. If this new direction in Saudi Arabia can truly be implemented and sustained, it will have enormous implications for both the country's immediate neighbors and the wider world. The Kingdom could become a source of capital and an economic engine to help reinvigorate the region. Failure could eventually usher in a new cycle of instability.

My limited experience reveals that while Saudis pay lip service to privatization and competition in the Kingdom, the government monopolies don't want it. Most of these state monopolies, such as Saudi Arabian Airlines and the telecommunication industry, even ARAMCO, have become liabilities stifling competition and discouraging investment.

The extreme wealth of certain Royal Family members does not go un-noticed. Fabulous palaces that stretch for half a kilometer in all four directions are common. It seems many of the Royals have such palaces in several cities throughout the kingdom. Many Saudis resent this ostentatious life style. Also, the intrusion of Royal Family members into certain private organizations is not the recipe for increased foreign investment.

Depending on rank and clout, each Royal Family member draws a stipend from the government. The minimum is about 3,000 dollars per month. Opposition groups say the royal stipend expenditures consume 40% of the entire government revenues each year, which if true would equal about 28 billion dollars in year 2000 alone. Others say the percentage is much less than this. Even more controversial, however, is the involvement of family members in commandeering land, taking over private businesses, and taking commissions on large contracts. Such practices have helped some Royal Family members assemble fortunes totaling billions of dollars.

In May 2000, gangs of Saudi youths clashed with the mutawas (religious police) in Riyadh. The arrest of a religious leader in a rural province near Yemen led protesters to fire on the home of the district governor, a member of the Royal Family. About the same time, news of a Saudi Arabian Airliner hijacked en route to London by some Saudi nationals claiming government repression was quickly silenced by the government. In a sign of unease, authorities have stepped up public executions, albeit that most of these have been for rape, murder, and drug trafficking. Since the events of 9/11, the situation has deteriorated greatly. Most of these recent incidents have been well documented and need no elaboration. The rise of the al Qaeda network and followers of Osama Bin Laden, with their extremist view of the world, have created urgency for changes to take place quickly. At least now the Royal Family understands the seriousness of the situation and readily admits that something must be done to curb these extremists.

The writing is on the wall. Many Saudi nationals resent the tremendous wealth that has been concentrated among the chosen few. There have been simply too many stories of one or two Royal Family members flying their 747 Jumbo aircraft over to the US or Europe for fabulous excursions and weekends where gambling losses total into the millions. It doesn't take many rotten apples in the barrel to spoil the whole lot.

Simultaneous with these excesses among the elite, locals are everywhere besieged by poor, handicapped beggars in desperate need.

As long as oil prices remain high, the overall economy will do well. Ex-patriots make up almost 35% of the population. These individuals would not be here if, financially, it was not worthwhile. With the recent kidnappings and other terrorist activities, however, many are now reconsidering their stays. At the same time, the majority of nationals are not happy with their standard of living and concerned with its slippage over the past several years. Continued high unemployment and the potential for major gyrations in the economy because of the present limited industry diversification are issues that could cause widespread unrest in the not too distant future.

It is my impression through many articles I have read and comments I have heard that Crown Prince Abdullah has avoided at least some of the trappings of wealth that other members have succumbed to. He is known to fly first class on Saudi Arabian Airline instead of reserving the whole aircraft for himself when his immediate family goes on a holiday. He seems to have a better understanding of the value of money and the responsibilities that come with it. He seems genuinely to care about the general population and their welfare.

Crown Prince Abdullah's attempted opening of Saudi Arabia is bound to be a slow and cautious process. The events of 9/11 have certainly slowed the process down. But despite the Saudis' conservative nature, sometimes infuriatingly so, they have come a very long way in a very short time.

The chosen few have an enormous responsibility on their shoulders. They should be quick to discipline family members who sometimes exploit their wealth and power for direct personal gain. They must also be quick to punish those radical Islamic clergy members who are encouraging extremist activities. Fortunately, they have a powerful political role model to look up to for guidance and wisdom in the founder of the country, King Abdul Aziz Al-Saad.

Chapter Ten

The Mirage

"As I grow older, I pay less attention to what men say.
I just watch what they do."

Adren Corregie
(August- December, 1999)

When I returned to the office after the Italian holiday, rumors were flying. Supposedly, a very wealthy Saudi businessman from the eastern province of the Kingdom was interested in buying Al-Salama Hospital.

My inquiries concerning a partner or a buyer in the U.S. had generated little response. Most of the U.S. private hospital companies were consolidating operations, not growing them, especially outside the U.S. The issue had not resurfaced. Frankly, I thought that perhaps A.R. had decided such action was premature. At least, that's what I hoped.

I visited with Dr. Rayes regarding the rumors of a potential buyer.

"Gordon, you know that the family has changed its position regarding the hospital now that Sheikh Khalid is not that involved. A.R. has told me that there is an interested party in the eastern province. That is about all that I have heard. He will be handling any such discussions himself. We will probably be the last ones to know."

The hospital Board of Directors had a regularly scheduled meeting in a couple of days. I mentioned to Dr. Rayes, "I hope Sheikh Sultan will be at the Board meeting. Perhaps he will be able to provide some type of status report."

"Don't get your hopes up. It's my understanding that Sheikh Sultan has a diving excursion planned somewhere off the coast of Africa. I doubt that he will make the meeting."

The hospital staff was buzzing. Doctors stood in the hallways in small groups discussing what scenarios might occur if the hospital was sold. Productivity was slipping and focusing on providing quality services was difficult.

The word on the street was that 1.8 billion riyals (480 million dollars) had been offered and A.R. and an unidentified Saudi businessman were negotiating the deal.

The Board meeting was completely consumed with speculations of what the outcome would be. The hospital was not even completed yet. What would happen with the gentlemen's agreement between Saudi ABV, the construction company, and the Al-Salama owner? A thousand such questions surfaced with no answers available.

Then as quickly as the rumor started, it stopped. I never received any information from A.R. that would either confirm or deny the rumors that had occurred during that two-week period.

About a week later in mid August, Dr. Rayes had just come back from visiting with A.R.

"Gordon, I have additional news. King Faisal Specialist Hospital and Research Center in Riyadh (KFSHRC) may be interested in some type of affiliation. We are unclear as to what type of affiliation they might have in mind. They wish us to pull together resumes of all of the physicians, head nurses, lab and x-ray technicians, and key administration staff as soon as possible and forward them to Riyadh."

"Dr. Rayes, you know how productivity has ground to a halt a couple of weeks ago with the last rumored buyer. The staff is going to be bewildered when we request them to update their curriculum vitae for KFSHRC. This type of thing is extremely disruptive to our operations. I know we don't have a choice, but perhaps it is time that A.R. addresses the Board and employees regarding his intentions."

Dr. Rayes agreed and was to ask A.R. about conducting such a meeting with the Board and the employees.

By this time, almost all communications between A.R. and the hospital were conducted through Dr. Rayes and visa versa. It seemed as though A.R. was beginning to distance himself from the hospital. I did not like what I was feeling, but there was little I could do about it.

Rose Stephens, the Nursing Director, was doing well. She had proven to be a "hands on" clinical nurse who was communicating with the physicians. The Filipino nursing personnel appeared to give her their full support; thus, nursing services were improving daily. Some of the U.S. and Canadian senior nursing personnel were a little uncomfortable with her rather formal British personality traits. She required all of her staff to address her as Mrs. Stephens and expected them not to wear an over- abundance of jewelry, which might suggest that they were anything other then the hospital's angels of mercy. As far as I was concerned, such discipline was quite positive.

One morning in early September, Mrs. Stephens came into my office.

"Mr. Utgard, I believe we have a narcotic problem in our surgical I.C.U. The pharmacy has stated that the use of pethidine has increased dramatically." Pethidine is a medicine that is distributed in sealed vials and given by injection.

After a thorough investigation, we discovered that one of the new South African nurses was the guilty party. She was taking the pethidine vials and replacing the pethidine with water; she then very cleverly heated the tip of the vial to the point that the needle puncture hole would close. Some patients were receiving injections of the distilled water while she was injecting herself with the pethidine. No wonder certain post-surgical patients were complaining of severe pain in spite of the pain killer injections. The vials come in standard numbers within each carton. She only performed this substitution on a small, random number of vials in each carton. Pethidin was a drug of choice when a patient complained of pain. When the first injection did not control the pain, a second injection, this time the real drug, would be given.

Once we had sufficient information, Mrs. Stephen and the personnel director confronted the nurse with the data. She confessed to what she had done.

We could have reported her to the government authorities, who would have immediately placed her behind bars most likely for several years, perhaps even given her the death penalty. In the interest of the hospital's publicity and for humanitarian reasons, we just quickly escorted her to the airport with a one-way ticket back to South Africa.

The hospital's financial problems remained the same even though the controllable expenses were being reduced. We had eliminated some sixty-five staff positions, some of which were high cost physicians who were low producers. The overall effect of the reduction was about half a million riyals savings per month. Our revenue per inpatient admission and outpatient visit was a little less than we had originally budgeted. This was due to the increased pressure by the insurance companies to save costs and because more and more cash patients were now being covered by the insurance schemes. While Saudi Arabian Airlines now considered the Al-Salama Hospital its facility of choice, we simply could not get the company to pay down its growing outstanding receivable.

With the airline's being a government entity, we found it difficult, if not impossible to turn its employees away. There were certain things that could have been done to discourage these patients from coming to the hospital. We simply were not as aggressive in applying these types of measures as other private hospitals.

Because of the lavish nature of the Al-Salama Hospital, we got more than our fair share of royal patients. They tended to be problematic patients in almost all aspects, especially when it came to paying their bills.

Princes Maha, the sister of Prince Naif, head of the Ministry of Interior, was admitted to Al-Salama Hospital in the early fall of 1999. Our gastro-interologist, an American Board Certified physician, was going to be working side by side with a world renowned G.I. physician Princess Maha had requested from Johns Hopkins University Medical Center in Baltimore.

Her entourage visited the hospital before her admission, meeting with Dr. Rayes and me. We assured them that all details of her treatment and stay at Al-Salama would be handled with the utmost care.

They requested the entire first floor of the VIP building. Each of the VIP floors contained nine suites, each group of rooms priced at about 2500 riyals per day. They outfitted the Princess's suite with all new drapes, carpets, pictures, and other amenities. The Princess's servants had all furniture replaced with dark black, soft leather chairs and sofas. We had to store all of our furniture on the fifth floor. Each day, the Intercontinental Hotel catered the food for the Princess and her entourage. Two Rolls Royce's were always parked just outside the VIP lobby for their use. She had her own security personnel stationed on the first floor. There were never fewer then twenty or thirty servants on the floor at all times.

The surgical procedure she had was fairly routine and progressed well. I visited her at least every other day. Although her English was poor, we got along well. I believe she truly liked me and did appreciate the attention the hospital's CEO was showing.

She ended up staying in the hospital for almost thirty days; I believe she liked Al-Salama better than her palace. An average length of stay for the type of procedure she had was about seven days maximum.

At our daily early bird meetings Mrs. Stephens always gave us an update on the Princess's health status; then, we would jokingly speculate on how much longer she would be with us. When she was finally discharged, it was a glorious day. There was much fanfare as the entire entourage and the Princess left the hospital. One of the last things she did was to donate to the hospital all the leather furniture she had brought in. Her medical bill was just under two million riyals.

Unfortunately, we were not getting paid by her palace for the services we had rendered. We had received a special letter of guaranty on file from one of her close friends prior to her admission to the hospital. Upon discharge, she had given explicit instructions not to send the bill to her friend, but rather to her business manager, which we did.

The primary problem of collecting funds that are owed by such Royals is that the hospital is required to deal with their business managers. One can never approach a Royal directly with any expected success regarding an outstanding payment. The business manager typically requires some type of cut before he will release any payment. And that was when payment was actually made, which was not very often.

I mentioned to Dr. Rayes, "I wonder how much we can get for all that black leather furniture Princes Maha gave us? We need to convert the furniture into cash so that we can pay our bills." We both laughed.

It was the same situation with Saudi Arabian Airlines, only on a very large scale. The airline allowed our staff to use its housing accommodations and provided them airline tickets that would go toward offsetting the receivables. With the amount of receivables that Saudi Arabian Airlines had with Al- Salama Hospital, we could have free airline tickets and free housing for the next ten years. What we really needed to do was to hijack a couple of its Boeing aircraft. Perhaps if we got a good price, it would come close to liquidating their receivables.

After some nine months, amazingly, we were successful in collecting most of Princess Maha's receivables.

The early bird meeting was held each morning at 8:15 am and generally lasted about thirty minutes. The Medical Director, Director of Nursing, Support Services Director and Night Duty Manager all attended. We went around the table and communicated important events that had occurred during the past twenty-four hours. I was briefed regarding VIP admissions and any unusual or significant events. If any deaths had occurred, they were reported. These early bird meetings proved to be an excellent communication tool. I then had information regarding the previous night's activity to pass on to Dr. Rayes when he arrived at the office, usually about nine am. I kept him well informed of VIP admissions and discharges, for his most significant role lay in serving as the Saudi patients and families' liaison officer.

In late September word came from Saudi ABV that our executive suites were ready for occupation. We had had our office in the temporary porta-cabins since my arrival almost a year and a half earlier. The new offices were lavish, and we quickly forgot about the modest offices and facilities we had been in for so long.

Dr. Rayes's office was huge. It was probably three times larger than what was really required. We had an executive conference room that was situated between my office and his, a location that worked out very well. Saudis are really impressed with spacious offices. They believe they must have such lavish offices, complete with tea boys, to receive guests and visitors. My office was not nearly as large as Dr.Rayes's, but just as lavishly decorated. Such lavish decorations and excessive space clearly demonstrated why this new hospital had cost so much.

One morning Dr. Rayes, a couple of other staff physicians, and I were informally meeting in the executive conference room. In came Dr. P.K. holding Dr Ashy's newborn girl all wrapped up in a pink blanket.

All of us men were goggled-eyed over the beautiful infant. Dr. Rayes and I took turns holding the baby before returning her to P.K.

Then as P.K. stood smiling and rocking the baby happily in her arms, she stated, "See that old man there," pointing at me, "he is the one who fired your daddy."

At that very moment, I saw the little baby frown, and I thought I heard her growl. It was probably some other noise I heard, for P.K. had quickly scooted out of the room.

This was a typical action by Dr. P.K. We all had come to expect the unexpected when it came to her.

The finance and marketing / business development departments were working closely with a large multi-specialty clinic known as the Dallah Group. This company cared for about 40,000 lives in Jeddah and had been using several local hospitals when their enrollees required inpatient care. The Dallah group was a large Saudi conglomerate and actually owned hospitals in Riyadh and another city in the Kingdom, but not in Jeddah. For several months, we had been in discussions with Dallah about some type of exclusive arrangement for their inpatients needs. Dallah was quite enthusiastic about this, for their clientele would like to be able to use such a splendid facility as Al-Salama Hospital. We also saw this as an opportunity to use our extra bed capacity.

The two parties had reached a tentative agreement that Dallah would be provided the entire fifth floor of the OPD tower. This floor contained two nursing stations with about thirty private rooms on each unit. The deal that had been worked out was that Dallah would lease one of the thirty bed units regardless of whether or not if they had patients. The daily rentals would cover our routine nursing services, house keeping, security, dietary, and other basic services. When these Dallah patients required diagnostic tests or surgery, we would give them such with a 30% discount off our usual and customary fee. The other nursing station was going to be rented and used for outpatient clinics and administration space. We anticipated this arrangement could provide more than a million riyals per month. This would go a long way in solving our cash flow needs, as a large percentage of these monies would be provided in advance each month.

At the same time the KFSHRC interest seemed to be rapidly heating up. The primary contacts we were working with were Directors Dr. David

Morehead and Dr. Saade Taher. These two KFSHRC senior officials were beginning to spend considerable time in Jeddah.

In a key meeting at Al-Salama, Dr. Rayes and I listened as Dr. Morehead stated what they were interested in.

Dr. Morehead began, "Gentlemen, we understand that you would like to know the extent of our intentions and what we have in mind. First of all, both Dr. Taher and I understand how disruptive this type of thing can be for your staff. We understand the importance of communications so the employees can function properly in such situations."

Over the previous three weeks, the entire hospital had been buzzing with rumors about KFSHRC's coming and taking over the place. With each passing day the tempo increased; very little information was being provided. I spent many hours each day assuring the staff that we would pass the extent of their intentions on as soon as we were informed.

A.R. and the private office had provided no information. It appeared to me that A.R. was giving KFSHRC complete freedom to evaluate the situation and decide what type of affiliation it desired.

Dr. Morehead continued, "We have a customer (King Fahad and senior Royal family members) who spends half its time in Jeddah. We have highly trained specialized physicians in various Jeddah palaces. These physicians are not being used. You have a unique hospital that happens to be located where we have a need. You also have extra bed capacity in the VIP bed tower and throughout the hospital. Your radiology department is only operating at about fifty percent capacity. We believe that we can develop a unique strategic collaboration where we will parlay each other's strength. This has the potential to be truly a win-win situation."

I responded, "Dr. Morehead, this is exactly what Dr. Rayes and I were hoping for. We do have location and extra capacity. Such collaboration with KFSHRC would be a tremendous marketing tool for us. Plus, the additional revenues generated by using the extra capacity would be great. We have high fixed cost. Additional use will have a small impact on our fixed costs. This additional revenue will only have limited incremental variable costs associated with it. Your plan sounds splendid at this point."

Dr. Morehead added, "We wish to place a project manager and a small staff on site immediately. Their task will be to review your operation and to see how best this affiliation can take place. We will send our consultants into the lab and pharmacy to work closely with your staff in this evaluation process. We ask that you provide necessary office space, furniture, and phone lines. We will provide the rest. Even if nothing develops as a result of this evaluation, you are going to be the recipient of several million riyals of free consultation services."

I stated that I was sure that we could arrange what they needed and asked when he wished to start.

"We are under orders by the Palace to have a recommendation within one month. We must start immediately. I would suggest that Dr. Tahar and I address your full staff in a presentation as soon as possible. I understand fully well the productivity issues and the poor morale that rumors can create. We will talk along the lines of a strategic collaboration between these two excellent health care organizations parlaying what each has to offer."

Dr. Rayes and I both agreed with Dr. Morehead and Dr. Taher that such a staff presentation needed to occur very soon.

We thanked both gentleman for the information they had shared and their preliminary plan on how they wished to proceed. Dr. Rayes stated that he would advise the owner immediately regarding this matter and if he had no objection, we would be ready to move forward rapidly. Rayes then turned to me and asked when I thought we could have the staff presentation.

"Gentlemen," I replied, "assuming we receive conformation from the private office, I would suggest at 1:30 pm tomorrow. We need to get this information out to the staff as soon as possible."

After the departure of the two senior KFSHRC officials, Dr. Rayes and I then reviewed what had been said. We both were elated at the prospects this would provide. KFSHRC's leasing some of our extra space and using our services could really help our financial picture. We would also be able to market this affiliation; probably the best marketing that could be done. Not only would we be having business from KFSHRC, but also our private business would increase because of the excellent reputation that both organizations enjoyed. It appeared, based on what Dr. Morehead and Dr. Taher envisioned there could not have been a more positive development for Al-Salama Hospital.

"Gordon, perhaps we need to place a clause in the Dallah contract that states if for some reasons the fifth floor of the OPD tower is required because of this affiliation, their agreement becomes null and void."

"Let's not do any thing yet, Dr. Rayes. We have a saying in Texas, "one bird in the pan is worth two birds in the bush." The Dallah deal is almost in the pan. Let us see what develops with KHSHRC before we say any thing at all to Dallah."

Dr. Rayes got the approval from the private office to move forward. I scheduled an all-key staff presentation for the following day. I was sure that the auditorium would be filled completely with the staff squeezing to get inside. Everyone was acutely anxious to hear what these two gentlemen had to say.

Between Mustafa and me, we managed to contact almost all staff members whom we wished to invite for the presentation that same afternoon.

During the following morning's early bird meeting, however, Dr. Mohsin was quite disturbed. He mentioned that he had never experienced anything like this. He went on to say that many of the Al-Salama physicians were quite worried and felt that KFSHRC had something up their sleeve. He had heard a rumor that in Riyadh KRSHRC was very much over- staffed and perhaps they would send their physicians here to replace ours.

Mrs. Stephens was also very concerned. It was a known fact that in Riyadh KFSHRC had insisted on having almost all western nurses. She commented that the Filipino nurses were extremely worried. She was worried herself for they might want to have their own Director of Nursing.

I tried to quell their fears. "What both gentlemen told Dr. Rayes and I yesterday was extremely positive. It appears they simply wish to lease a couple of floors of the VIP building, which are empty at this time. We would sell them our diagnostic services such as lab and radiology. Such an affiliation would be an outstanding marketing tool to attract more private patients to Al-Salama Hospital. The ability to tie in with their medical telemedicine communications services could provide tremendous educational benefits for our doctors and nurses. All I can say is that we have to believe what they tell us until proved otherwise."

The KFSHRC in Riyadh is, indeed, a world-class hospital. It was created almost thirty years ago for the purpose of serving the members of the Royal Family and other dignitaries such as ambassadors and key Saudi commercial families. It is also a place where the Ministry of Health can refer their patients when special tertiary care is needed. The Royal Commission works directly for the King and his royal cabinet. The KFSHRC is funded almost exclusively by the Royal Commission and serves basically as a subcontractor to the Royal Commission.

Over the years this Riyadh hospital continued to grow in size, stature, and cost. Because of the direct funding by the Royal Commission, it was known to pay some of the best salaries and to attract the best talent from around the world. It was never seen as a threat to the private sector; this was not the mission of the KFHSRC.

In recent years as the Royal Commission started to cut back on funding as a result of government deficits, KFSHRC tried to make up some of the lost revenues by creating medical outreach services that could be sold to the private sector. Education programs and second opinions through their telemedicine were available to the private sector for a price. Such revenue generation replaced only a very small part of what was being cut back by the Royal Commission. Still, these medical outreach services were definitely worthwhile and fairly well received by the private sector. Al-Salama Hospital had come close to signing an education training contact with KFSHRC the year before, but had decided upon the JCAHO initiative instead.

KFSHRC was well known to be low in productivity and efficiency. The facility was grossly overstaffed with relatively highly paid individuals.

As a result, KFSHRC found itself with the problem of having to reduce expenses and somehow generate additional non-government revenue. Being required to have a presence in Jeddah would also require additional funding that probably would have to come out of the hospital's Riyadh budget.

It appeared that most of the senior Riyadh staff from KFSHRC realized this and were not that excited about the Jeddah initiative. Dr. Morehead had simply responded to the demands of the Palace, which was the organization's primary reason for existence. At least, this is what he had said.

He reported directly to Dr. Anwar Jabarti, who was the official liaison between KFSHRC and the Royal Commission and the Palace.

At 1:30 pm the auditorium was overflowing. We had to ask some of the late arrivals to wait outside. I had also invited the hospital Board members, who all had special seating behind a long podium that faced the audience. Sheikh Sultan, our Chairman, was not present. This obvious lack of involvement by the private office continued to bother me.

I called the meeting to order.

"Good afternoon. I wish to thank each one of you, and especially our hospital Board of Directors, for attending this important meeting. I would like to introduce Dr. David Morehead, Executive Director Medical and Clinical Operations at KFSHRC in Riyadh and Dr. Saade Taher, Medical Director. As you all are aware, over the past several weeks we have been involved with KFSHRC in coming up with ideas regarding how we can work together to the benefit of both. Yesterday, Dr.Rayes and I visited with these gentlemen, who presented a preliminary plan of how they see a formal affiliation developing. What I heard yesterday was exciting and will, I believe, be extremely beneficial for the future of Al-Salama Hospital. Without further ado, I will now turn the podium over to Dr. Morehead and Dr. Taher. After their presentation, they will attempt to answer any questions you might have."

Dr. Morehead took the podium. He thanked Dr. Rayes and me for arranging the meeting and thanked all present for their attendance. He mentioned that KFSHRC was extremely excited about the possibilities of affiliating with Al-Salama Hospital. He complimented Al-Salama as a remarkable facility with a reputation for excellence in private healthcare that was growing every day.

Dr. Morehead continued, "In a nutshell, what we desire to do is to develop a strategic collaboration that parlays each other's strengths. You have location and excess capacity. We have a customer group who spends half the time in Jeddah and desires to have health care services available here. We also have necessary resources to accommodate their request. We believe such collaboration will allow us to accommodate the Royal Family desires and will help propel your practice of private medicine.

"We have some preliminary ideas regarding how to proceed, but it is premature to discuss them now. Dr. Rayes and Mr. Utgard have very generously provided us necessary office space in this building to open up a KFSHRC project office. During the next month, you will see many of our personnel in most all disciplines rotating to your hospital from Riyadh. The objective will be to work very closely with your various department heads and their designees in coming up with a formalized plan of how best to execute this strategic collaboration. Dr.Taher and I are under orders to bring a plan approved by Al-Salama Hospital and KFSHRC back to the Palace within one month. We all have a mammoth task ahead of us to meet this deadline."

Dr. Morehead went on to speak about the importance of communication while this plan was being formalized. He pledged, with Dr. Rayes and my approval, to provide to the staff a weekly briefing of the status of the project. He stated that he hoped to be able to address this audience next week at the same time.

After Dr. Morehead's presentation, the podium was opened for questions. The Al-Salama physicians have never been known for their shyness. Several very pointed questions were asked of Dr. Morehead. To one degree or another, all questions centered on the following response given by Dr. Morehead:

"Let me make it absolutely clear that we have no intentions of becoming involved in your private practice of medicine. We have no intentions of becoming involved in any of your supplier contracting or hospital operational processes. In absolutely no way will we be involved in Al- Salama Hospital personnel issues. You are going to be the benefactors of our best personnel in almost all disciplines visiting with you during this next thirty days. You should look upon these individuals strictly as consultants; they have absolutely no line authority. All of these KFSHRC visitors will be reporting to our Project Director that will be on site in the next couple of days. Your management has also committed to appointing one individual as a liaison with our Project Director. If any particular problems are at issue, these two individuals will solve them on site or bring them to the attention of Mr. Utgard and me for resolution. Let me repeat—read my lips—we view this as a strategic collaboration parlaying each other's strengths."

The presentation had the desired outcome of communicating the present situation. But it greatly escalated the speculation of how all this was going to turn out. I had to keep reminding my direct reports that they had heard the same thing I had, and this was totally consistent with what the two men had stated to Dr. Rayes and me the day before.

We decided that Mr. Safar Abu Milha would be the Al-Salama liaison with their Project Director. Mr. Safar was a Saudi and a member of the senior management team. It made sense that we should use him in this capacity.

Early the following morning, Dr. Rayes had just returned from visiting with A.R. He mentioned to me that A.R. wanted us to be fully cooperative with KFSHRC. It was no longer necessary to have discussions with any other parties regarding a joint venture relationship, lease, or sale. We needed an escape clause that allowed us not to lease to Dallah the fifth floor of the OPD tower, depending on how this strategic collaboration developed.

I had no problem canceling any further joint venture discussions. As far as I was aware, there were no other discussions in process. At least from the U.S. side, there had proven to be little interest.

I was, however, concerned about the Dallah contract. They were ready to move ahead rapidly beginning the first of October. Any such stipulation might very well lead them to postpone the contract date until we had a clear picture of the KFSHRC affiliation. We really needed those additional two million riyals per month that the Dallah contract would generate immediately.

After I contacted Dallah, it became quite evident that they were not interested in having such an exclusive arrangement if there were any possibilities that the deal might be canceled. After all, they would have burned their bridges with the other participating hospitals. They felt it best to postpone the effective start date of the contract until January 1, 2000. Surely by then, a clear picture would be present which would determine whether or not the fifth floor of the O.P.D. tower was still available for Dallah patients.

As far as I was concerned, this was the first major casualty of the planned affiliation. By postponing this Dallah contract, we would lose at least five-six million riyals during this time.

I was also personally contemplating a certain loss or at least a sharing of authority with Dr. Morehead. He undoubtedly would have to become more and more involved. Any such true strategic collaboration would, indeed, affect our operational processes. But sometimes one has to give up something to gain more. Based upon all outward evidence and declarations, this arrangement with KFSHRC could be extremely beneficial to Al-Salama Hospital over the long term. Anyway, this was how the owner desired us to proceed and that was that.

KFSHRC appointed a very well qualified and professional Saudi as their Project Director. Suliman Al-Salama had started his career with KFSHRC as a pharmacist. Over the years, he had moved up into the more senior level management positions. They obviously had a lot of confidence in Mr. Al-Salama to assign him this importance task. He and his small semi-permanent project staff were on site within a couple of days. The only negative thing about this individual that I could tell was his last name. "Was this an omen of what was to come?" We all joked.

The entire month of October and most of November was a rush of activity. At times there were twenty-five to thirty KFSHRC key department heads at our hospital gathering information. The common joke contemplated how they could allow so many staff to be here at Al-Salama in Jeddah and still keep their Riyadh hospital operational.

Dr. Morehead and Dr. Taher's weekly commitment of addressing the key staff of Al-Salama with status report activities was taking place about every second week. I could feel myself taking more and more of a back seat to these two KFSHRC officials. Throughout their communication presentations the same consistent theme of a strategic collaboration parlaying each other's strengths continued to be preached by them and supported by us.

There were several KFSHRC consultants who were spending almost their entire time in Jeddah. Their pharmacy, lab, and nursing consultants seemed more like our own staff. We truly were the beneficiaries of some excellent consultation from these individuals free of charge.

The Al-Salama senior management consisted of about one-third of my direct reports. I considered the CFO, Director of Nursing, Medical Director, and a couple of other directors as my senior management team. Dr. Rayes was looked upon more as a consultant to the senior team. He rarely attended joint meetings. Since he was now reporting to A.R. and the private office, his clout had increased significantly. Any actions regarding the affiliation with KFSHRC were discussed with him to make sure they aligned with the desires of the owner.

The affiliation process continued to take on a life of its own. At least half of my time was dedicated to helping KFSHRC develop their plan. Mr. Safar was spending all of his time with the affiliation processes.

There were only a couple of incidences in which the KFSHRC consultants overstepped their staff responsibilities. When this did occur, we notified Suliman Al-Salama and the situation was quickly rectified.

At the same time, Dr. Morehead was becoming tenser about the time it was taking the KFSHRC project team to submit their plans. The thirty-day deadline had already come and gone, and I was guessing that the Palace had him under considerable pressure to provide a plan quickly.

We had decided that other than providing them our full cooperation, we'd best wait for them to come up with what they needed in writing and then we would respond.

In the meantime we had been doing considerable study regarding how to charge them for our services and facility space. We had already thought about basing the rent on the amount of square meters that they had decided to occupy. It would be a simple calculation of figuring the depreciation and utility cost per square meter and then multiplying that by the square meters they desired to occupy. We thought this was a fair approach. There would be no more added on top of these two basic items. Our services, such as diagnostic lab and radiology, would be based on our full usual and customary fee. We knew the type of patients they served would be extremely demanding. We also anticipated having to spend considerably more than normal for these Royal patients in the area of dietary, laundry, housekeeping and the general hotel aspects of the care provided. Simply because of the demands we knew KFSHRC patients would require, we felt it would not be appropriate to give a discount on our fees, as we were going to do for Dallah. At least this was to be our initial negotiation strategy.

The KFSHRC project team and the relentless flow of their consultants continued for another month. At first, the KFSHRC Project Director, Suliman Al-Salama, provided us a list on Wednesday afternoon of which Riyadh consultants would be arriving the following week. This would allow us to advise our respective department heads so they could be ready for the visit. But it got to the point where there were so many coming from Riyadh without any notice that Suliman simply could not provide us names. KFSHRC consultants must have felt that a visit to Al-Salama Hospital was an inherited right and short holiday where they could experience Jeddah, the "Jewel of the Red Sea."

On only one incident during this two and a half month period did we put down our foot. One of the consultants they were sending us had been a previous Medical Records Department head at Al-Salama Hospital. We had decided not to renew this employee's contract and had recruited an American as head. Some problems had cropped up with the previous employee just before she left Al-Salama Hospital. We now heard that she had secured a new position in the medical records department at KFSHRC in Riyadh and was coming to evaluate the staff of our medical records department with the idea of seeing who had the last laugh. We decided it would not be appropriate for her to come. It would have been problematic for our new department head; KFSHRC respected our concern.

We all had an excellent opportunity to see the casual work ethic of the KFSHRC employees. The primary disadvantage of having these employees and temporary consultants working in our hospital was their negative influence concerning working hours and the salaries. Many arrived at work about 9 am, took at least an hour for lunch, and then disappeared as early as 4:30 pm. They always took Thursday and Friday off. Their salaries were considerably higher then ours, especially in such areas as nursing, pharmacy, and radiology technology. Their Filipino staff received almost three times more than our nurses. It did not take long for these issues to start raising their heads.

Our response to the questions by our employees regarding such matters was always the same: "As a private hospital, we have to compete against other hospitals regarding our productivity and cost. Please compare your schedule, pay, and benefits with other private hospitals."

We knew that we compared very favorably with the other private hospitals and in some categories, such as the consultant physicians, our salaries were much too high even compared to the KFSHRC consultant physicians.

Such matters would have long-term effects regarding this strategic collaboration. I began to think about the success percentage back in the U.S. when a government academic institution merges with a private institute. It typically does not happen, and when it does happen, even more typically it does not work.

Sometimes at night I woke up and thought about the many problems that would have to be worked out with this affiliation. For example, we would have to develop employee non-compete policies for any Al-Salama staff member who might be clamoring to apply for any of the KFSHRC open positions.

During the early bird meetings, almost all the time was spent discussing "what if" scenarios. I daily reminded my senior management team that we needed to sit back and wait for them to present their proposals. We would then respond accordingly. Until that time, we needed to do our best to keep the employees, including ourselves, focused upon the Al-Salama mission.

One morning in late October, we received a call that Prince Sultan Bin Abdul Aziz was coming to the hospital for an M.R.I. investigation of his shoulder. Prince Sultan was responsible for the Department of Aviation and Defense and was the third in line in the Royal family after King Fahad and Crown Prince Abdullah.

We spent the morning preparing for the Prince and the large entourage that would surely accompany him. Dr. Mamoon, Chief of Radiology, was a nervous wreck preparing to receive the Prince.

A couple of hours later the entourage arrived in a fleet of Rolls Royce's with the Prince coming a little later. I shook his hand along with the other dignitaries, and we escorted the entire group to the radiology department. There must have been two hundred people accompanying the Prince for his simple M.R.I. procedure.

Dr. Mamoon gave him the choice of the closed or open M.R.I. machine. Of course, he chose the open, which generally takes a little longer. After about ten minutes, one of the escorts stated to me that it was taking too long, that the Prince wanted to hurry it up so he could get on board the royal yacht for his weekly cruise.

Having seen the yacht from a distance, I regarded it as more of a full-scale ocean liner equipped with a helicopter and several lifeboats. I engaged a brief conversation with this special escort, asking him if the Prince liked to fish or dive when he took his weekly cruises.

Abdul responded, "No he really does not do much fishing. One wall in his large estate room is a huge TV screen. We just lower a robot that has video capabilities over the side, and the underwater scenes are then transmitted from the robot by video to the large screen in the Prince's chamber. He can experience the many treasures of the Red Sea without ever having one drop of salt water on him."

Refreshments were offered to the Prince and his entourage, and they left in the same ostentatious manner in which they had arrived.

Dr. Rayes, Mr. Safar, and I scratched our heads. If this was a prelude of what was to come as a result of the collaboration with KFSHRC, we needed to triple our usual fees. The M.R.I. result was normal, simply reflecting the typical age-related wear and tear of the shoulder.

One evening in late November, Dr. Rayes, several KFSHRC staff, and I were invited for supper to a prominent Saudi's home. It was a beautiful home with the lavish food in great quantities served outside around the large swimming pool. There were probably thirty guests that evening. Paula Bond, the nurse consultant; Sarah Dawson, lab consultant technician; and two or three other female KFSHRC consultants were invited.

Before dinner several of the guests were seated in traditional Saudi style in one of the large rooms inside the house.

The traditional way such rooms are furnished is that all sofa or cushions are pushed up against at least three, sometimes all four, walls within the room. We were all seated on cushions. Sarah was on my right and one of the other consultant females was on my left. Mrs. Bond was a couple of cushions further away. Dr. Rayes happened to be out visiting with some of the other guests around the swimming pool at that time.

The room was laid out in such a manner that there was a very large full screen TV against the fourth wall in this room. The TV was on with volume off, featuring a Saudi football game. The host was sitting on a cushion with his back to the football game being broadcasted, facing his guests and engaged in pre-dinner informal conversations.

I was talking to Sarah, not paying any attention to the TV, when suddenly she seemed to lose interest in what I was saying and began staring straight ahead with a strange look on her face. When I looked away to see what had caught her attention, I quickly saw that the football game was no longer being broadcasted. There, bigger than life, were three couples enthusiastically engaged in various sex acts and positions I did not believe possible. There was still no sound; the host wasn't aware that the TV somehow had switched over to this triple X movie. For some time he did not realize what had happened. Finally, he noticed that his guests were squirming on their cushions, all intensely gazing in disbelief at the large TV screen behind him. When he turned around and saw what was occurring, he very nonchalantly said "Sorry," turned off the TV, and continued to talk without missing a beat.

Later that evening at dinner, I said to Dr. Rayes, "Well sir, you missed all the action. Our host really gave the KFSHRC people something to talk about back in Riyadh."

Dr. Rayes could only smile. Half seriously, he said, "That's hard to believe. Perhaps our host did not want his guests to get bored. Or maybe they were just provided a prelude for what he expected to happen after dinner."

This unusual dinner party was the subject of hot conversation for the next couple of days.

In early December, the KFSHRC project team was almost finished with their plans for the affiliation. Several times Dr. Morehead had stated that the plan would be presented to us that we might give our input back in writing. Through this process, we would develop a mutually satisfactory strategic partnership.

Finally, after taking much longer than any of us anticipated, Dr. Morehead and Dr. Taher requested a meeting with Rayes and me to present their plan.

Dr. Morehead started the conversation, "Gentleman, this project of developing a strategic written collaboration between our two institutes has taken much longer than we expected. The Palace is not happy with our progress to date, even though I do not see how it could go any faster. Our preliminary plans, pending approval by the Palace, are that we will require about fifty inpatient beds. We believe we will need all of the fifth floor and fourth floor of the VIP tower. We will also require the fifth floor of the OPD tower. In addition we will need at least the fifth and fourth south balconies that connect the bed towers for office space. We will have to do considerable modifications to the royal suites on the fifth floor for this will be reserved for the King and immediate family members. All windows will need to be bulletproof glass. We will have to have a special I.C.U. and certain elevators will need to be exclusively dedicated for serving only this floor. Somehow we will have to arrange the VIP lobby so that Royal family patients and your regular VIPs can be separated. Also, the E.R. will have to have major modifications, including its access from the street.

"All these modifications have to be completed by March 1, 2000."

Dr. Rayes and I looked at each other in disbelief. We had no problem providing to them the space they had requested in the VIP tower; indeed, this was what we had expected. But I was disappointed that they were requesting the use of the fifth floor of the OPD tower. That meant the Dallah arrangement would not be feasible. Plus, the modifications that were being suggested were extremely major. This was a brand new facility; Saudi ABV had not even turned some of the spaces, such as the royal suites, over to us. Our E.R. was the most up-to-date and lavish in the Kingdom. Why would they need to modify that? The modifications requested would take at least eight months and would be very expensive.

We requested a brief caucus. Dr. Rayes and I contacted A.R. to inform him of their preliminary plan. After about fifteen minutes we resumed the meeting.

Dr. Rayes began, "We have spoken to the private office about your ideas. In principle we agree with what you desire to do. We need you to give this plan in writing. Any modification to this building will have to be at your cost. Such modifications will need to result in a longer lease period as well." He asked if I had anything to add.

I replied to Dr Morehead, "Once we get your plan in writing, we will immediately ask Saudi ABV to provide a gross estimate of what such modifications will cost. I assume this information will be helpful to you. We will also provide you with what our lease fee will be based upon the square meter of space you have indicated you will need. We will pledge to have our response back to you within one week after we receive your written plan."

Dr. Morehead concluded happily that the meeting was very positive; he was pleased to report how close we really were to being able to present an affiliation plan to the Palace. He concluded, "Let us get this plan from our side documented and to you so you can officially respond."

I mentioned that it would be best not to discuss this meeting with anyone else until we had the written plan presented. Once we had that, and assuming we were in agreement, we could announce our intentions.

Everyone agreed that this would be the best approach.

Linda had been in Jeddah for the past couple of weeks. Mark and Emily had stayed in Texas, as they were busy with their education and sport activities. Linda had kept herself busy with the various shopping trips to the souqs that she enjoyed so much. The weather this time of the year in Jeddah was also very good, unlike the summer when she was here last.

She and I were to leave together after a week to return to Texas. I had to be back in Jeddah no later then December 31st because of the Y2-K concerns. There would be no ski vacation this Christmas because of the timing. I planned to attend a three-day international health care financing symposium in Miami on the return home. Linda would be with me and could enjoy the amenities of the Miami Sheraton Beach Hotel while I was attending the seminar.

I scheduled an all-staff presentation in mid December just before I was to leave. We had had numerous positive developments during the first half of 1999. But beginning in late August, with the arrival of KFSHRC, it had been extremely difficult to keep the employees focused on our mission. I felt that this particular presentation was critical in both acknowledging our accomplishments and setting out clear objectives and action plans for year 2000. I had to get the staff refocused on taking care of patients and somehow keep them from continually being distracted by this affiliation of the two hospitals.

I decided to invite Linda to hear the presentation. I felt this would provide me the opportunity to introduce her to the staff. She would be seated next to Dr. P.K.

The evening before the presentation, Linda and I were invited to a party in my residential compound, Nueva Andalucia. This party was one of the quarterly flings that Shiekh Mohammad, the compound owner, threw. It was always a great party with plenty of drinks, food, and music. Unlike the one the Brass Eagle held each month at the American Consulate, this party was usually limited to the compound residents, except for a busload of the Moroccan flight attendants who worked for Saudi Arabian Airline that Sheikh Mohammad always brought in. These girls would perform some extremely erotic dances once they had had a few drinks. I don't know if he paid these girls to show up or not, but they all seemed to enjoy themselves.

Typically, by midnight the wives were pissed off that their husbands were drooling over these young girls as they gyrated to the music. Most of the bachelors would usually leave the party late, alone, and quite frustrated. A few, however, would wake up the next morning and think how wonderful and generous Shiekh Mohammad was. Unfortunately or fortunately, I was always in one of the first two categories of males described above.

The all-staff presentation was held the following evening in the auditorium at 9:30 pm. Dinner was to be served at its conclusion.

I started the presentation in the usual manner of welcoming all who were present. I then asked Linda to stand and introduced her as my lovely wife. Linda looked very dignified and attractive. I was proud of her.

I had convinced Dr. Rayes that he should say a few opening remarks. He asked that I prepare a statement for him to read, which I did.

After this, I presented plaques to the best all-round administrative, clinical, and nursing department recipients who had been voted on by the various department heads. All staff present felt that the respective department heads very well deserved the awards.

I then spent some time praising all staff for their excellent work during 1999. I reviewed the many accomplishments that had occurred during the year. Most of these had been presented as action items during the similar presentation the year before.

The rest of the introductory comments detailed the importance of staying focused upon the hospital's mission. I talked about our vision as a private hospital, about how important it was to be willing to change the way we do business and about certain processes that would result in the strategic collaboration being worked out with KFSRC. I discussed the many positive points that would come about as a result of this collaboration.

I then spent considerable time outlining the year 2000 goals, measurements, and action plans that had been approved by the hospital's Board of Directors. These goals were as follows:

+ To develop a long-term, mutually beneficial strategic collaboration with KFSHRC;

+ To fund hospital operations through hospital-generated cash or financial arrangements and achieve a break-even net from operations after deleting depreciation expenses;

+ To complete the total turnkey hospital project expansion and activate all new facility and equipment;

+ To work towards accreditation by the Joint Commission of Health Care Organization International (JCI) and improve the quality of care provided;

+ To become more patient friendly and focus on the hotel aspect of costumer satisfaction;

+ To complete the Oasis I.T. implementation project;

+ To establish new services beneficial in meeting our customer's demands that also proved financial viable; and

+ To develop a more aggressive marketing program by the hospital.

Each of these goals had specific measurements, time frames, and action plans required that were also included in the presentation.

At that time, there was no way of knowing that all these goals and action plans would become totally useless within a month.

Later that evening after Linda and I dropped Dr. P.K. at her compound and returned to our villa, I asked Linda what she thought of the presentation and if she thought the evening had been productive.

"Honey," she said, "even if you were not my husband, I would have thought you did a wonderful job. The presentation of those awards at the beginning of the program was really appreciated by everyone there.

The next day while visiting with Dr. Rays, I mentioned that we still had not received the written proposal from KFSHRC. I had hoped we would have received this so that we could formulate our response before I left for the states. Dr. Rayes reminded me that Ramadan was fast approaching; he doubted seriously if we would receive anything until after I returned.

"You know, Dr. Rayes, there is no way that those modifications can be completed by March 1st. It will take probably at least six to eight months to make those changes and that is if we start immediately. I can see already how Saudi ABV will respond to this. It will be very expensive."

I was beginning to look at this proposed affiliation in the manner of the desert travelers of old trying to make their way across the vast expanse of sand. They could look in the distance and imagine they saw blue water lusciously quenching the landscape's thirst. Perhaps this affiliation proposal by KFSHRC was also nothing more than a mirage that vanished as one got closer.

Chapter Eleven

Betrayals

"Return to the root and you will find the meaning."

Sergston.

(January–February, 2000)

This year's holiday would be short. I flew direct from Jeddah to New York and then to Miami for the three-day International Summit on Managed Care. Linda accompanied me on this leg of the trip. The summit was excellent and I saw several of my old acquaintances. Dr. Yazid O'Haly, Hospital General Director of the Saudi Arabian Ministry of Health, and Jim Janeski of Joint Commission International were there. Both of these gentlemen represented organizations that had been previous clients of Utgard Associates.

I have found that the most valuable element of such seminars is the renewing of one's network and the realization that one's colleagues all have their own unique set of work related problems.

By the time Linda and I reached Grapevine, it was the second week of December. Although we were booked for a week of skiing in Colorado, I really just did not feel up to it and ended up canceling. I would have to leave for Jeddah on December 30th because of Y2K. I had requested that all key hospital staff members be on duty the evening of the December 31st, just in case problems did develop.

Despite Mark and Emily's disappointment at not going skiing, the two weeks back in Texas spending Christmas at home were quite relaxing.

I arrived back in Jeddah about 4 pm on December 31st.

The Nueva Andalucia was having a first class New Year's Eve party. This was not one of the typical Sheikh's parties. We had a formal sit-down dinner by the pool while a band played to our delight. About ten pm the party guests moved to the dance floor, signaling time for me to depart for the hospital for potential Y2K problems at midnight.

I, along with many others, spent the eve of the new millennium at the Al-Salama Hospital waiting to see what type of problems would ring in at midnight. To everyone's relief, there were absolutely no glitches pertaining to Y2K issues. This reconfirmed the right choice staff had made in selecting the hospital's bio-medical engineering services as the best performing administrative department. Mr. Raafal, the Saudi national who headed this department, provided an excellent example of the manner in which some of the Saudis were assuming key positions at the hospital and doing outstanding jobs in their areas of responsibility.

Throughout the Kingdom, it was evident that the entire Y2K scare had been blown out of proportion. Perhaps because of all the dire predictions, organizations had taken the proper steps early.

By now, it was the middle of January, and we still had not received any-thing in writing from Dr. Morehead and the KFSHRC project team. During my absence over Christmas, they had opened up a small primary care outpatient clinic and were seeing only one or two patients per day.

"Dr. Rayes, what do you think is going on with KFSHRC? I know that Ramadan has just concluded, but their activity here, other than the small clinic, has come to a standstill. What has happened to the written plan that Dr. Morehead promised?"

He had no idea why they had not contacted us other than Ramadan had just ended and perhaps they were a bit behind because of that. He suggested that I try to contact Dr. Morehead again. I had already tried a couple of times only to be informed by KFSHRC that he had left the Kingdom during Ramadan and should be returning soon. This was certainly a believable reason, and I simply needed to wait for his return.

During the next week, I was unsuccessful in making contact with either Dr. Morehead or Dr. Taher. I had been informed that they both were back in Riyadh but were in meetings. I suspected that they were implementing the final touches of the plan before submitting it to us for our review and response.

By now the apprehension among the hospital physicians and general staff had settled back down. There really had been very little activity by KFSHRC during the past month. To our knowledge, very few of their project team members had been in Jeddah during Ramadan. The numerous consultants that had bomb-barded us during the past three months were also almost non-existent at this time. The activation of the small outpatient primary care clinic was the only evidence that they were at Al-Salama Hospital at all.

About the fourth week of January, we started hearing the rumor that KFSHRC was not going to affiliate with Al-Salama Hospital. The rumor was coming from some of the Saudi physicians who worked at the Jeddah University Hospital, ones who had good contacts in Riyadh. The grapevine had it that a decision had been made by the Royals to use the new military hospital that was being built. It would not be completed for another eighteen months, however.

This rumor was quite strong. Within a couple of days it had spread throughout the hospital. I still was unable to contact Dr. Morehead, and the KFSHRC project team was still in Riyadh.

"Dr. Rayes, something is happening. I hope they aren't changing their minds about the strategic collaboration. As you know, the rumor the past couple of days suggests they may be considering the new wing of the Military Hospital."

He replied, "Yes I know, it does seem that something is going on. I am also unable to make contact with Anwar Jabarti in Riyadh. The new military hospital would make sense except it is still many months away from completion. The way Dr. Morehead stated how important it was to have this hospital ready by March 1, 2000; it just does not make sense."

Within a couple of days, just as quickly as the first rumor surfaced, a second rumor came from the same group of university physicians. I had no idea why these particular individuals would have any better information sources than we did. Perhaps some had family members who were working closely with the Palace or with KFSHRC in Riyadh.

This particular rumor was considerably more disturbing than the first. By the end of week, the hospital was buzzing that KFSHRC was taking over the entire hospital.

I informed my senior management team at the early bird meeting. "Folks, we have absolutely no information from KFSHRC that indicates that their intentions are different from what they have repeatedly told us. We continue to await their written proposal concerning a strategic affiliation by which they will lease certain parts of the hospital and we will sell back to them various services."

I was really becoming irritated with Dr. Morehead. I had been unable to contact him for the past couple of weeks; he was not returning my calls. The entire hospital was again at a high pitch because of the rumors that kept coming from the university physicians. I thought to myself that surely if they had decided upon another course of action, they would have informed Dr. Rayes and me.

Finally, I went to Dr. Rayes. "Enough is enough. The hospital staff's productivity level has hit rock bottom. My senior team cannot keep the employees focused upon our mission. You and I need to travel to Riyadh to visit with Dr. Morehead and Dr. Jabarty to find out exactly what is going on. There is no way we could have all that activity for three months, then have everything just come to a standstill unless something is up."

Almost unbelievably, in the midst of my conversation with Dr. Rayes, Mustafa interrupted, "Mr. Gordon, Dr. Morehead is on the phone and wants to talk to you."

"Amazing," I said, and quickly left Dr. Rayes's office to take the call. "Maybe we will be able to find out what is going on now."

Picking up the phone, I asked David Morehead how his holidays had been. After some small talk, I mentioned that we had been trying to contact him over the past couple of weeks with no success. He acknowledged this and apologized for not returning the calls with the excuse being his extremely heavy workload and focus regarding another new project he had been assigned to. He then revealed that he and Dr. Taher were just leaving KFSHRC en route to the airport. He said they were on their way to Jeddah and requested a meeting with Dr. Rayes and me at about 2 pm. I thanked David for his call and said that we were looking forward to seeing both him and Dr. Taher and getting a status report regarding the yet-to-be-received written proposal. It was six weeks late by this time.

I went back into Dr. Rayes' office. "Rayes, Dr. Morehead and Dr. Taher will be here about 2 pm and have requested to meet with us. To tell you the truth, I don't like the feel of Morehead's telephone call. I believe we are going to get some type of bombshell delivered. Have you heard from A.R. at the private office? Perhaps he has heard something."

Dr. Rayes replied that he had talked with A.R. that morning and nothing new had been mentioned. If he had known of anything new, he would have said something. Rayes then immediately called A.R. to advise him of the 2 pm meeting with Drs. Morehead and Taher.

At precisely 2 pm, Dr. Morehead and Dr. Taher walked briskly into Dr. Rayes office where I was also seated. The next half hour was to be absolutely unbelievable.

Dr. Morehead began, "Good afternoon, gentlemen. I understand that both of you are legitimately wondering what has been going on with the project? The Palace has made a new decision. KFSHRC, Riyadh has been instructed to take over operations of the entire hospital immediately. We plan to operate the hospital as a satellite facility of KFSHRC in Riyadh. Both Dr. Taher and I will be here full time until the change has stabilized. We will need to begin the transition immediately. We must be completed by the end of the first week in March.

"Dr. Taher and I must visit with a couple of our project team personnel on the fourth floor. Perhaps you two need to visit for a while. We can come back down in about an hour to see what the next steps are from your vantage point."

They then left the room. "Dr. Rayes," I howled, "do you mean to say that you were not aware of what they have said? This is unbelievable that Morehead would have the gall to march in here and advise us that KFSHRC is taking over the entire hospital immediately. What's going on here?"

"Gordon, I'm heading to the private office to talk to A.R. I will call you as soon as I have information. I will not be meeting with Dr. Morehead and Dr. Taher again today. Let's keep this meeting with these two guys just between us until I can brief A.R. to see what he wants to do. Gordon, other than the rumors of the past week, I had no advanced information regarding what we have just heard."

I left the hospital early that day, went home, and had a long run. As I was running, I kept thinking that I had been lied to and set up. I simply could not believe that A.R. had not known about this situation. What was I going to say to the staff?

Later that evening Dr. Rayes called me at home and informed me that he had spoken in detail to A.R. about the meeting. He stated that A.R.'s instructions were for us to cooperate fully with the KFSHRC officials. He went on to say that there had been a change and we had no choice but to cooperate. A.R. had only been notified just before our meeting with Morehead and Taher that the Royals wanted the hospital. Apparently, they would be working directly with A.R. regarding the details of the purchase or lease transaction.

"Rayes, you and I need to visit first thing tomorrow morning before this information gets out to our staff."

After this relatively brief telephone conversation, I could not sleep. How could A.R. allow this to happen? Did he really want to get rid of the hospital that badly? Why weren't Dr. Rayes and I informed of what was happening? We had been made to look like complete fools.

There was nothing more that could be done until the morning. I thought about informing Dr. Mohsin Hussien, but decided it could wait until then.

The following morning, I was at the office early. To my surprise, at about 7 am Dr. Morehead knocked on my office door (which was open) and came in.

"Good morning, Gordon. I want you to know that I didn't know about this change until last week. We felt best to keep it completely confidential until the official Royal decree was released."

"Dammit, David, how can I believe you? Dr. Taher and you have given us the wrong picture completely. What happened to our strategic collaboration that would parlay each other's strengths? If I heard you say that phrase about strategic collaboration and affiliation once, I heard you say it a hundred times."

Dr. Morehead calmly replied, "The Palace, meaning the King or his Royal cabinet, issued a Royal decree for Al-Salama Hospital operations to cease on March the 6th and for KFSHRC to take over operations on March the 7th. Gordon, we will be coming up with a plan on how best to proceed. I would like for Dr. Taher and me to visit with you and Dr. Rayes this morning."

"David, I feel violated and at the moment completely numb. I have not been informed of any Royal decree regarding the hospital. I have been instructed to cooperate with you fully until further notice. Between you and me, I can't even express my total disappointment at how this is coming down. I cannot respond to you at the moment until I have more information from my side."

"I know how you must feel, Gordon. We must now put the feelings behind and move rapidly ahead to activate this management transition. I believe we need to call an all-staff meeting to announce it."

"What are you going to tell them? That our strategic collaboration has reverted to reverse privatization? We do not need a meeting for that. I am absolutely sure that the word will already be out this morning. If we call an all-staff meeting, you need to have a lot of answers of how this take- over is going to proceed."

Dr. Morehead curtly replied, "Very well, Gordon, you can believe what you wish. I did not know about these changes until last week. This is Saudi Arabia you know. The Palace will do things without informing me."

"David, if you knew last week, why didn't you call me last week? You wouldn't even return my calls to your office. If what you say about Al-Salama Hospital's ceasing operations on March 6th is correct, that's only five weeks off. This is no normal management transition. It's rape. As far as I'm concerned, I will notify my management team officials this morning after I discuss the matter with Dr. Rayes. I am against having an all-staff meeting until you have details to share with the staff, which as far as I can tell, you don't. Also, remember that at any such meeting relating to this matter, you will be addressing the staff, not I."

From our very first introduction, Morehead had made me uncomfortable. He was an American trained pediatric urologist, turned administrator. I am sure he was a very smart individual. But I am always suspicious when a physician specialist decides to leave his practice in his prime to move over into the administration side. Was he not happy as a physician or perhaps not successful? Maybe he just wanted something different and there is nothing wrong with that. He was a small-framed individual, who, in my opinion, had a Napoleon complex. This was simply my opinion; perhaps it was wrong. Maybe our chemistry just did not match.

Dr. Rayes came to the office late that morning and seemed quite sad. I advised him of the meeting with Morehead that I had that morning. I asked him about the staff meeting and the alleged Royal decree.

Rayes replied, "The reason I am late is that I have been at the private office with A.R. Yes, there appears that there has been some type of decree as mentioned by Dr. Morehead. We must now co-operate the best we can; A.R. has the task of getting the most he can out of the transaction. The problem with these deals with the Royals is that there is only one-sided negotiation. There is basically nothing we can do but hope the owner is able to get a decent price for the facility. That piece is completely out of our hands. We have to focus on what we do have influence over. Gordon, I am in total agreement with you regarding your statements to Dr. Morehead. I see no benefit in calling an all-staff meeting until he has some concrete details regarding the many questions he will be asked."

"Rayes, I have had previous experience involving company takeovers. I was involved with the merger of the Blue Cross and Blue Shield of Texas and the Illinois Blue Cross and Blue Shield Plans. I was also with Hospital Affiliates when it was taken over by Hospital Corporation of America (HCA) several years ago. What should happen, even in a hostile takeover, which I would definitely classify this to be, is that senior management of KFSHRC (Dr. Morehead, Dr.Taher, and Dr. Jabarti) should discuss their plans with us. How do they want you and me to be involved? Do they even want us to be a part of the transaction? What will our roles, if any, be after March 6th? These are all legitimate questions that should have already been communicated to us. What about our Board of Directors? They should be actively involved with this matter."

"You are absolutely right, Gordon. Even though we have been instructed to cooperate fully with KFSHRC officials, let's make sure they understand that we are still responsible and in charge of Al-Salama Hospital until March 6th. Let's put Dr. Morehead and Dr.Taher in the hot seat for a change. Since they apparently have decided to keep us on the sidelines, let them come up with the answers."

"Rayes, I am going to call the other two Board members who are not associated with the private office to inform them. I have to assume that Sheikh Sultan, our Chairman, is already aware through A.R. I also have to believe that Jamal in the private office knows of this by now. I will also call a meeting this morning of my direct reports to advise them. I'm sure the information has already been leaked out, but I need to inform them officially."

"I would not necessarily conclude that Sheikh Sultan or Jamal are aware of the situation," Dr. Rayes stated. "I believe Sultan is on another one of his diving excursions at the moment."

The meeting with my direct reports was held at 12 noon.

As I had expected, some information had already been leaked out. I officially advised them of what I had been told. I said that we had not been given any additional information from Dr. Morehead, but we were opposed to calling a meeting until he was in a position to answer questions.

Dr. Mohsin commented, "Mr. Gordon, this is what we were all afraid might happen in the end. You cannot trust the KFSHRC motives. What is important now is what will happen to our employees. Dr. Morehead must be in a position to discuss these issues. Has he not at least informed you and Dr. Rayes of their intentions?"

"They have not told Rayes and me anything. Dr. Morehead claims he was not aware of the changes until last week. Frankly, I do not believe him. There is nothing more we can tell our staff at this time. I believe the full responsibility falls upon KFSHRC to be able to provide the answers, since they have elected not to share information with either Dr. Rayes or me. Unfortunately, it appears they are not comfortable with or perhaps they simply do not know the answers to share at the moment."

Later that day Dr. Morehead again contacted my office. "Gordon, I believe you need to call the all-staff presentation to discuss the situation."

I replied, "David, let me remind you that until March 7th, we are still in charge of Al-Salama Hospital. Unless you have the necessary information to answer questions of the staff, Rayes and I believe such a meeting will do more harm than good. Once you have answers how to proceed, I believe it is appropriate to share them with Dr. Rayes and me first, and then we can call the meeting and let you address the staff."

I did not hear from Morehead for the next couple of days.

By the end of the week, the hospital was in a total uproar. The employees were continuing to look to Al-Salama senior management, and rightfully so, to provide them answers of what was going to happen to them.

It was amazing how quickly alliances changed. Many of the staff were trying to realign themselves politically with the management-to-be. Some of my senior staff, such as Mr. Safar, was the worst. The "sucking up" to the KFSHRC senior management was so obvious it was actually sickening to me. But, people were apprehensive about their livelihoods. How would they take care of their families? Would they be fired and sent back to a third world country life again where they could earn but a fourth of what they were making in Saudi Arabia. Despite my disgust, I could understand why such obvious switching of alliances was quickly occurring.

The following morning Mrs. Rose Stephens, Director of Nursing, came to my office.

"Gordon, I thought I should tell you that Dr. Morehead and Mrs. Paula Bond have offered me the position of the new Director of Nursing for KFSHRC. They have asked me not to share this with you, but I believe you need to know what is going on. I'm sure there are others who have also been offered positions."

"Thank you for telling me, Rose. Yes, I do need to know."

I immediately called up to the KFSHRC project office and asked to speak to Dr. Morehead.

"Hello, David, this is Gordon. I need to meet with you at your earliest convenience."

"Sure Gordon, I can come down to your office at 10 am. See you then."

Promptly at 10 am, David stepped in to my office.

"David," I began, "I have been reluctant to talk with you about how I believe you are handling this situation during the past week. Something has been brought to my attention that troubles me greatly, however, and I believe it is time to talk very frankly. For whatever the reason, you have decided to keep me in the dark regarding your plans and immediate action. I simply have two questions to ask you at this time. Both questions have as their basis the desire to cooperate fully with you as per my instructions from the Al-Salama Hospital owner.

"First question is what role does KFSHRC desire for Dr. Rayes and me to play under the new management after March 6th, if any? The second question is what role do you wish us to play during the next four to five weeks until 6th of March? I ask the second with the understanding that as CEO, I am still responsible for the operation of this hospital until that time."

Dr. Morehead looked at me. "Let me answer the second question first. We believe that all Al-Salama Hospital staff must be terminated no later then March 6th .We will decide which of these ex-employees we will rehire. We also believe that all suppliers, sub-contractors, and other contractual arrangements such as Joint Commission International must be terminated no later than March 6th. Again, we will decide whom we wish to re-contract with. As I have been requesting, I again ask that you call an all-staff meeting so this can be articulated.

"As per your first question, I do not see how we can use your services after March 6th. Regarding Dr. Rayes, as far as I know he has not expressed any interest in joining KFSHRC. As a Saudi, if he desires, he can be assigned a responsible position, I'm sure."

"That's what I needed to hear. David, you should have discussed these items with me immediately after you heard that the strategic collaboration was no longer going to occur. I can appreciate your position as it relates to having little control over what the Palace may or may not do. What I cannot appreciate is the sloppy, insensitive manner you have dealt with the senior management of this hospital regarding this power grab. I will talk to Dr. Rayes again concerning your request for the all-staff meeting. I think you know our position."

During the next couple of days, Dr. Rayes spent most of his time meeting with A.R. at the private office. I was beginning to resent the fact that I had no contact whatsoever with A.R., who was now calling all the shots regarding what we would and would not do. Dr. Rayes was simply a messenger who brought back information and passed on to me for necessary action.

He and I met on February 5th to discuss what A.R. now wanted to do.

"Gordon, A.R. is not happy with the progress being made with the royal representatives regarding the official hospital transaction. He is getting fed-up with their arrogances and obvious delays. But, that is his area of responsibility not ours, Al-Hamdulliah. We need to take the following course of immediate action that is within our control:

(1) Contact Saudi ABV and have them stop delivery on all medical equipment that has not yet been delivered on-site;

(2) Remove as much of the supply items and pharmaceutical items as we can. These items are not part of the transaction and will continue to belong to Al-Salama Hospital. Ideally, on March 7th, there will not be so much as a bandage left in the hospital;

(3) Prepare a termination letter with an effective date of midnight March 6th for all Al-Salama employees, including you and me;

(4) Send a letter to all suppliers, subcontractors, and any other party that we may have a contract with, formal or informal, explaining the situation and terminating these agreements as of midnight March 6th; and

(5) Set up immediately the all-staff meeting that Dr. Morehead has been requesting."

I countered, "The hospital's Board Chairman, Sheikh Sultan, should sign the termination letters. The letter has to go out at least thirty days in advance of the termination date. This letter will need to be distributed tomorrow to comply with the employment terms of the contracts if we are going to pay salaries only up to midnight March 6th. Also, many of the subcontractors have termination notice requirements of ninety-days; else there are significant penalties that may be applied."

I thought about my previous experiences concerning such matters as when one organization takes over the assets of another. The surviving organization must assume the liabilities of the one being taken over. Now, seeing first hand how the Palace was dealing with A.R., who was representing his father and also the owner of the Al-Salama Hospital, I wondered if they would be responsible for paying the employees accrued service award benefits. If not, would the owner take on this responsibility?

The all-staff meeting was set for the next day in the hospital's auditorium.

The auditorium was packed, a nervous noise level several decibels louder than usual. I opened the meeting with Dr. Morehead and Dr. Taher seated behind me. Several of the KFSHRC staff were seated in the auditorium. I couldn't help but notice that Mrs. Stephens was setting next to Paula Bond and that Mr. Safar was seated with the KFSHRC project staff. Such was to be expected, as Al-Salama staffs were maneuvering for new positions with KFSHRC.

After a very brief opening, I turned the podium over to Dr. Morehead. He spent the next half an hour explaining why KFSHRC had been instructed to take over the hospital. He did his best to play down the previous meetings where he had preached the benefits of a strategic collaboration. He encouraged Al-Salama Hospital staff to apply for positions at KFSHRC for a hire date of March 7th. He then mentioned that there were numerous unanswered questions and he would do his best to answer them or to get an answer. What he intentionally avoided was the issue of the termination notice, craftily letting that subject slide for me to discuss.

After his presentation, he was bomb-barded by all types of questions with most having the theme of "what is going to happen to me."

When I took the podium, the audience was angry, disappointed, and totally insecure about their futures.

I had to advise them that all employees, including myself, would be receiving termination letters. Dr. Tahar Hassan asked who would be responsible for paying the service awards. Most of the questions that were fired at me had to do with salaries from February 1st through March 12th, and payment of service award benefits. The private office, through Dr. Rayes, had already several times assured me that such payments due would not be a problem. Either Al-Salama or KFSHRC would pay them no later than one week following the March 7th takeover.

I couldn't help but reflect on how just six weeks before in this same auditorium, I was presenting to these same people the year 2000 goals and action plans and handing out awards for the best performing departments. Things can change very rapidly in Saudi Arabia.

"Please do not be concerned about your benefits that are owed. Over the years, has the Bin Mahfouz family ever been anything but generous to a fault? I have been assured over and again that benefits will be paid within one week after March 6th."

Shortly after this, we adjourned the meeting. Dr. Rayes had elected not to be present at the meeting. This was his typical approach. He just disappeared, taking himself out of awkward situations.

I felt depressed and had a hollow pit in my stomach as I observed the employees congregating around the new hospital leaders. Everyone was trying to score points with the KFSHRC leaders. I walked over to the elevators, entered one by myself, unnoticed, and went back to the office in a very melancholy state of mind.

Later that evening I called Dr. Rayes to brief him on the meeting. I also gently criticized his absence from the meeting. Either A.R. or Sheikh Sultan, the so-called Board Chairman, should have been present to provide assurances regarding the employees service award benefits. I was inwardly distraught over the way A.R. and Sultan had distanced themselves from the Al-Salama Hospital employees. Outwardly, I was determined to see the transition through and to do my best to represent the hospital.

I reiterated to Dr. Rayes that I had not received approval from Sultan or A.R. regarding the draft termination letter they were sent. "Dr. Rayes, they should know that we must provide 30 days notice as per Saudi labor law. For each day that this letter is delayed, they will be responsible for an additional hundred and seventy-five thousand riyals of salary cost, even though the employees' last day of work will be March 6th."

Amazingly, the private office did not approve the draft and sign the original letter until February 12th. As a result of this delay on their part, salaries and benefits would be due through March 12th instead of March 6th when the Al-Salama ceased operations. This avoidable delay cost the owner more than a million riyals, or close to two hundred and seventy thousand dollars.

I knew the last four weeks of Al-Salama Hospital operations were going to be extremely difficult. Our inpatient census was still quite high and the outpatient clinics quite busy. Dr. Mohsin was doing his best to keep the physician staff motivated to see and take care of patients. We were beginning to get numerous patient complaints about poor nurse and physician attitudes, no surprise under the current situation.

During the morning meetings we discussed the many issues of closing down Al-Salama Hospital. We had been instructed by KFSHRC that by close of business on March 6th, there should be absolutely no patients in the hospital. This would be extremely difficult for OB patients and patients who might be in the ICU. KFSHRC senior management was showing no compassion at all towards our private patients. As far as they were concerned, come March 7th, the patients did not exist. All of them would have to find new doctors within days.

Dr. Mohsin gave me reports that Dr. Morehead and other KFSHRC key physicians were treating our doctors in a very unprofessional and demeaning manner. It was as though the somehow superior KFSHRC staff had to go through the exercise of interviewing the vastly inferior Al-Salama Hospital physicians. I kept hearing from my staff that some statements being made by KFSHRC were totally unprofessional, such as "there is the right way of doing things, and then there is the Al-Salama way." Within a couple of weeks, most of the Al-Salama Hospital physicians, including Dr. Mohsin, were fed up with the arrogance and began making their plans to join other private hospitals in Jeddah.

Insurance companies, employer groups, suppliers, and sub-contractors were all totally shocked when they received their contract termination letters. Many of these demanded early termination penalty payments and complete liquidation of their payables.

I quickly came to realize that KFSHRC had a notoriously poor record for paying its bills. In some cases, its payables with equipment suppliers, such as Siemens, were five years old. All of these contracted companies and suppliers were extremely concerned that once KFSHRC took over, they might very well never be paid what they were owed. It was still unclear who would have the responsibility of the hospital's liabilities after March 6th. Most of the suppliers and vendors did not wish to take a chance. They were offering us as much as forty percent discounts off the amounts due if we would pay before the March 6th date. With only a few exceptions, however, these payables were not liquidated even with the offers that had been put on the table. This revelation concerning the way KFSHRC paid its debts made me realize that even if they had leased the two floors in the VIP tower, we probably would not have received our rent monies. The old Dallah deal was really looking good at this time.

About ten days after the takeover announcement, Dr. Morehead called me for a meeting.

"Gordon, I have been made aware that some of the computers and other light office equipment are walking off. I would like to place our security personnel on-duty alongside yours immediately. Do you have any objection to this?"

Suspecting that some of this was taking place, I told David that I had no problems with his request.

I knew that we would need to create a demobilization team to take care of the many requirements after March 7th. A completed equipment inventory listing was required as soon as possible. There were literally a thousand items to be addressed in a matter of about two weeks.

David Lane, from Saudi ABV Construction Company, came to my office.

"Gordon, our work is for Sheikh Khalid Bin Mahfouz. We are not interested in working for KFSHRC or their sub-contractor Saudi Oger. We still have probably six months of work left before the project is complete. What is going to be our situation after the take over?"

"David," I replied, "There will be some type of demobilization team or "wrap-up team" for Al-Salama. I am sure that one of its areas of responsibility will include the continued liaison with Saudi ABV until such time as the project is complete."

I had instructed the purchasing department manager to start returning supplies to the manufacturers for credit. The hospital had an inventory of supplies and pharmaceuticals that was close to seven million riyals. We only wished to maintain enough of these items to see us through March 6th.

The purchasing manager, who had been offered a position by KFSHRC, quickly announced our intentions to the KFSHRC senior management.

Dr. Morehead and one other KFSHRC manager came storming into my office.

Dr. Morehead began, "Look here Gordon, I'm sick and tired of your staff systematically stripping this hospital of its supplies and equipment. Where have the ambulances gone? Why are supply levels at half of what they were last week? I am holding you personally responsible for potentially jeopardizing the safety of the Royal Family members by removing these items."

I countered, "As far as the ambulances, I am unaware of what you are talking about. I will certainly check, for that is an equipment asset that should be part of the transaction. Regarding the supplies, David, I have been instructed that the supplies and pharmaceuticals are not part of the transaction and that they should be removed and sent back to suppliers for credit."

"Well, Gordon, that's exactly opposite of what I have been told. I've been told that you would be handing over a fully stocked hospital. I will immediately make contact with the Palace to clarify this issue."

This was the first of many serious misunderstandings between Dr. Morehead and me. He was trying to do his job and I was trying to do mine. We were both caught in the middle as a result of the dealings between the powers-that-be. His boss, Dr Anwar Jabarti representing the Palace, told him one thing. The private office told me something else. These misunderstandings were all the result of having no formal agreement concerning the hospital transaction.

By February 20th, the hospital's census had dropped to about forty patients. The outpatient visits had fallen from 1200 per day to about 300 per day. Most of the insurance companies and employer groups, such as ARAMCO, were making their arrangements with other doctors and hospitals. We were satisfied that by the takeover date we would have virtually no patients in the hospital, except true emergency or ICU patients that could not be transferred immediately to other facilities.

Dr. Mohsin, representing the medical staff, convinced me that the last outpatient service should be concluded on the last day of February. We also informed the local Ministry of Health (MOH) that the emergency room would be closed effective March 1st. Even with all these actions, we continued to be hassled by Dr. Morehead about the importance of having no Al-Salama Hospital private patients in the hospital past March 6th.

Word was beginning to get back to Dr. Morehead and his boss Dr. Jabarti in Riyadh that the physicians at Al-Salama Hospital were very dissatisfied in the manner that they were being handled by KFSHRC. The Al-Salama staff had been provided conflicting information regarding the process of applying to KFSHRC. There was obvious confusion and growing resentment by the Al-Salama employees, especially among the physicians. It was extremely important to KFSHRC that they be able to recruit a large number of nurses and at least some physicians from the Al-Salama staff to have the resources available to reopen on March 7th.

Dr. Morehead approached me again about another meeting with the general staff to "calm the troops" as he put it and to articulate what the hiring process was.

Again, the auditorium was completely full with much discussion taking place among the staff.

It was easy to see which members of the Al-Salama staff had secured new positions with KFSHRC. Either those employees were not at this meeting, or if they were, they were seated next to their soon-to-be new colleagues.

I immediately turned the podium over to Dr. Morehead. I had noticed that Dr. Taher, KFSHRC Medical Director, was less and less present with Dr. Morehead in such general staff meetings. I could have been wrong, but

I was beginning to sense that Dr. Taher was distancing himself from Dr. Morehead, who seemed to be getting less popular by the minute.

This particular all-staff meeting had the opposite effect of what KFSHRC had hoped for. Dr. Morehead had really nothing new to report and was becoming agitated at the many duplicate questions that were being asked. The epitome of this meeting occurred when one of our senior consultant physicians asked an elementary, but sincere, question.

"Dr. Morehead, I am still a little confused about the formal application form versus a simple letter that indicates our interest in employment with KFSHRC."

"Your name, sir?"

"Yes, I'm sorry; my name is Dr. Mohamed Tarkhan, Consultant in Neurology."

"Dr.Tarkhan, you must complete the application form as I have already indicated several times. A letter of interest is not sufficient. Now sir, are you less confused?" You could have heard a pin drop after this comment.

Once Dr. Morehead had turned the podium back to me, the staff took this opportunity to question again the status of the salary and service award payouts. I reconfirmed what I had stated in the previous presentation that according to the private office, this would occur about one week after the turnover date. I anticipated a March 15th payout date.

After this meeting, many of the Al-Salama physicians made up their minds not to apply to KFSHRC. They immediately began to talk with the other private hospitals to secure their futures.

As far as I can remember, this was the last general meeting of the staff before the takeover date. Also, from this time on in private conversations, Dr. Morehead was frequently referred to by most of the Al-Salama physicians, including myself, as Dr. Lesserhead.

Most of the private independent physicians were Saudi nationals who practiced only part-time at Al-Salama with the balance of their time spent at the University. There were two exceptions, Dr. P.K., and an American Board Certified pediatrician. These two were the only private independent physicians practicing full-time at Al-Salama Hospital.

With the exception of Dr. P.K.'s clinic, all the other private independent clinics were located on the third floor of the utility building. Extra space on the third floor of the utility building, immediately above the parking garage, had been converted to private doctor clinic space. The third floor area had also served as the temporary location for the hospital's finance department while their permanent space was being constructed in the main facility.

These clinics were designed to be temporary, but they served the private independent physicians very well. There was very easy access to these clinics, allowing their patients to bypass the standard ground floor outpatient registration process. The utility building was connected to the main hospital by a bridge that traversed the city boulevard running in front of the main entrance of the hospital. Thus, it was very easy for these private doctors and their patients to go from their clinic to the hospital and visa versa.

The private independent physicians, like our employed physicians, were very concerned about whether or not they would be allowed to continue to use these clinics after March 6th.

A meeting was held between the fifteen private independent physicians and Dr. Morehead. These were some of the best-known and most prestigious physicians in Jeddah; most were Saudis. It would be politically important for Dr. Morehead to do what he could to accommodate them for at least the short term. I had advised him of this and had suggested KFSHRC should, for public relations purposes, consider not charging rent to these doctors.

The meeting with these physicians went well. They were all informed that they could continue to use the clinics until September 30th. They could also use the hospital's diagnostic services if they desired, for a fee. Their private patients, however, would have to be admitted to some other hospital, for they would not be eligible for inpatient services at KFSHRC. This meeting was documented by minutes that proved to be quite important a couple of months later.

The private doctors were happy with this approach. It took the pressure off their having to find new clinic space immediately.

Because of not being able to use the hospital's inpatient services after the March 7th takeover date, all the private independent physicians, with the exception of Dr. P.K., elected to find new clinic space in Jeddah and vacated their clinics on the third floor by May. This was unfortunate for KFSHRC. If they truly intended to get involved with the private practice of medicine, they would have done themselves a great favor by maintaining these private doctors' association with KFSHRC.

I felt it was a good time to ask Dr. Morehead about the vacant space on the third floor, adjacent to these clinics that had recently been used by the finance department.

"David, you know we are going to appoint an Al-Salama Hospital demobilization team that will probably be functional for up to five to six months after the takeover. Can that group of individuals use the vacant finance space on the third floor?"

He replied that he understood the importance of such a wrap up team and volunteered the space, committing it to our use until September 30th, just like the private physician's space on that floor.

I felt very good about this, for I was worried about where this demobilization team would be located. Because of the type of activities this team would be involved in, the location needed to be on the Al- Salama campus. At that time, I thought September 30th should be ample time for the team to complete its wrap-up activities. As far as I can remember, after the takeover announcement, this was the only time that Dr. Morehead accommodated any of my requests.

Shortly thereafter, Dr. P.K. came to my office.

"Mr. Gordon, I had an official meeting with Dr. Morehead, and we have agreed that I should relocate my clinic to the third floor of the utility building where the other private physician clinics are located."

I responded that there was some vacate space on the third floor of the utility building where the other private physicians had their offices and clinics. I was certain that KFSHRC would not allow her to remain in her present clinic on the first floor. Every one of the KFSHRC physicians would be vying for that location. It was right next to labor and delivery and thus, prime space. I mentioned to P.K. that I knew how fond she was of her clinic and I knew that she had been awarded this location because of her hard work and dedication to Al-Salama Hospital. But, if I were she, I would immediately go ahead and relocate to that vacant clinic space on the third floor while it was still available. This is exactly what she did.

The termination letters to all staff that had evidentially been signed by Sheikh Sultan had been out for about two weeks. Front-page feature articles in both the English and Arabic version of the *Saudi Gazette* and *Arab News* had been published: "Al-Salama Hospital's Fired Staff Face Uncertain Future," "Hospital Sacks All Staff," "KFSHRC to Take over Al-Salama

Hospital On March 7th." These were the headline articles. This takeover of Al-Salama was receiving much publicity, much more than what the National Commercial Bank (NCB) had received several months previously when it was taken over.

I called Jerry Mc Duffy at the private office to see if he would like to have lunch. This was one of the few times in the past two years that I had visited with Jerry. I talked with him about what had happened and what the current status of the hospital was.

"Gordon, I do not have anything to do with the hospital as far as the private office goes. What you have told me is basically what I know. I will say this. As bad as this sounds regarding Al-Salama Hospital, it pales against what happened to NCB. With all due respect regarding this situation with your hospital, the bank takeover hurts me much more, as I'm sure it does the owner, Sheikh Khalid, and his sons A.R. and Sultan."

By the first week of March patient care activity had almost completely stopped. There were only about a dozen inpatients; we anticipated that all of these would be discharged before March 7th. There was one exception, that being a staff member's premature newborn baby in the NICU.

I had presented a plan to Dr. Rayes concerning the formation of a demobilization team that would go into action on March 7th. Fortunately, Dr. Morehead had agreed to the space on the third floor where this team would be located. The function of this team would be quite varied with the major activities being as follows: (1) acting as a liaison between KFSHRC and Saudi ABV; (2) securing and moving all 300,000 Al- Salama active patient medical records out of the hospital; (3) distributing the final salaries and accrued service awards; (4) securing exit visas; (5) transferring Igamas (employer sponsorship letters); (6) conducting equipment and supply inventories; (7) collecting account receivables; (8) paying account payables; (9) completing the final audit for the hospital; (10) helping the ex-Al-Salama employees make the transition to new jobs and helping with housing, air transportation, and anything else we could during this difficult time.

The plan called for about fifty remaining employees for the first month with the number rapidly decreasing each month until by August 1st there would only be about six left. The team was to be completely dismantled by August 15th, 2000. Ex-Al-Salama staff who had the necessary skill levels and who had not already secured new employment would fill all positions recommended. I had recommended that I direct this team for the primary reason that I wanted to see it through to its completion.

Dr. Rayes had to get approval from A.R. for the demobilization team. It still had not been given.

One evening during the first week of March as I was driving down to the old souq in central Jeddah, I received a call on my cellular phone from Dr. Morehead.

"Hello, Gordon, this is David Morehead. I have been informed that sometime later this evening a semi-trailer will be pulling up to the hospital's warehouse and loading up the remaining supplies and disposables. I have ordered a legion of soldiers to surround the hospital. They have strict instructions to stop any such truck and take those involved into custody. The Royal Palace has stated that the supplies stay and that what you all are doing is stealing from the Royal Family."

I couldn't believe what I was hearing. I pulled my Land Rover over to the side of the road and responded.

"David, as for as I know, there is no semi-truck en route to the hospital to load up the supplies. If there were, we would do it in the light of day not during the night. By the way, have you considered sending in armored tanks and air support as well?"

He replied, "Well, I hope you are telling me the truth and that I have been misinformed. Consider you and your staff warned regarding this matter."

I sat there for a while contemplating how this situation had deteriorated so far so fast. Just six weeks ago, we were blissfully happy to be moving towards a strategic collaboration with KFSHRC. Now, they were stating they had called in a legion of soldiers to surround our hospital and were accusing us of stealing from the Royal Family. Wow! How things had changed!

I drove back towards Al-Salama at about 10 pm to see if, in fact, there was any unusual activity. To my surprise, there were military personnel at the hospital stationed at all the various entrances and exits and at the main warehouse. This was really too much.

I called Dr. Rayes at home and gave him the entire story about what Dr. Morehead had said and about seeing the military personnel outside the hospital.

"Gordon, this is the last straw. I am going to contact A.R. immediately. If it is the last thing we do, we are going to get Dr. Morehead out of Saudi Arabia. To save time, please construct for my signature a strong letter addressed to Dr. Jabarti requesting Dr. Morehead's immediate removal from this site and giving the various reasons for such. I will sign it tomorrow morning and we will fax it to Dr. Jabarti. I'm sure A.R. will support this action."

Dr Rayes signed the letter the next morning, and we faxed it to Dr. Jabarti in Riyadh as planned.

Later that day, Dr. Rayes called me by phone.

"It worked! Dr. Jabarti has said that he will be removing Dr. Lesserhead (even Dr. Rayes was now referring to David as Dr. Lesserhead) from the site immediately. Our new contact will be Mr. Suliman Al Salama until further notice."

I was delighted with the news. David had become a real pain in the ass. KFSHRC officials were definitely doing themselves a favor by pulling him out. We had previous experience working with Suliman who had been the initial KFSHRC project manager until January and found him a very sensible individual who got along well with most everyone.

When I announced this news to my senior management at the following morning's meeting, they were all elated as I had been. Dr. Mohsin was especially happy to hear that Dr. Morehead was being removed from the KFSHRC transition team.

We all assumed that Dr Jabarti had advised David of this matter, for he was not on site the following Saturday or Sunday. I had been trying to reach Suliman Al-Salama, our newly appointed KFSHRC contact person, who also was apparently still in Riyadh.

On Monday morning about 9:15 immediately following the early bird meeting, to my surprise David walked into the executive conference room and sat down. As my senior management team was leaving, they were as surprised to see him as I was. He began by inquiring how many inpatients we had and if we still felt confident that the hospital would be empty by midnight March 6th. There were only about four more days before the takeover was effective.

I responded to David that I had been trying to reach Mr. Suliman Al-Salama, but I had been unsuccessful in doing so. He asked why it was necessary for me to contact him. Was this something personal or business related? I replied that it was business related.

"Gordon, you should know by now that anything having to do with Al-Salama Hospital and KFSHRC needs to go through me."

"David," I replied, "have you not heard; have you spoken with Dr. Jabarti?"

David asked what I was talking about and told me to quit talking in circles.

"Ok, David, I will be quite blunt. We have been informed that your ass is out of here and not a minute too soon as for as I'm concerned. We were advised that Mr.Suliman Al-Salama is taking your place temporarily and that he is our new contact man. Frankly, I'm surprised as hell to see you here."

Dr. Morehead's face became white. He stood up. "Gordon, I have not been advised of this, and until such time as I am by Dr. Jabarti, I am the one in charge here for KFSHRC."

I replied, "Perhaps you should talk with Dr.Jabarti, not me."

One half hour later, David came storming back into my office.

"Gordon, your information is incorrect. I have spoken with Dr.Jabarti. I am still in charge of this transition and you need to continue to work only through me as it relates to KFSHRC." He then stormed out.

I went in to see Dr. Rayes to advise him of this encounter. I mentioned that it appeared as though Dr. Jabarti had told him one thing and Dr. Morehead something else.

After I related what had just occurred, we both just shook our heads in disbelief. Unfortunately, this type of approach seems to be a standard way many Saudis go about doing their business. Depending upon whom they are speaking to, they may say one thing to one individual or group and exactly the opposite to another individual or group. For this very reason, it is best to have any thing of significance in writing.

This fiasco did not improve the situation with David.

The private office had requested that we produce a professionally filmed video of Al-Salama Hospital within forty-eight hours. The purpose of the video was to be able to demonstrate to the palace representatives that this facility was worth a lot of money. The use of this video would be effective in introducing Al-Salama Hospital to individuals representing the Palace who might not have been that familiar with the facility. The sound track, background features, and overall production turned out to be excellent.

On the day before the takeover, I had the last direct report meeting. It was a very sad occasion for several of the key staff had been at Al-Salama from its beginning. Everyone was wishing each other the best of luck, for many had uncertain futures. We showed the newly produced video. Several individuals simply broke down and cried while watching the video. The work that had been put forth by these individuals to make this a world-class hospital cannot be adequately conveyed. We all had the same sinking feeling that we had been betrayed. The uncertain part was that we were not altogether convinced that the betrayal was totally at the hands of the Palace and KFSHRC. Every one of the hospital's employees was totally numb over what had happened. We had absolutely no control over the situation.

Each of the direct reports at the meeting was provided a complimentary copy of this well-done video.

I still had not received approval to activate the demobilization team. The hospital employees were very concerned about who would look after their interests and take care of the many outstanding issues after the takeover date.

On the afternoon of March 5th, Dr. Rayes asked that I visit with him concerning activities after March 6th.

"Gordon," he began, "A.R. and I have reviewed your plan concerning the demobilization team and its responsibilities. We want you to head this team up with certain provisos."

It was now common knowledge that Dr.Rayes had secured a position at the private office working with A.R. and Sultan. Rayes had shared this with me in confidence three weeks earlier. The private office had under-gone a restructuring and had created a new name for the family business headquarters, Al Murjan ("pearl of the sea" in Arabic).

Rayes continued, "A.R. has given me the chance to manage a significant part of the family businesses related to health care services and products, plus some of the family's private affairs. None of us would have ever predicted that Sheikh Khalid's hospital would have been taken over by the Palace in this fashion. But it has happened and now we must move on and simply make the best of it.

"The family is interested in having another hospital. They actually own a building that was designed to be a hotel. The building has never been used and could be converted into a small hospital with several outpatient clinics. The new hospital we envision will be much smaller and considerably less grandiose than this hospital.

"I am offering you the position of CEO at the new Al-Salama Hospital. The compensation package cannot be as generous, but you would be in full control. I will not even have an office in the hospital. The stipulation to this offer, assuming we can work out the compensation details, is that I do want to be quite involved with any financial issues that may arise in the operation of the hospital."

My mind was rushing at this moment. Dr. Rayes had stated that I would have full control, yet he wanted to be in charge of the financial issues. This seemed like a significant dichotomy, but this was not the time to question his provisos.

We agreed that the duties of the demobilization team would be those that I had previously recommended. In addition, a small number of employees would begin planning for the new hospital and would become part of the demobilization team as well.

Dr. Rayes continued, "A.R. will not be paying the ex-employee service awards quite as quickly as initially planed. This is one of the issues that he is negotiating with the palace representatives. Also, the total funding for the demobilization team must come from the collections of the outstanding receivables. On March 7th, your demobilization team operational account will have zero funds. Incidentally, the February employee payroll will also be delayed, except for the members of the demobilization team, assuming you can collect enough money."

This news about delaying the service award payouts and the last paychecks was very disturbing to me. We had decided that instead of paying the February salaries on March 1st, which would have been the usual process, we would pay it no later than one week after the March 7th along with the service award benefits due. Salaries due would be for the period of February 1st through March 12th (42 days of salary) plus the service awards. The total amount of funds required to make these payments was about 27 million riyals or about 7.2 million dollars. I had been told several times by the private office that there would be no problem with this, and I had told the hospital staff the same on at least two separate occasions. I was now beginning to understand why the employees had been so concerned about the issue even as I tried to convince them that their concerns were totally unfounded. Perhaps my naivety in believing what I had been told was beginning to surface.

I asked Dr. Rayes how long he thought this delay would be. I reiterated that I had stood in front of an auditorium full of employees and conveyed the message that the final salary and accrued service award benefits would be paid no later than one week after the takeover date. He assured me that any delay would not be for long that A.R. was simply trying to get the hospital transaction with the Royals down in writing. Verbally, they had agreed to the key transaction details, but he was having a little difficulty in getting it reduced to a written contract. Rayes reminded me that one of the outstanding issues was who would be responsible for paying the liabilities.

"Rayes," I responded, "If the delay is more than a couple of weeks, we are going to have some serious problems with these ex-employees. I want to bring you a proposal, for a very quick response, before I agree to direct this demobilization team and start the planning for a new hospital."

I was not overly concerned about starting the demobilization team with absolutely no funding. I anticipated that we would collect at least 1.5 million riyals before the end of March and probably at least that much again in April. I knew that to pay the demobilization team their soon-to-be delayed salaries of February 1st through March 12th plus their new salaries for the period through March 31st would require the availability of some 1.1 million riyals on April 1st.

For the past week, I had been trying to get the hospital Board to meet for the last time. Resolutions needed to be made and written into the records. One of the resolutions was the dissolution of the Board as of midnight, March 6th. Other resolutions gave thanks to its members for their support and guidance over the past eighteen months.

With great effort on my part, and, likewise, great reluctance by the Board members, we did meet on the late afternoon of March 6th, naturally with the exception of Chairman Sultan. The necessary business was conducted and resolutions presented and approved to be recorded into the annals of the history of Al-Salama Hospital. After the meeting was adjourned, a photo session was held. We had engaged the services of a professional photographer to take several pictures of the medical staff and other key employees earlier that day. The employee pictures were taken outside with the magnificent Al-Salama Hospital VIP bed tower and fountains in the background.

Someday in the distant future when former employees may be looking through some old Saudi albums, they may stumble upon these photographs. I am sure at that time an intense nostalgia will rise when they ponder their experiences at Al-Salama Hospital.

After the Board meeting, I visited with Dr. Rayes regarding the proposal concerning the demobilization team.

"Dr. Rayes, in order for me to be interested in serving on this team and in order for me to be able to recruit the required ex-employees, I must have agreement on two issues. One, I need enough funding placed in the demobilization operational account to cover the back salaries of team members for the period of February 1st through March 12th. This will amount to about six hundred and fifty thousand riyals. I have no concerns about covering all the team's expenses after the start date. But I do not believe it is fair to have to pay the teams pre-operational salaries with no funds to start with. Second, I want a commitment that if for some reason accrued service award payments continue to be delayed, as soon as we have collected enough funds, the demobilization team members will be paid out first."

Dr. Rayes responded that he felt my two requests were very reasonable. We then negotiated my specific arrangements, including the modified package once the demobilization team functions ended and the new hospital developmental team started.

The agreements that were offered to the demobilization team candidates were referred to as independent casual contracts. These agreements represented significant reductions in the monthly salaries for several of the members, including me. There were no vacation benefits, no health benefits, no sick leave, and no housing benefits. Each of us could be terminated with one day's notice. The only incentive I could offer was the guarantee that they would be paid their contracted salaries as long as funds were available and the team members would have first priority for the accrued service award benefit payments that were due when enough funds were collected by the demobilization team.

At midnight on March 6th, there were no Al-Salama Hospital patients in the hospital. Even the tiny baby who was in critical condition in the NICU had been transferred to the University Hospital upon the insistence of KFSHRC.

The following morning at 9 am, Dr. Morehead came to the executive suite and entered. I ordered coffee for both of us and we went into the executive conference room for a brief discussion. I spent a few minutes advising Dr. Morehead of the responsibilities of the newly formed demobilization team. Once he realized that I would be directing the team, he probably regretted that he had already promised space on the third floor of the utility building for this activity.

I handed over the keys to the executive suite to David, shook his hand, and wished him good luck. Al-Salama Hospital was no more. It was now a satellite facility of KFSHRC, Riyadh.

Chapter Twelve

Aftermath

"Acceptance of what has happened is the first step to overcoming the consequences of any misfortune."

William James
(March 7th, 2000–November 15th, 2000)

When I look back at the demise of Al-Salama Hospital and dissect the chain of events that lead to this outcome, in summary, this is what happened as I perceived it.

+ Sheikh Khalid builds a lavish five star hospital with more of a benevolent mission than other private hospitals. This hospital has tremendous fixed costs.

+ As a result of the on-going BCCI problems and ultimate collapse, Sheikh Khalid steadily loses power and influence with the ruling family, who acquire 50% control of NCB in 1999 and the balance of control in 2002. Sheikh Khalid virtually disappears from Jeddah with various rumors associated with his disappearance to Taif, Saudi Arabia. The Sheikh's various business interests, including the NCB and sole ownership of the Al-Salama Hospital are handed over to his sons, A.R. and Sultan to oversee.

+ The older son, Sheikh A.R. assumes the role of owner's representative for the hospital even though Sheikh Sultan, the younger son, is the hospital's official Chairman. Sheikh Sultan has little interest in the hospital. Neither son has the affinity towards the hospital that Sheikh Khalid had.

+ The sons discover that the return on investment for Al-Salama Hospital is not going to meet their expectations. They are much more short-term focused than their father and do not have the same affinities for the hospital as their father. When they decide to lease or sell the hospital, they discover that there are very few interested parties because of the high cost.

+ The Royal Family desires to have a similar type of health care hospital available to them in Jeddah as they have in Riyadh. They hear about Al-Salama Hospital's being on the market.

+ The Royal Family instructs their health care sub-contractor, King Faisal Specialist Hospital and Research Center (KFSHRC), in Riyadh to evaluate Al-Salama Hospital to see if an affiliation or strategic collaboration is feasible.

+ KFSHRC, looking after its own interests, suggests to Prince Abdul Aziz Bin Fahad (youngest son of King Fahad) that the hospital could also serve private patients and, thus, could be a good business.

+ Representatives of Prince Abdul Aziz discuss possible hospital transactions with A.R. The Royals are not happy with the sale price as presented. A.R. refuses to accept the terms of their offer. A Royal decree is issued to the legal owner, Sheikh Khalid, to vacate the hospital within six-weeks with the details of the transaction to be worked out later. The Royal representatives make some type of verbal commitment to A.R.

+ On behalf of Prince Abdul Aziz, KFSHRC takes over the hospital operations as the Palace's healthcare sub-contractor. The name of the Al Salama Hospital is officially changed to KFSHRC-Jeddah. The verbal agreement between the Royals and Sheikh A.R. is never converted into a written agreement, resulting in the Royals paying the owner, Sheikh Khalid, or owner's representative, Sheikh A.R., very little, if anything, for the facility.

What remains unclear (and will probably be forever) are three primary issues involving the takeover: How much was due to the problems Sheikh Khalid had with the Royal Family concerning NCB and other concerns? Did the sons simply wish to unload the hospital prematurely? How aggressive were certain Royal Family members in commandeering a high potential private business? Perhaps the takeover was a combination of all three.

Sheikh A.R. and Sheikh Sultan proved to be generous regarding the housing benefits for the ex-employees. I had suggested to Dr. Rayes that we should try to extend the period for ex-employees to be able to stay in their hospital- provided accommodations, especially those with kids in school. All such housing was leased from other individuals or compounds such as Saudi City, which was owned by Saudi Arabian Airlines. In most of these cases other than Saudi City, the housing owners had already been paid up for six months to a year in advance. This is common practice in the Kingdom. Many of the employees with families lived in Saudi City compound. We did not have to pay rent there as it was simply offset against the huge receivable that was owed to us by Saudi Arabian Airlines. At least this arrangement with Saudi City compound did not require a cash outlay. The way I saw it, if we did not treat another Saudi airline patient, we would have cash free housing for the next thirty years. For this reason we had begun to place almost all family employees into the Saudi City compound.

The private office agreed to the extended housing benefits. The final outcome agreed that all family contracted employees could remain in their hospital-provided housing free of charge until July 1st. For those employees who received housing allowances, the allowance would be paid through May 31st. The only legal obligation required of the private office was to provide housing or to pay housing allowance through March 12th.

This positive and generous gesture by A.R. and Sheikh Sultan was very well received. The families with children could allow them to complete the school term without having to worry about housing. Unknown at the time, this gesture would play a major role in helping to keep the lid on in the very difficult days to come.

I had decided that with my significant reduction in income I did not need to continue to live in such an expensive compound as the Nueva Andalucia. The villa was also much larger than I required. Effective April 1st, I signed a three month contract that could be extended on a month-to-month basis with Arabian Homes, whose one-bed room accommodation was more of an apartment or flat than it was a villa. Arabian Homes is one of the more up-scale western housing compounds in Jeddah. My new flat proved to be quite satisfactory at one-third the cost of where I had been living. Although it would have been too small had the family been there any length of time, for my situation it worked out fine.

For the past six months, I had been trying to get my parents to come visit me in Jeddah. Although they are fortunate to be in excellent health and have the means to travel extensively, they have tended to shy away from overseas ventures. Dr. P. K. had tried to bring them to Jeddah when she visited with them on a sailing cruise the previous October. She teased my father as a man who called himself a sailor and yet didn't like adventure. She challenged him to see Saudi Arabia.

Dad usually commented to us that he had no interest in going to Saudi Arabia, that those Arabs wouldn't have a pot to piss in if it were not for their oil, that the only thing over there was sand and camels. P.K. simply replied, "I want to change your wrong opinion."

One day in January, the Saudi Gazette carried a front-page article on the first European cruise liner that had stopped at the port of Jeddah a couple days before. The newspaper picture depicted a rather large group of older European tourists walking down in the souqs of old Jeddah. The article went on to state how much this tourist group had enjoyed their stop in Jeddah. This was a sign of the times. The Kingdom was really serious about opening up the tourism industry to outsiders. I faxed the article to Dad.

Between this article and Dr. P.K.'s relentless coaxing to visit Jeddah, they finally agreed to come during the second and third week of March. In many ways, it was a bad time for me because the takeover had just been completed and the demobilization team activities had just begun. Offsetting these negatives were the facts that I was still living at the luxurious Nueva Andalucia, the weather in March is great, and this might be their last opportunity to visit.

Once they arrived, they had a wonderful time. Dr. P.K. took them under her wing and cooked up several of her delicious Indian meals for them. She also showed them around while I was busy at the hospital. She was happy to have them as they filled the void of her own parents, whom she missed a lot. Her love for them was genuine.

On one Thursday afternoon, P.K. and I drove my parents to Taif, and we all spent the night at the Al Hada Sheraton. The drive up the escarpment was quite fascinating and exciting as it would be for anyone's first time ascent to the top. We arrived early enough that same afternoon to take them to the top of the Camel Trail near Harithi. The fifteen kilometer four wheel drive adventure to our designation is always a true test for the Land Rover. The view of the mountains was breathtaking especially in the cool, clear weather. Hiking all around the area, we saw several of the large, beautifully colored blue lizards basking in the sun. My parents enjoyed it tremendously; P.K. did not let them forget their reluctance before they agreed to visit Jeddah.

The next morning we got up early, had our breakfast, retrieved the free picnic lunch the hotel had so generously prepared, and departed for the Wahba Crater. The scenery was a total contrast to what they had seen the previous day in the mountain range of Taif.

We arrived back to Jeddah late that evening after a great adventure.

During their visit, they took a couple of short excursions to the souqs of old Jeddah. My mom got a kick out of bargaining with one of the elderly gold souq owners. To her delight, she negotiated a good deal (so she thought) for a gold bracelet and earrings. She was surprised to see so much gold hanging all over the shop.

The following week, I took off one workday for another combination snorkeling / fishing excursion. My parents had a great time snorkeling. I caught a small sea turtle while scuba diving at five-mile reef. When I bought the turtle up to the boat to show them, my mom said to P.K., "He's been catching turtles since he was a little boy." They swore they saw a large shark trailing me while I was diving in relatively shallow water (30 feet) directly under the boat.

Later that day, Dad caught a couple of nice Jackfish that gave him quite a battle. They thoroughly enjoyed the outing on the Red Sea. That evening, back at the Nueva Andalucia we barbequed the fresh fish.

While they were there, I introduced them to Dr. Rayes, who always took time to be gracious with guests. His greatest attribute is how he can make people feel welcomed. He is an individual impossible to dislike or to feel uncomfortable with during an initial introduction.

Dad kidded with him. "Gordon here tells me that you are in training to be a Sheikh, which means that you cannot work more than three hours a day."

In his good-natured way, he showed those sparkling white teeth in a broad smile and responded. "Well, with Gordon here doing all the work, I have plenty of time for Sheikh training."

We had a difficult time securing seats on their departure flights. The Hajj was just over, jamming the airport with pilgrims trying to return to their homes all over the world. Millions of Hajj pilgrims visit Mecca during the season, paying their respect and worshiping Allah. Other than dealing with this particular problem, my parents really enjoyed their trip to the Kingdom. They had seen much more of the country in a two-week period than most expats would see in a year.

My problems with the takeover went on unabated during this time. After the previous fiasco with Dr. Morehead, he was coolly avoiding contact with me for the most part. By now I had moved from the executive suite in the hospital to the third floor of the utility building where the demobilization team was located.

He quickly moved into my old office and was making sure that all knew that he was still in charge of the takeover. He continued to upset people, including some of the newly arrived King Faisal staff from Riyadh. I believed it would only be a matter of time before he was removed.

Mr. Safar introduced me to the head of the new maintenance sub-contractor, Saudi Oger. He indicated that Saudi Oger was removing the three large Al-Salama signs on the outside of the building and asked where we would like to have them stored.

I looked outside and saw the large construction crane in the process of removing our signs. Another deep, sinking feeling hit my stomach. The change of the name of the hospital and the removing of the Al Salama Hospital logo signs clearly demonstrated that our hospital was no more. All of the ex-employees felt the same way. It was like a bad dream from which I expected to awaken and find that all this had gone away and things were back to normal. Unfortunately, it was reality. The removal of the Al-Salama signs confirmed the reality of the matter. So many of the ex-employees had been here since the original hospital had opened; some eleven years previously. The sense of great loss created numbness in everyone. Some had tears rolling down their cheeks. It felt like a funeral.

By the middle of March, the ex-employees were becoming impatient with the delayed final salary and service award benefit payments.

I went to Dr. Rayes office, that had also been relocated to the third floor of the utility building.

"What have you heard about the payments due to the ex-employees? This delay is now starting to get a little serious. The extension of the housing benefits was much appreciated by the ex-staff, but what have we done for them lately? If we do not receive funds to pay out everyone due by April 1st, we are going to be in big trouble. You know, Dr. Rayes, I am the one that stated to them that they should have no worries regarding this matter. They are expecting this issue to be resolved."

"Gordon, I'm sure that the issue will be solved before April 1st. There are still two weeks before that time. By the way, my office at the new private office is ready. I will be moving out there next week."

The Al-Muujan private office had changed locations, having secured a new one-story office complex. Dr. Rayes had secured a new position, Head of Medical Sector. Under the new organizational structure it was very clear that the Director of the Al Salama demobilization team reported to the Head of Medical Sector at Al-Murjan. But based on the short-term nature and the responsibilities of the wrap up assignment, this new hierarchy caused me absolutely no concerns.

The first week of April came and went, and we still had not received the necessary funds for payment of back salaries and service award benefits. We did have enough funds in the demobilization team account to pay the salaries of the members of this team, but this caused even greater concerns among many other ex-employees regarding why their back salaries were still delinquent while the demobilization team members received theirs. These ex-employees had no way of knowing that the guaranteed payout was one of the stipulated prerequisites to recruiting the demobilization team members. We began to refer to this team as DMT for short.

Our initial collection efforts were going well. I anticipated that there would be sufficient funds in the DMT account by the third or fourth week of April to make the service award payouts to the DMT members, even if special funding was not received. As with the salaries, this had also been a stipulated prerequisite for those on the DMT. I was sure that the necessary funds to pay all the other ex-employees' back salaries and service awards would surely be made available before mid-April. After all, that would be more than a month late, a ridiculous delay.

We had presented a complete inventory of capital assets to Dr. Morehead the last week of March. These assets included all medical and non-medical equipment that had been delivered on site by Saudi ABV. The listing did not contain certain non-medical equipment such as desks and old computers that were more than five years old. This inventory listing had a value of about two hundred million riyals.

Dr. Morehead contacted me, "Gordon, how do we know that this inventory listing is correct? Our people were not involved. As far as we are concerned, we cannot accept this."

"David, your people were asked to be a part of this endeavor and decided not to participate fully in the process. As far as I'm concerned, this represents the most accurate inventory available as of midnight March 6th. I am not in favor of doing another inventory. I have been informed that some of this equipment has already been shipped to your Riyadh facility."

An accurate equipment inventory listing was quite important. If the hospital transaction turned out to be a lease agreement, a listing of what we were leasing would be critical. If it were an outright sale, perhaps it would not be as important but would still help support the asking price.

Dr. Morehead stared at me. "Well Gordon, I cannot recommend that the Palace accept this and that's final."

The following day Dr. Anwar Jabarti was escorting a Saudi named Dr. Sultan Bahabri through the hospital. I had known Dr. Bahabri previously because he headed up the KFSHRC Medical Outreach program in Riyadh. I had dealt with him the previous year when we were considering a contract with KFSHRC for education training. We had developed a good rapport with each other during that time.

That very morning a rumor emerged that Dr. Bahabri would be taking Dr. Morehead's place as interim CEO of the Jeddah facility. I wished that were the case, but I doubted that it were so.

Later that afternoon, I received a call from Dr. Morehead. "Hello, Gordon, this is David. I'm going to make your day. I'm going back to the KFSHRC in Riyadh and Dr. Bahabri will be taking my place immediately."

I sat up straight. "Is that a fact? Well, I want to wish you the best of luck David. I know that many of the disagreements we had were because of the ambiguous demands that we both faced during this time period. Perhaps in the future we will work together again under different circumstances."

I doubted very seriously if either one of us would be able to work together in the future. Lord, I hoped not.

At the end of the first week of April, Dr. Sultan Bahabri arrived in Jeddah. He and I met on the second day of his new assignment as interim CEO.

Within one month after returning to Riyadh, Dr. Morehead was released by KFSHRC. I guess he returned to the USA. I have not heard from him since.

After some brief discussions surrounding our past endeavors working together, Dr. Bahabri got right down to business.

"Gordon, I understand that the working relationship between KFSHRC and Al-Salama has not been good. Frankly, that is why I have been assigned this position and Dr. Morehead has been sent back to Riyadh. Gordon, my style is completely different from David's. I believe in teamwork, open communications, and building relationships. I hope to make the transaction as smooth as possible, and I know that you feel the same. I'm sure we will have our disagreements; after all, we are on opposite sides of the fence. But Gordon, I believe that as professionals we can work through our differences to arrive at what's best for both organizations."

I responded, "Dr. Bahabri, I feel as you do. I'm glad you're here. I have been given instructions to cooperate fully with whoever is in charge. I know that we can bridge a lot of gaps that have occurred since January."

"Gordon, here are my main concerns as they relate to the activities that you may have some control over: (1) completion of the hospital construction by Saudi ABV, under our supervision; (2) payment of the ex-employee's back salaries and service award benefits for many of these individuals have or will be joining us; (3) resolution of the equipment inventory listing; (4)

resolution of the supply and disposable issues; (5) recruitment of selected ex-Al-Salama employees.

"By the way, Gordon, a decision has been made that this hospital will not be a satellite facility of the KFSHRC in Riyadh. It will be a freestanding facility separate from Riyadh. I'm sure we will continue to borrow resources from there at least in the short term. Being separate from KFSHRC, Riyadh is sort of a mixed blessing. We will have much more control, but also we will be held solely responsible for making this a successful venture for the Palace. The hospital's official name has been changed to King Faisal Specialist Hospital and Research Center (KFSHRC), Jeddah, and this name will soon appear on the out-side of the building, our stationary, envelopes, and other printed materials."

We were able to agree on two of the five concerns Dr. Bahabri raised during this initial meeting.

The KFSHRC, Jeddah would evaluate all supplies, disposables, and pharmaceuticals on-site and determine what they desired to keep. They would then purchase these from us. The rest we could remove and do with as we pleased. This was a great start; they would probably buy at least 1.5 million worth of supplies, and we could probably get another 2 million as credits against our payables for the items they did not want. The monies from KFSHRC, Jeddah, would go directly into the DMT operational account, I thought. The credits would help relieve the payment pressures from some of the main suppliers.

The second issue we resolved was agreeing to support their efforts to hire specific ex-Al-Salama hospital staff. It was going to be extremely important that they employ a significant number of our Asian nursing personnel in order to operate the hospital. The DMT desired to do whatever we could to help secure new employment for those of our ex-employees who wanted to stay in the Kingdom. Dr. Bahabri and I discussed how best to reopen discussions with our physicians, who had become very disenchanted with the way they had initially been approached. Eventually, almost thirty percent of the old Al-Salama staff were rehired by King Faisal Hospital, Jeddah, with most being nurses and technicians. Some physicians and administrative personnel, such as Mr. Safar and Mr. Dunn, the ex-CFO, joined the KFSHRC, Jeddah.

The other three issues were much more difficult.

"Dr. Bahabri, Saudi ABV refuses to place itself under the supervision of KFSHRC, Jeddah or your new facility sub-contractor, Saudi Oger. There is intense competition between Saudi ABV and Saudi Oger and Saudi ABV will simply not work under the other company. Saudi ABV has already been paid the full amount for the project, with the exception of a meager 10 million riyal withhold. They have indicated that they will still work directly with me and the other DMT members, since we represent Al-Salama Hospital, whom they were dealing with even though there was never a signed formal contract. If you insist on Saudi ABV's working directly under KFSHRC, Jeddah or Saudi Oger company, they have stated they will shutdown and leave the site uncompleted. I definitely believe they will do just that; it would be to their advantage financially. I'm sure they will have to pay considerably more than 10 million riyals to their sub-contractors to complete this project.

"Regarding the medical and non-medical equipment inventory issue, we feel strongly that this listing is the absolute most accurate there is available representing what was here at mid-night March 6th. I hope that KFSHRC, Jeddah will concur with the listing. It is not appropriate to conduct a new inventory a month after the takeover date.

"Regarding the overdue salaries and service award benefits, Dr. Bahabri, believe me when I say this is my most pressing concern. Unfortunately, it is completely out of my hands. The funds required to accomplish this is a little more than 27 million riyals. These funds have to come either from the old Al-Salama owner or the new owner for this to be completed. Whatever influence you may exert with the Palace through Dr. Jabarti will be very much appreciated."

The two-hour meeting concluded with a sense of understanding between Dr. Bahabri and me. We had many problems yet to solve. We both understood the importance of a professional working relationship in solving difficult problems, even if we were on different sides of the fence.

By mid April necessary funds had still not been received to pay the overdue salaries and service award benefits. I knew that extremely serious problems were developing with the ex-employees.

Dr. Rayes had informed me that A.R. was not having any success with the Palace representatives in getting them to sign a contract to specify what had apparently already been verbally agreed to. The Palace had not paid one halala thus far. Yet their contracted medical care provider, KFSHRC, Jeddah, had occupied Sheikh Khalid's facility for almost six-weeks.

"Gordon," Dr. Rayes began, "A.R. is not going to provide the funds to pay the ex-employees what is owed until the Palace signs a formal contract. He has also instructed me not to release any sponsorship changes for the ex-staff until the contract is signed. Further, he is not going to pay any funds to the vendors for the same reasons. He believes that the ex-employees are really the only leverage he might have in getting the Palace to conclude the transaction."

This position taken by A.R. was extremely bad news. I understood the strategy, but I was having a difficult time agreeing with it. The problems associated with completion of the transaction between A.R. and the Palace did not involve our ex-employees. Why should they continue to suffer because of this issue? Why should we use their shoulders to fire our guns? This was an expression I would hear many times from the ex-employees.

"Dr. Rayes, with all due respect to A.R. and understanding of the frustration he must be experiencing at the hands of the Palace, I fail to see why we should continue to make our ex-employees suffer. Let's face it, the Bin Mahfouz family, as ex-owners of NCB, are not exactly paupers. This approach makes me look like an idiot or liar. I was the one who twice stood before the staff, representing the private office on their instructions, to reassure them that there would be no problem concerning this issue. I really don't appreciate being used in this fashion."

"Gordon, we need to get our ex-employees behind us in raising this issue to a high profile level. We should indirectly suggest that they complain to the Saudi Labor office, their individual consulates, and the newspapers. The only thing that will get the attention of the Royals is bad publicity. Once the newspapers and consulates realize that the nonpayment of back salaries and service award benefits is the direct cause of the Royals' failure to keep a previous commitment, I believe the issue will quickly be resolved."

"OK, I can see the rationale of this strategy, but I am not so sure that the ex-employees will be supporting the Bin Mahfouz family in this matter. I can assure you that they will complain to whoever will listen. Their intent will not be for the reason of supporting the family. Granted, it may produce the desired effect. But at what cost? In my opinion it is going to damage the reputation of the family.

"This is an attempt to get the ex-employees fired up and indirectly helping us solve the problem with the Palace. Between the non-payment issues and the no-Igama transfer stance, we will see our ex-employees take the type of action that should catch the attention of the Palace."

This was probably the lowest point in my career at Al-Salama Hospital. I had told all the staff that these payment issues would not be problematic. I was now beginning to wonder if the ex-employees would ever be paid what they were owed.

When I returned to the DMT offices, I called a meeting of the five key DMT personnel and discussed the matter. All felt very bad, as I did. They even felt that the ex-employees' anger might be taken out against the DMT members. We agreed that we would get the message out indirectly to the ex-employees as requested by the private office.

At the conclusion of these discussions, I probed another area. "Gentlemen, we have another issue we need to discuss. We now have enough funds in the DMT operational account to pay all benefits due to our DMT members. As you are aware, this was an agreement made with each member that once funds became available, DMT members would receive priority. You know the issues that came up when we paid the DMT salaries for February and March and how upset the ex-employees were regarding that matter. They are going to be livid when they hear that we have received all monies due and they have nothing."

Discussion followed regarding the pros and cons of making the payout to the DMT members. In the end, it was unanimously agreed that we should proceed, for this was part of the contract between the DMT members and the private office. After discussing the issue with Dr. Rayes, I decided to proceed with the payout as previously committed.

In retrospect, this decision may have been a mistake. It was certainly one of those damned-if-you-do-and-damned-if-you-don't situations. Legally, by contract, this was a prerequisite offered to get the DMT members to sign their agreements. On the other hand, I knew that to try to keep the payments a secret would not work. I also knew that the ex-employees would probably feel betrayed by the DMT when we took the money.

I ordered the cheques, totaling approximately 2.5 million riyals, to be cut for all DMT members. This would take our DMT operational budget down to about 900,000 riyals, still enough for routine operations.

I then called a meeting of all DMT staff members.

"Folks, I have news for all of us. As you know, one of the incentives of joining this team in early March was that once sufficient funds were collected, DMT members would have service award payout priority. I am happy to report to you that we have sufficient funds and the payout will be made as promised. Mr. Abdullah Harandah, our H.R. specialist and I have received approval from the labor office to fulfill our DMT commitment regarding service awards priority."

There was a great cheer and excitement in the meeting area where some forty-five DMT members had gathered.

I continued, "You all know the criticism we received four weeks ago when our salaries were paid up-to-date while other ex-employees had not been paid. I believe we all recognize that the other ex-Al-Salama Hospital employees, once they hear this news, will respond in a very negative manner. We are considering this payout to represent a one hundred percent loan, interest free, from the DMT against your future service award payment. If we receive the special funding for payment of service awards, we must distribute those funds to you as well. Thus, you would have received a double payment, and in this scenario you will be required to turn those monies back to us. Returning these monies to us will liquidate your DMT loan. On the other hand, if we do not receive the special funding, we will not consider this distribution a loan at all, but rather your direct payout. Frankly, I'm not sure when we will receive necessary special funds, or even if we will receive funds, to pay the others. It will not matter to the others if you had a previous agreement as a DMT member or not. They will be very upset that you have been paid and they have not. I would not openly discuss this issue or flout the fact that you have been paid out. On the other hand, I am not naïve enough to think that this payment will remain hushed. When the others ask you why you were paid, you look them straight in the eyes and tell them that this was part of the agreement when you accepted the scaled-down DMT casual contract. Don't lie about it. You have no reason to feel guilty or to hide this fact. It will not be a matter of if you will be asked; it will be a matter of when. Don't volunteer information, but don't lie about it either."

At this point, the cheques were distributed to the DMT members. Everyone was required to sign a document that stated that this distribution was considered a loan against the eventual service award monies yet to be received.

Even before this distribution to the DMT members, we had already made several small loans to ex-employees who were not working. These loans would be deducted from what was actually owed them once the separate service award funding was received. The DMT operational account was never intended to be used to pay-off the ex-employees benefit payments. When funds were taken out of this account for such purposes, they had to be reimbursed later for the account to remain viable.

We began to meet informally with the ex-employees to discuss the problem the private office was having with the Palace. We indirectly encouraged them to complain to their consulates and to whoever else would listen. A couple of the key DMT staff lived in Saudia City compound where many of the other ex-employees lived. They had nightly gatherings of between sixty to hundred people who were becoming extremely upset with the continued delay in payments.

Newspaper articles started to appear. One front-page article in the Saudi Gazette was entitled "Al Salama Staff Go To Court For Salaries." The following published story provides an excellent account of the situation in late April 2000.

"About 300 employees of Al-Salama Hospital filed a complaint with the Labor Court Tuesday seeking SR 70 million in back salaries and end of service awards. Gordon Utgard, Chief Executive Officer of the hospital, disclosed this to the Gazette.

"Some other employees have taken their complaints to their consulates, he said. A takeover of Al-Salama by King Faisal Specialist Hospital (KFSHRC) was announced a few months ago. According to insiders, the deal has not been finalized yet.

"The Gazette learned Tuesday that some 800 plus employees have not been paid their salaries for the months of February and March, and their end-of-service awards. About 70 workers are now jobless. The others are scouting for jobs.

"At the Labor Court Tuesday, the hospital workers were asked to hold on for a week by which time a decision on a timeframe to discuss the case would be decided.

"A Filipino nurse, who asked not to be identified, said the situation is causing her and her family a lot of distress. She had served the hospital for the past seven years. Her two children who live in the Philippines depend on her for their expenses. They received nothing from her over the past months and have financial commitments they cannot meet. The hospital owes her an estimated SR 65,000, she said.

"At the SR1.5 billion hospital, the salary issue was the talk. The Employees Affair department was a beehive of activity. Employees were seen moving from one office to another trying to get a hearing.

"'Unfortunately, nothing can be done,' one staff said. 'We went to the Labor Court this morning but you know how things are. We will be paid eventually, we know, but we do not expect it soon.'"

The article was right on target, except the amount was 27 million instead of 70 million. The larger figure also included vendor and sub-contractor liabilities.

Several of the hospital physicians had taken jobs at Bakhsh Hospital, another private hospital. I received a telephone call from the hospital's owner, Dr. Abdul Rahman Bakhsh.

"Hello, Mr. Gordon, this is Dr. Bakhsh. I know that you have many difficult problems that you are dealing with. I need your help. The Ministry of Health (MOH) has informed me that if we do not bring these ex-Al-Salama physicians under our sponsorship by May 15th, they will fine me a hundred thousand riyals per physician. We need you to release the sponsorships of these physicians to us, or I will have no choice but to discharge them."

I told Dr. Bakhsh that I understood his predicament. I believed by then at least the issue concerning the Igama transfers would be settled. I assured him that this particular issue was one where instructions from the owner's representative, Sheik A.R., were very clear. I mentioned that I would pass his concerns on to the private office and hopefully the issue would be resolved before the deadline imposed by the MOH.

The non-payment issue and tough stance on the Igama transfers was taking up the vast majority of the DMT staff's time.

Simultaneously, we were still trying to resolve problems between Saudi ABV and KFSHRC, Jeddah. We were also diligently working on the plans for the new Al-Salama Hospital. A facility design-consulting firm was involved with the modification designs of the vacant hotel building that A.R.

wanted to be used as the new hospital. We also had hired Arthur Anderson Company to conduct a marketing survey and feasibility study. All of these issues were beginning to come together, and it was my responsibility to provide the private office a new hospital proposal sometime within the next thirty days.

The DMT team was extremely busy during these days, often working seven days a week twelve hours each day. We were receiving almost daily visits from the various consulates, the Labor office, MOH, and even the local representatives from the mayor's office. All of these individuals demanded time and wanted to know what we were doing to help solve the payment and Igama transfer problems.

I received a call from Dr. Mohsin Hussein, who was now employed as a neurosurgeon at Bakhsh Hospital.

"Hello, Gordon, this is Dr. Mohsin. I know you are aware of the problem that we physicians are facing here. Unless Al-Salama releases the sponsorships, Dr. Bakhsh will have no choice but to terminate our contracts. Not paying us what is owed is one thing. Keeping us from earning our livelihood is quite another."

I mentioned to Dr. Mohsin that I had already received a call from Dr. Bakhsh regarding this matter and had already informed the private office of this dilemma. I stated to Dr. Mohsin that he knew that I must wait for instructions from A.R. before I could release any sponsorship.

"Tomorrow evening the ex-Al-Salama physicians working here at Bakhsh would like for you to attend a meeting. I believe, Gordon, that communicating with you directly will help relieve the tension. There will be about twelve to fifteen doctors present at 9 pm in the hospital's conference room on the third floor."

I mentioned to Dr. Mohsin that if he believed such a meeting would be helpful, I would certainly come to it, Inshalla.

When I told Dr. P.K. about the meeting, she tried to convince me that nothing good would come out of the meeting, considering the hopeless situation. She thought that I should not attend the meeting. I really saw no particular problem in accommodating Dr. Mohsin's request. I wanted the DMT members to be as accessible to the ex-staff as possible. As it turned out, I should have listened to Dr. P.K.'s advice on this matter.

The next evening I went to the meeting. It was much more hostile than I had expected. The physicians directed their frustrations and anger at me since they had no access to the private office. I encouraged them to contact their respective consulates.

They all knew that until I received instructions from A.R., sponsorships would not be transferred; and until special funding was received, back salaries and service award benefits could not be paid. I promised them that I would make sure that their concerns were provided to the private office the following morning. In my heart I believed that the private office would continue on the same course until A.R. made some progress with the Palace representatives regarding the hospital transaction.

One of the more out-spoken physicians angrily spoke. I anticipated that some time during the meeting that this particular physician would claim center stage. He began to express himself in the outrageous fashion that he was so known for.

"Mr. Gordon, we have been informed that you and the rest of the DMT have already received your service award monies. Is that true?"

I expected that this topic might come up, but I was not expecting such a foul mood displayed by all present. The non-payment and non-sponsorship transfer issues had shattered past friendships and working relationships and trust that had been developed over the past two years.

I responded to the physician, "Doctor, when the DMT members were appointed, the only incentive that we could offer was service award priority once funds were available. Yes, the DMT members have been made loans that are the equivalent to their service awards. These loans will be paid back into the DMT operational account once special funding for the service awards is received. By the way, the DMT contracts provide very poor benefits."

The doctor continued, "Well, it seems to me that the DMT members are all living and working in paradise. They have already been paid. We poor old physicians who produced all the funds will be the last on the totem pole."

Then the others chimed in, supporting the physician.

I tried to cool the reaction down, but it was futile. "Gentleman, we have made numerous loans against the service awards due to many ex-employees who have demonstrated that a true emergency exists. Such a loan was made to one of the physicians who presently is sitting at this table."

The same doctor then angrily blurted out, "Hey, that's great news; we will all come over tomorrow to receive a loan that is equal to our service award benefits. Is that ok? This whole thing stinks. What do you mean "loans"? It's our money. How do you lend someone his or her own money?"

Another physician interrupted, "Gordon, you have let us down. Why wasn't the money distributed equally amongst all of the ex-employees."

By now, I was getting fed up with the abuse. I understood their frustrations and why they were directing their anger at me. But enough is enough.

"Gentleman, I came here this evening at your request to try to provide you the answers the best I could. I was not expecting this type of attack. Obviously, it was a mistake to have come."

As a parting blow, Dr. Mohsin said, "Gordon, you should have not taken the money. That money will not give you any happiness. The captain should not be the first to abandon his sinking ship."

I made one final reply. "Gentleman, believe what you want, but the ship sank at midnight March 6th. Inshalla, special funds will be received to pay all ex-employees their benefits due. Hopefully, I can convince the private office of the importance of releasing your sponsorships. It would seem to me that this issue is the most serious for you at the moment."

I then stood to excuse myself.

Dr. Mohsin also stood and said, "Gordon, you are a brave man and we appreciate your telling the truth. At least you did not lie as other DMT members have. Regardless though, we feel that receiving those benefits before the others was wrong."

I knew this issue would be problematic regardless of the previous agreements made. Criticism would be forthcoming. I still believe that the service award priority given to the DMT was justified as per the pre-contractual agreements made with those members and approved by the labor office. Others did not see it that way.

The first thing the next morning, I visited with Dr. Rayes at his office at Al-Murjan.

"Dr. Rayes," I started, "the situation has reached an explosive level. We must convince A.R. that the release of the sponsorship transfers is critical, especially if we are going to continue to hold up the benefits due. We have pushed the ex-employees to the limit. They have done what we had hoped they would do; it's our turn to respond."

By now a formal class action complaint had been registered with the Labor Court. The Labor Office was demanding that the ex-employees be paid. They were also demanding that Igama transfers take place or exit only visas issued.

The Egyptian and Philippine General Consulate officials had visited with us trying to put political pressure on the Bin Mahfouz family. There was a threat by the Philippine consulate to blackball the entire Bin Mahfouz enterprises if they did not correct these problems.

All of the newspapers continued to carry the Al-Salama saga with articles appearing quite often.

The only party who appeared nonchalant about the whole ordeal was the Palace.

A.R. still refused to succumb, even to these pressures.

"Gordon," Dr. Rayes replied, "I have already heard about the doctors' meeting you attended last night. Perhaps you should have not gone. The only thing A.R. is seeking is a signed document with the Royals. Once he receives that, even if the funds are not immediately forthcoming, he will provide special funding for all ex-employee benefits due and we will also release all sponsorship transfer request. Until that happens, he has instructed us to hold to the present course."

"Dr. Rayes, we have been more successful than I had anticipated with our collections. We should also be receiving about 1.5 million riyals from KFSHRC, Jeddah, for the supplies they have bought from us. I believe we should open up the ex-employee loan program for all those who fall into pre-determined criteria. I believe we could make additional loans out of the DMT operational account up to two million riyals without jeopardizing its operational budget. Many of the Filipino nursing staff who have not secured new jobs don't even have money for food. Rumors are that some of our ex-nurses are even prostituting themselves to earn money to get by."

We decided that we had to do at least this much, even though it was not sanctioned by A.R. We established specific guidelines regarding loan priority and amounts that could be loaned out.

The word "loan" was probably a misnomer, as so graphically stated by the doctor at the infamous Bakhsh physician meeting I had attended. These were actually advances against benefits due. One of the guidelines established that to all ex-employees leaving the Kingdom on an exit-only visa, we could advance payment up to a maximum of SR7500. Any amounts owed over this amount would be paid to the individual only when funds became available. The ex-employee would be required to provide us his/her bank wiring instructions or appoint an official caretaker who would receive the funds on the departed ex- employee's behalf. Most were very leery to leave the Kingdom without having collected all benefits due, a legal requirement that we had chosen to ignore. Some was better than none at all. Another of our guidelines was that if an ex-employee had not secured new employment, we would advance about fifty percent of the benefits due, not to exceed 20000 riyals. From time to time a call would come in from the private office to advance certain ex-staff the entire or almost the entire amount due. The final figure depended upon how successful the individual had been in reaching Dr. Rayes. For the most part, he kept out of the loan program.

We started this formal loan program in the first week of May and had planned on its continuing only until June 1st.

As the weeks continued to roll by without resolution to the problems, it became obvious that the program would have to be extended. Knowing that the other key DMT members would be placed under great pressure to advance funds to all that requested such, I spent my entire days during this period administering the program. I was reluctant to delegate this task to anyone else. If that were to occur, the DMT operational funds would quickly be depleted. Ex-employees were required to place their loan requests in writing. I limited the number of interviews per day to forty-five as the DMT office location was flooded with ex-employees striving to have loan requests approved. During this period, we advanced about 2.5 million riyals to ex-employees out of the DMT operational account. This program had literally kept the ex-employees from having a true revolution against the DMT and the private office.

In late June, I visited with Dr. Rayes regarding the DMT loan program.

"Dr. Rayes, between the service awards paid to the DMT and loans (advances) to other ex-employees, we have paid out about 5 million riyals or some twenty percent of the total amount due. As you know, this money has come directly out of the DMT operational account. I do not believe we can lend much more without jeopardizing the viability of the DMT operations. Until some of this is reimbursed, we'd best discontinue the loan program now. We should be able to fund the DMT through August as it now stands."

We both agreed that no additional loans would be made except in truly emergent life threatening situations. The private office was surely not going to provide the DMT with any operational funds if we ran out.

In late June, Dr. Bahabri contacted me and set up an emergency meeting at KFSHRC, Jeddah.

"Gordon, I have outstanding news for you. The Palace is going to deposit enough monies into a special King Faisal Hospital account to pay off the 27 million in back salaries and benefits due to ex-Al-Salama staff. We will receive this special funding within twenty-four hours. We will then transfer it to your account so that the payment can be made."

Dr. Bahabri had a vested interest in seeing this payment issue resolved. Many of the ex-Al-Salama nurses and technical staff had joined KFSHRC, Jeddah. They complained daily about the situation, their morale continuing to decline. Dr. Bahabri would be perceived as a hero to these employees if he were able to pull this off with the Palace. It would be considered a major early success for him.

I was elated. The entire DMT staff and Dr. Rayes felt that at least this important issue had been resolved.

That very evening, I received a call from Dr. Rayes.

"Gordon, I have some bad news. A.R. has instructed me not to accept the money. He is unwilling to move forward in solving the problems until he has some type of written document from the Palace regarding the hospital transaction. In addition, he is taking himself out of the picture. The owner of the hospital is his father, Sheikh Khalid Bin Mahfouz, and A.R. does not have the legal authority to act on the owner's behalf. There will be an owner's trustee appointed that will have total responsibility for the hospital transaction. We will be receiving all future instructions from the owner's trustee regarding matters of service award payments and Igama transfers."

"Dr. Rayes, the word is already out that the Palace is providing the necessary funds. We all, especially A.R., are going to look very bad if we do not accept these funds so the payment issues can be resolved. Frankly, I believe we will be placing our DMT members in harm's way by this approach. A.R. and you are isolated from the day-to-day attacks that we are being subjected to. This action may very well send them over the edge. I believe it is a serious mistake to turn this down."

Dr. Rayes agreed with me but indicated that there was nothing he could do unless A.R. changed his mind. We had our orders and that was that. I inquired who the new owner's trustee might be and if A.R. had simply given up on the whole thing since this appeared to be a total reversal in strategy. Dr. Rayes assured me that A.R. hadn't given up but rather felt that he had been violated and mislead by the Palace representatives. Seeing that an impasse had been reached, he suggested that someone else could be more effective working on behalf of the owner. Also, legally he could not act on behalf of Sheikh Khalid, even if an agreement was reached, for he was not legally designated as the owner's representative.

"Gordon, the Saudi gentleman who has been selected as the owner's trustee is Sheikh Ibrahim Afandi."

Sheikh Afandi was a very well known respected and influential Saudi attorney. He was one of the "big hitters" and dealt with the senior Royal Family members often. Sheikh Khalid could not have chosen a more high profile Saudi outside of the Royal family members themselves.

The following morning, I called the key DMT members together and briefed them on the previous evening's discussions with Dr. Rayes. There was a deep disappointment and a foreboding atmosphere in the room. We all knew the problems that were getting ready to hit with the ex- employees once they heard the news. I actually had to plead with a couple of members not to quit the DMT team. We all were beginning to fear for our own safety once this information was out.

Immediately after the meeting with the DMT team, I went to see Dr. Bahabri. Having previously pleaded with him to see what he could do with the Palace in helping resolve the issue, I felt embarrassed about having to decline what had previously been offered. He had been successful with the Palace representatives; I'm sure, only after exhausting discussions. Now, I had to tell him that we could not accept the funds. Like me, he could not believe what he heard.

"Gordon, does A.R. and the owner's trustee understand whom they are dealing with? Has A.R. lost his mind? I believe your private office has made a politically dangerous gamble regarding this matter. I'm sure the offer from the Palace, once turned down, will not come again."

We all knew that Prince Abdul Aziz Bin Fahad was the Royal family member who had wanted Al-Salama Hospital. He is the youngest son of the King and rumor has it that he is also his favorite. He was the individual to whom Dr. Bahabri referred when he asked if the private office and the owner's new trustee knew with whom they were dealing.

The ex-employees were livid. They were beginning to understand clearly that the DMT's hands were tied regarding these problems. In fact, we now referred all complaints to the new owner's trustee, Sheikh Afandi.

After several unsuccessful attempts to contact Sheikh Afandi, both Dr. Rayes and I sent him a fax. Both of us articulated the acute importance of the non-payment and Igama transfer problems. The faxes further stated that we were no longer assuming responsibility for future actions that might occur as a result of the unresolved issues, including the safety of the DMT members. We were equally frustrated with what appeared to be total inaction by the owner's new trustee. It had also appeared that A.R. had gone into complete hibernation.

By now, it was the first week of July. I'm sure that irate telephone calls and all sorts of visitors were besieging Sheikh Afandi's office due to our referral of all vendor and ex-employee complaints and all government officials to his office. The DMT offices became a revolving door. Everyone who came in was immediately referred to Sheikh Afandi's office.

I finally received a return call from the Sheikh. He wanted to meet with Dr. Rayes, eight of the ex-Al-Salama physicians who were now employed at Bakhsh Hospital and me in his home the following evening at 10 pm. I contacted Dr Rayes, who refused to be present and asked that I mention that he was out of the country. The eight physicians invited were mostly the same ones that had roasted me at the meeting at Bakhsh hospital a couple of weeks previously.

The ex-Al-Salama physician who by now had informally assumed the role of physician spokesman was Dr. Taher Hassan, previous head of cardiology services at the old Al-Salama Hospital. He was a good choice to be the spokesman for the physicians since he was well liked and politically astute. He had not been present at the meeting I had attended at Bakhsh Hospital.

"Dr. Taher, this is Mr. Gordon. I have some good news, I think. We have been requested to meet Sheikh Afandi tomorrow evening. He has also requested the presence of several other specific Bakhsh physicians. I will send you a fax with the names of the physicians he has invited. Please inform the others. Please note that it's important that Dr. Omayer and Dr. Saber do not start complaining about the DMT members. I have been requested to be the spokesman for this group by the private office. We all must remember that we desire the same thing. The payment of all benefits due and the Igama transfers are paramount."

"I totally agree with what you say, Mr. Gordon, and will contact the others. I cannot guarantee you that Dr. Omayer and Dr Saber will not verbally attack you during the meeting. I agree that if they do, it will be counter-productive. But everyone knows those two are a couple of loose cannons."

The following evening's meeting with Sheikh Afandi provided the illusion of a very successful meeting. The Sheikh had a distinct presence about him that conveyed action and confidence. He assured us that he would be meeting with Prince Abdul Aziz Bin Fahad within two days. He stated that the outstanding benefit payments and the Igama transfer issues would be resolved within one week after his meeting with the Prince.

We all left the Sheikh's villa with new hope and a feeling that Sheikh Khalid had selected the right individual as his trustee. The two doctors that I was concerned about had, for the most part, behaved themselves and had not gone off on a tantrum.

Another couple of weeks rolled by without any resolution of the problems. At least now the Sheikh returned my calls after a couple days. I was keeping Dr. Taher informed daily so he could pass on the information to the physicians.

Sheikh Afandi's excuse for not having resolved the problems was that Prince Abdul Aziz was out of the Kingdom. It would not be resolved before he was able to meet with the Prince. This information was quickly disseminated and at least provided a glimmer of hope.

At this point, I really was not much involved with the private office since A.R. had turned everything over to Sheikh Afandi. Dr. Rayes and I visited by phone every other day or so. I attempted to keep him informed of the pulse of the ex-employees, vendors, and the like.

The MOH had backed off their threats to fine Dr. Bakhsh if the ex Al-Salama physicians did not get their Igamas transferred. Even the MOH, recognizing the matter was not in our hands, had to make exceptions because of who was involved in the dispute.

My working relationship with Dr. Bahabri, interim CEO of KFSHRC, Jeddah was becoming a little strained. Several of his lieutenants, some of whom had been previous Al-Salama Hospital employees, were demonstrating more open signs of dislike with the DMT members. We started getting requests to vacate the third floor. We were also informed that all previous Al-Salama patient medical records had to be removed from the KFSHRC, Jeddah campus in a very short time frame.

It was becoming more difficult to remove off-site the supply items that the hospital had not wanted. KFSHRC representatives continually asked about the Saudi ABV undelivered equipment that by now was being stored mostly in our off-site warehouse. They were frustrated that anything having to do with Saudi ABV hospital construction had to be routed through the DMT before Saudi ABV responded. Most of the time, Dr. Bahabri and I could work out some type of compromise, but these issues were placing a strain on both of us.

Two particular issues caused strong disagreements. One was that he refused to pay the DMT cash for the Al-Salama supplies and disposables that KFSHRC, Jeddah had requested. His response was that these monies would be offset against the eventual sale or lease of the hospital. This wouldn't help me any. I had planned for these 1.5 million riyals to go directly into the DMT operational account, not to be offset sometime in the future. Hell, the transaction with the hospital might never be accomplished. A second issue evolved when he requested that we sub-lease several empty Saudia City villas to KFSHRC, Jeddah. When I refused to do so because, again, he would not pay cash and wanted the rent payments to go against the future hospital transaction, he became quite upset. I needed cash now, and we were able to rent those villas to tenants who would pay up front.

I had asked Dr. P.K. to move from her clinic space to another location on the third floor. With the third floor's having three corridors, such a move would pose no serious problems. Her office had been on the first corridor while the DMT location was on the third corridor. Moving her clinic to the third corridor, immediately adjacent to the DMT location, freed the entire first and second corridors for use by KFSHRC, Jeddah.

Mr. Safar was relocating his office from the main hospital to the first corridor where Dr. P.K.'s clinic was previously located. He became upset with Dr. P.K. when she did not leave her personal indoor plants and other office décor for his use. These two had not gotten along very well in the past anyway. At the same time, there was, on the third floor, a well-known, somewhat arrogant Saudi physician, previously a private independent physician at Al-Salama Hospital, who continued to store his office furniture there. When he was asked to vacate these items so KFSHRC could take over the space, he became very angry. "Why do they let that Indian, non-Muslim, female doctor continue to have her clinic here, while at the same time you are kicking me out? As a well-known Saudi national physician, I damn well should have preference over her."

"Dr. Sindi," I responded, "I'm sure if you were practicing in your clinic here, instead of using the space to store your furniture, KFSHRC would not have any problem in providing you space until the end of September. Dr. Kaushik is conducting her clinic here; you are not. Perhaps you should talk with them instead of me about the matter."

Dr. Sindi and Mr. Safar (now working for KFSHRC) were both upset with Dr. P.K. I have no solid proof but I highly speculate that they contrived a plan to get her out of the building and in trouble with the MOH. There was circumstantial evidence later on, which suggested this was the case.

In early July, the MOH paid a surprise visit to the third floor of the utility building. Three individuals marched down to Dr. P.K.'s clinic where her nurse was telephoning patients to remind them of appointments. They demanded to see and then took her appointment book. They also took her license for Al-Salama Hospital. Then they locked and sealed her clinic. She did not even have time to remove her personal belongings before the clinic was locked up.

Two of the inspectors were from the MOH, and the third was from the police. Most of the activity between these individuals and Dr. P.K.'s nurse occurred before I walked down to the clinic to see what all the commotion was. At the same time I arrived, so did Dr. P.K. She talked to one of the MOH officers whose wife was her patient.

When we asked the representatives what was going on, they stated that Dr. Kaushik had been practicing under the license of Al-Salama Hospital, which was now closed, and asked why she was practicing in KFSHRC unless she was their employee.

All of the ex-Al-Salama physicians had the same problem associated with their medical licenses. Since no sponsorships were being released to other employers, medical licenses were expiring. It was no longer possible for Al-Salama Hospital to renew these licenses since the hospital was no longer in business. In order to have a medical license renewed by the MOH, the practicing physician had to be under the sponsorship of a hospital or clinic that was operational. It was a genuine "catch 22" situation. Even the MOH recognized the dilemma and did not push the licenses issue. The business about Dr. P.K.'s being asked to leave the third floor and refusing this request by KFSHRC, Jeddah was ludicrous and a result of conspiracy. She had been given the space until September 30th just like all the other private independent physicians. Unlike the others, she had elected to take KFSHRC's offer to stay put in the clinic until September 30th thus giving her more time to decide to which other private hospital she would relocate. She showed them the official minutes of her previous meeting with Dr. Morehead of KFSHRC, and I also showed them the minutes of the meeting conducted with the private physicians in which Morehead had stated that they could remain in the clinics until September 30th.

A couple of days later an article appeared in the Saudi Gazette about a physician's clinic being closed down by the MOH. Even though the article did not mention her specifically by name, all associated with the medical profession in Jeddah were aware of who it was. All these actions, not to mention the loss of her patients with her clinic's closure, placed Dr. PK under great stress.

Dr. Rayes and I worked very hard with the MOH to convince them that their action against Dr. PK had been unfair. It was simply a matter of providing evidence that she had permission from KFSHRC, Jeddah to be there and to demonstrate to the MOH that many other ex-Al-Salama Hospital physicians were in the same boat regarding the expired licenses.

We produced copies of meeting minutes in which Dr. Morehead had previously given permission for all private independent physicians to remain in their 3rd floor clinics up to September 30th. Amazingly, KFSHRC, Jeddah seemed not to be aware those minutes had been taken. The matter of the license was more difficult. Even though the MOH was not enforcing the licensing issue with other ex-Al-Salama physicians, they were very reluctant to show this lack of enforcement by reversing what they had already done pertaining to Dr. P.K.'s licenses. It was unfair that she had been singled out, but technically, the MOH had taken the correct action. The private office ultimately authorized me to grant an exception to our transfer policy. This allowed her to change her sponsorship to another local private hospital employer. Soon after that she received her new licenses from the MOH under the sponsorship of the Bakhsh private hospital.

This was a dramatic ordeal for her to go through and was completely unconscionable as she had not yet recovered from losing Al-Salama Hospital after working there for nine years. I have reason to believe that this underhanded act was orchestrated by the disgruntled Saudi physician and the ex-Al-Salama employee whom she had asked to return the plants that he had taken.

Almost all of the ex-Al-Salama Hospital physicians were facing problems. Because of the number of doctors who were suddenly seeking new positions, the Jeddah market place became quickly saturated. Most had to accept jobs at one-half to one-third of their previous salaries. I do not believe, however, that any of the other doctors experienced the degree of difficulties and emotional stress that Dr. P.K. had with the closure of Al-Salama Hospital.

Ex-Al-Salama patients were also suffering from the closure of the hospital. All of them had to find other doctors and hospitals, which were now becoming over-crowded. When such a large, active, private health care provider is suddenly closed, it greatly disturbs the marketplace. The other private hospitals absorbed the patients that had been using Al-Salama. These hospitals were having a bonanza. Their inpatient and outpatient workload skyrocketed. With the reduced competition, prices soared. The net result was a decrease in services and options with a simultaneous increase in cost for private patients. KFSHRC, Jeddah was only going to provide services to the Royals and other dignitaries at first. They had plans to offer their services to private patients, but this was a secondary purpose. When they did finally get around to serving the private market, their prices were more than double what other hospitals were charging. Their mind set was also foreign to the private practice of medicine. For the most part, private patients were very reluctant to use KFSHRC, Jeddah.

The general populace was also upset that such a beautiful five star hospital serving the needs of the private market place could suddenly be snatched away to become so underused by a chosen few. This certainly didn't go unnoticed. Very little was said openly by the Saudis regarding this act of reverse privatization. In guarded conversations, however, this was the hot topic at the time. The takeover of Al-Salama Hospital received much more attention than the NCB takeover. At least with NCB, the general public was not affected. Their banking activities went on as usually. This was not the case with the takeover of the Al-Salama Hospital.

Linda, Mark, and Emily were back in Jeddah for their usual summer vacation. This year Linda had come several weeks earlier than the kids. Mark and Emily came over together much later because of their summer activities back at home. Emily was heavily involved with her cheerleading activities, and Mark was preparing for graduate school. Because of these factors, the kids would only be in the Kingdom about one week. The plan was that we would all leave together the first week of August and travel to Switzerland for five days. The family would than go back to Texas and I would return to Jeddah.

Allowing Emily to spend most of her summer back in Grapevine paid off for her. She was selected as an All-American high school cheerleader during the competitions she was in. Mark graduated from Baylor University in late May and came to Grapevine to stay with Emily so Linda could come to the Kingdom. Mark was accepted to graduate school at Rice University in Houston to study mechanical engineering and would be starting in mid-August.

Before the kids arrived in late July, Linda and I had taken a brief trip to Dubai, UAE. The three-day get away was fun and relaxing. Dubai is an ultramodern city with fabulous hotels and restaurants. We took a desert safari one late afternoon on which the four-wheel drive vehicles all ended up at a typical Bedouin camp. The small tour group experienced a traditional Arabic dinner and enjoyed watching the Arabic dances and listening to songs and music under a gorgeous starlight night.

After we returned to Jeddah, Linda kept herself quite busy shopping at the souqs and visiting with the other ladies in the compound.

Once Mark and Emily arrived, I tried to schedule as many activities as possible within the short time they would be in Kingdom. We were able to take only one dive in the Red Sea.

The kids and I did take a three-day driving excursion to the city of Abha in the Assir region of Saudi Arabia. Linda decided to stay back in Jeddah for the drive was going to be quite long.

I didn't realize that it was going to take fourteen hours of driving to get to Abha. The highway was a two lane, winding mountainous route that was slow and demanded much driver concentration. On the other hand, the scenery was outstanding and the weather very pleasant. Abha is almost 3000 meters high and offers a great escape from the smothering heat of Jeddah in the summer months. It is a popular place for Saudis from all over the Kingdom to come for summer family vacations.

I had reserved the services of a couple of experienced French mountain climbers who were staying in Abha. They had been hired by the local Prince to be on call when he or his family wanted to do some climbing. The professional climbers had plenty of time on their hands, so the Prince had given them permission to take others out when he or his family wasn't using them. These two guys were put up in the beautiful Abha Palace Hotel with all expenses paid and a fat salary. It seemed to me like the perfect job.

We reserved their services for two days and took two different climbs. The first day was more of a practice climb, learning how to "rope up" and scale rocks and cliffs. It was quite strenuous but also quite safe. We had the right type of equipment and experienced climbers to help us learn. The second day we went to a location called Al-Habula about fifty kilometers outside of Abba. There, we negotiated a vertical cliff that was about two hundred meters high. The climb took two hours to complete. In the more difficult sections, steel rods had previously been hammered into the rock wall that made it possible for novices like us to climb. At the top of the cliff, the view looking towards the west and seeing the desert some 3,000 meters below was spectacular. The Red Sea was only about another eighty kilometer due west, but was not visible from this vantage.

The Al Hubula climb was exhilarating, but exhausting. We did not get back to Abha until 3 pm where we immediately checked out of the hotel and departed for Jeddah. While driving through a dark tunnel on the way down the escarpment, we narrowly escaped a serious accident. Finally, we arrived back in Jeddah about 3 am the following morning. I was totally exhausted and swore that if there were a next time to Abba, I would take at least two more days off or fly instead of drive.

The following day, I heard unfortunate news about a situation that involved one American and three British ex-pats regarding a major alcohol bust. I did not know any of the people involved, although the American and one of the Brits lived at the Arabian Homes compound where I lived.

They were involved in smuggling in two containers of liquor through the Jeddah Port Authority. Even though alcohol beverages are prohibited in the Kingdom, there is a strong black market for brand name liquors such as Black Label Whiskey, Gordon's Gin, and several brands of Scotch. Where there is demand, there will be product, legal or not. The ex-pat community consumes its fair share of alcohol, but the big black market is in supplying certain rich Saudis. I have been told by reliable sources that it is not uncommon for individual Saudis to order a hundred and fifty thousand riyals of booze at a time. There is a very lucrative illicit market for such products. The consequences can be extremely bad for those who take the risk and get caught. It is said that Saudi Arabia is the largest market for illegal import of Scotch whisky.

These particular individuals had gotten into big time smuggling and had stepped on some toes. Rumor had it that because they were playing out of their league, they were set-up at the port. I am convinced that corruption with port inspectors is rampant. At any rate, these guys got caught and were placed into prison for a long period of time. Under the circumstances, the death penalty would not have been out of the question. In some ways, perhaps they would have been better off. I was told that one of the British guys attempted suicide twice during his jail term. One cannot expect any help whatsoever from his consulate if caught in this type of illegal activity.

The sad thing is that while they were caught and thrown into prison, the booze made it through and was distributed by the party that had set them up. These poor souls might be rotting away in prison for many years while others on the outside enjoyed their illicit products. The American chap had a beautiful, young Filipino wife who didn't waste any time in becoming involved with someone else who could maintain her in the way she had become accustomed. So goes life in the Kingdom, on the dark side.

Linda, Mark, Emily, and I left together for Zurich, Switzerland the last day of July. This is a great place for a holiday during the summer. We spent two beautiful days in Zurich, two days in Lucerne, and one day on a tour through the Alps. It was great to get out of the heat and humidity of Jeddah in August, even if only for five days.

Again, Mark and Emily completely wore me out, this time with their desire to hike up almost every mountain they saw. After these five days in Switzerland, they departed for the states and I went back to Jeddah. It had been a memorable five days.

When I returned, I discovered that a lot had happened while I had been out of the Kingdom. My key DMT staff members caught me as I was entering my office the first day back.

"Gordon, two days ago a Memorandum of Understanding was signed between Sheikh Afandi, representing our owner, Prince Abdul Aziz at the Palace, and KFSHRC, Jeddah. This memorandum states that the Palace will transfer twenty-seven million riyals into a special account at KFSHRC, Jeddah to be specifically used for paying the back salaries and service awards. It goes on to say that the three parties have agreed to complete the details of the transaction within ninety days from the date that the document was signed."

"This is great; it's what we have been waiting for. What are the snags as you all see them?"

They indicated that the only problem that they could see was that KFSHRC; Jeddah was not transferring the funds into our account. They were to be responsible for all payments made and would come up with the administrative details of how best to go about the distribution.

I was concerned about this approach. How would they know what to pay each person? The only thing we had provided to them was the gross amount due employees. They had no idea of what the net due to each employee was as a result of advances, loans, telephone bills owed, and other expenditures. For their plan to work we would need to turn this information over to them. I was not at all sure if the owner's representative, Sheikh Afandi, would allow us to do this.

After this brief meeting with the key staff, I called Dr. Rayes. He confirmed what the DMT team had told me.

"Dr. Rayes, this twenty-seven million is serving as a deposit, as I see it, with the balance of the hospital transaction due once the details are completed between the Palace and Sheikh Afandi. Is that correct?"

He responded that this was precisely correct and at least now the Palace would be paying enough out for us to pay off our ex-employees.

"Dr. Rayes, I am not comfortable with KFSHRC, Jeddah's being responsible for the distribution. We have already paid out more than five million riyals to the ex-employees as loans against the service awards due. Once they have completed the distribution correctly, they will have about five million riyals leftover. Can we trust KFSHRC, Jeddah to give us back that leftover balance to reimburse the DMT operational funds that were used to make these loans?"

"Well, Gordon, that's a very good point. They certainly should. I'm afraid that there's no way around their making the distribution. The Memorandum of Understanding specifically states that these funds will go directly into a special KFSHRC, Jeddah account only to be distributed by them to our ex-employees. In order for them to do this accurately, we must provide them the correct net amount due ex-employees.

"By the way, I failed to mention that we have been given the go-ahead for release of sponsorships for those ex-employees who can provide us demand letters from their new employers."

This news about the release of sponsorships was great. It appeared that both major issues concerning our ex-employees were being solved.

I was beginning to feel better about KFSHRC, Jeddah being responsible for the fund distributions. In some aspects, it took the pressure off the DMT staff, for it was going to be a major administrative headache to make the distribution. Close to eight hundred ex-employees would be coming to receive what was due them. With this decision, the only thing required of us now was to release the listing that reflected the net amount due each ex-employee.

I contacted Dr. Bahabri for a meeting later that day.

"Good afternoon, Sir," I began, "well this news is great about the Memorandum of Understanding being signed. It looks as though we will finally be able to take care of the overdue payments and sponsorship transfer problems concerning our ex-employees."

"Yes, this is great news. Gordon, you need to go on vacation more often. See, you leave and all the major problems get resolved."

I laughed and agreed.

He went on to mention that for them to do the distribution, they needed the information from the DMT immediately regarding what we owe each ex-Al Salama employee. He stated that the money should be in KFSHRC's special account by the end of the day so that they could start the payouts within twenty-four hours.

I mentioned that we had the information available and it should take no more than one day to refine the numbers and provide the refined listing reflecting the net amount due each ex-employee. I went on to state that there was one point that was very important to me. "Dr. Bahabri I know that you are aware that over the past couple of months many ex-employees, including the DMT members, have been paid all or a part of their monies due. Actually, we have paid out about twenty percent of the total amount owed. These funds came out of the Al-Salama DMT operational account in the form of loans or advances against the benefits owed. These monies need to be paid back into the DMT account. Once your finance department has completed the distribution, you will have a balance of about five million riyals left. It's critical that this balance be transferred to us so that the DMT operational account is reimbursed."

"Gordon, I doubt if that will occur. I understand your reasoning and I will check with Dr. Jabarti about it, but I would not be optimistic if I were you."

I stated that we felt very strongly about this matter and before we would provide the listing, we had to have a clear understanding that the balance leftover would be transferred to the Al-Salama DMT operational account without delay.

The following day we heard a rumor that only seven million riyals had been transferred into the KFSHRC, Jeddah special account. We had decided not to provide Dr. Bahabri the ex-employee information until we could get some type of response from him regarding the balance of the funds that would eventually be left in the special account. But if this rumor were true, there wouldn't be any balance left anyway.

DMT Finance manager Ehab Sabri came into my office.

"Gordon, I need to speak to you about two items. One is that it is now common knowledge that only about twenty-five percent of the back salaries and service award monies have hit the KFSHRC special account. All the ex-employees feel that this seven million-riyal transfer from the Palace will be all that comes. Everyone is once again very upset and frustrated. Second, I hear that Dr. Bahabri has instructed his finance manager, against his advice, to begin paying immediately twenty-five percent of each ex-employee's gross amount due. This will mean that there will be many staff, including all the DMT members, who will be overpaid. How will we get this money back once it is paid out?"

Once again it seemed that KFSHRC was screwing things up. After confirming the rumor was correct, I called Dr. Bahabri and mentioned that this approach would lead to many ex-employees being overpaid thus depleting the available funds before others were paid what was due. He responded that the Palace had placed severe pressure on him to distribute the funds immediately. Since I had elected not to provide him the net due listing, the only listing he had available was the gross amount due each ex-employee. Since KFSHRC had received a little more than twenty-five percent of the total gross due, he believed distribution of the same percentage out to each ex-employee to be justified. He refused to consider that many of the ex-employees had already received a good part of what was owed. I reminded him that if he continued with this approach, we would never be able to collect the overpayments made; as a result, some ex-employees would be cheated while others would have been overpaid. I pleaded with him to reconsider.

"Gordon, that's your problem. I am not going to risk criticism from the Palace for delaying the distributions. By the way, we expect the additional twenty million balances to hit our special account within one week."

The good news that had come out of the discussion with Dr. Bahrabi was that he sounded confident that the balance of the funds would soon arrive. The bad news was that I anticipated severe problems in coaxing the overpaid ex-employees to return the overpayment. There would be no serious problems with the current DMT members returning the overpayments, but with the others, now scattered all over the Kingdom, there would. They would probably feel that these extra funds were justified for all the problems they had encountered as a result of the several months delay in payment. Frankly, I couldn't blame them.

After conferring with Dr. Rayes, we decided to immediately provide Dr. Bahrabi the information regarding the total net due each ex-employee. Unfortunately, he had already begun the distribution.

"By the way, Gordon, Dr. Bahrabi sent me a fax yesterday complaining about your lack of cooperation. Just thought you should know."

I mentioned that he was just upset that we didn't jump regarding his net due listing request, adding that I felt that KFSHRC had no intention of transferring the ending balance in their special account to us once these payouts had been made.

The issue turned out to be not quite as serious as it had initially seemed. The only ex-employees who had already received more than what they were due were those who had loan advances that amounted to seventy five percent or more of their net due. Not that many ex-employees were in this category. A week later after the second distribution was completed, there were only about twenty ex-employees who had been overpaid and would not return the over payments. Most of these were lower paid individuals and the amount was insignificant.

For the entire month of August and first two-weeks of September, we worked very closely with the KFSHRC, Jeddah finance department in assisting their distribution of the funds. At the same time, we were aggressively involved in the Igama transfer process for those ex-employees who had provided demand letters from their new employers.

By mid-September, most ex-employees had been paid all benefits owed. The one exception was those ex-employees who could not demonstrate proof of sponsorship transfer to their new employers. KFSHRC, Jeddah continued to hold back twenty-five percent of the benefit due until proof of sponsorship change was made. This was at our request, for it was important at this stage to encourage the ex-staff to change their sponsorships as quickly as possible or to leave the Kingdom.

The payment of the back salaries and service award benefits to the ex-employees was originally supposed to occur no later than March 15th. This six-month delay in paying ex-employees had been a nightmare.

KFSHRC, Jeddah was left with a balance of about five million riyals in their special account, as we had predicted. They would not transfer the excess funds to the DMT operational account. In addition, they were one of the last employers to accept the sponsorship transfers making our ex-employees their responsibility instead of Al-Salama's. This delay continued to upset the old Al-Salama staff that was now working for KFSHRC, Jeddah; they still had twenty-five percent of their benefits withheld until the process was completed.

Throughout the six-month period the DMT had been functioning, a significant amount of work had gone into planning for a new Al-Salama Hospital. We had given a presentation to the private office with both our design consultant and Arthur Andersen Company represented at the presentation. I was discouraged when neither A.R. nor Sheikh Sultan attended the presentation. The individuals from the private office who did attend did not seem that interested in the new project.

By now, it was mid-September. I had originally planned that the DMT functions would be completed a month earlier. The original plan was that a few of its members would sign conforming contracts funded out of a new Al-Salama Hospital developmental budget. It seemed that the Bin Mahfouz family was just not that interested in a new project; it was not likely the new hospital would become a reality any time soon.

There had not been one meeting between the Palace representatives and Sheikh Afandi to work out the hospital transaction. The Memorandum of Understanding that had been signed stated that the transaction would be completed within three months after it was signed. Those three months were only days away with absolutely no activity concerning the transaction. Sheikh Afandi seemed to have disappeared into the sunset.

Saudi ABV construction firm had declared the project complete, which in reality it was. Nevertheless, I was instructed not to accept the project as complete, and the ten million riyal withhold was never paid to Saudi ABV. They packed up and pulled off the project site. When KFSHRC, Jeddah kept calling the DMT regarding various small construction items, we simply referred them to Saudi ABV, who never responded.

With vendor account payables of some twenty million riyals, we continually informed them that no payments could be forthcoming until the hospital transaction was complete. Only then would we know if the liability belonged to Al-Salama or to KFSHRC, Jeddah. Some of the suppliers took us to court. As soon as the courts understood that the dispute over payments involved the Royal Family, they simply dismissed the case. Nothing was going to happen regarding vendor payments until someone provided the DMT necessary funds.

By mid-September we had reduced the DMT to about twelve full time equivalent employees. I anticipated that there would be DMT functions required until December or January. The primary items that were still left to be completed were the Igama transfers, relocation of the old Al-Salama patient medical records, and relocation of the DMT office. I was convinced that KFSHRC, Jeddah would not be reimbursing the DMT operational account the five million riyals they owed to us. As for me personally, I anticipated that my duties would be completed by the first or second week of October.

The one last major task that I wished to see completed before I left was the relocation of the DMT offices and old patient medical records. KFSHRC, Jeddah had kept their commitment of allowing us to remain on the third floor until September 30th, but not a day beyond. Originally, I thought the wrap up activities would be finished by mid-August. When I realized that certain activities would probably continue until the first of the year, I had requested Dr. Bahabri to allow us limited space for a while longer. They refused this simple request and demanded that we be off the campus by close of business, September 30th.

After looking at several options, the private office gave us permission to use a small part of the vacant hotel building that was owned by the Bin Mahfouz family. This was the same building that we were planning to convert into a new Al-Salama Hospital if approved by A.R. The building location, space provided, and layout of the area were all quite satisfactory for us. There was enough open space available here to relocate the entire active Al-Salama hospital patient medical records from KFSHRC, Jeddah. It also contained enough office space to accommodate the remaining DMT members. At least all remaining DMT functions could be performed from one location.

My main concern was how we would be able to get the furniture—desks, computers, copiers, shelving—and other needed assets relocated to the new location. None of these items had been included on the asset inventory listing that had previously been provided to KFSHRC, Jeddah. They took the position that all old Al-Salama assets, regardless of whether or not they were on the inventory listing, were now their property. If we could not get these items moved to our new location, we would be sitting on the floor with nothing to work with. To re-outfit the DMT offices, even with the reduced employee count, would have been quite expensive. We certainly were not going to receive any funds from the private office for this purpose.

In addition to these office assets, there were two expensive IBM servers that we needed for the new hospital, if there was going to be one. These had intentionally been omitted from the inventory listing.

Somehow, we had to demonstrate to KFSHRC, Jeddah, that all these items were not their property, nor were they DMT property.

We developed what we called the "blue dot" strategy. We purchased a bunch of blue dot decals about the size of a dime from a local office supply store. We then made sure that all assets we intended to move had a blue dot affixed to them. With some extra stationary from Saudi ABV, we constructed a letter using their letterhead and stating that they had loaned the DMT these assets back in March when the team was being established. The letter also stated that Saudi ABV expected to have these assets returned by January and that all such assets loaned were designated by a blue dot decal.

I did not feel guilty about this at all. All of the items, with few exceptions, were quite old and none were on the inventory listing. We had previously been given verbal permission from KFSHRC, Jeddah that we could take these assets with us. They later changed their minds, which was not unusual. Anyway, we had to have these items to function.

When moving day came on September 29th, we had employed Four Winds Moving Company to assist in the office move. KFSHRC, Jeddah had placed several of their security personnel on the third floor to check all items being taken out by Four Winds.

They looked for the blue dot. If they saw one, no problem. If not, the item was immediately taken out and put aside. They were even checking our staplers. Of course, we had not placed the blue decal on mere office supplies. The comment made by one of the security personnel was, "See there, if we had not checked these items, Al-Salama would have stolen all these supplies right out from under our noses."

Amazingly, the trick worked. All it would have taken was one call to Saudi ABV to discover that the blue dot scenario was only a ruse.

As a parting gesture, after the last truckload pulled out of the utility building en route to our new location, several mysterious blue dots appeared upon the office doors of selected KFSHRC, Jeddah lieutenant employees.

By the close of the first week of October, the DMT office relocation had been completed and routines were almost back to normal.

I paid a visit to Dr. Rayes. We discussed what I saw as outstanding issues to be accomplished and the prospects for a new Al-Salama Hospital. I also submitted to him a proposal that contained several options as to how certain DMT members, including myself, might function until the first of the year.

"Dr. Rayes, very few items pertaining to the wrap up are still outstanding. The vendor payment problem will not be resolved until funds are provided. It is almost impossible to collect any more of the receivables. The Igama transfers will have to continue for the next couple of months. You know the situation concerning the old Al-Salama patient medical records and how that activity must continue for some time, requiring one full and one part time employee. Dr. Rayes, my question to you is are we or are we not going to have a new Al-Salama?"

I knew before asking the question that the Bin Mahfouz family had experienced many disappointments and setbacks concerning the Al-Salama Hospital transaction with the Royals. I had sensed for some time that the family was becoming "fed up" with the whole mess. It seemed to me that the entire transaction was completely stalled. Even the funds provided by the Palace to take care of the ex-employee service award benefits had been shorted by 5 million riyals. When one considered that Sheikh Khalid had spent so much money on the hospital and had had it taken from him for a fraction of its cost, it must have been extremely painful. I thought back to the days shortly before the so-called strategic collaboration days with KFSHRC when a qualified Saudi businessman had supposebly offered close to 1.8 billion riyals to buy the hospital and what might have taken place if that transaction had been completed.

Dr. Rayes responded, "I do not see the interest from key members of the family to build a new hospital at this time. They could, although unlikely, have the Al-Salama Hospital dumped back in their laps. When Crown Prince Abdullah officially becomes King, there is that possibility. He was against this transaction from the beginning and felt that the new Jeddah Military Hospital expansion should have been the site of choice instead of the Al-Salama Hospital. Rumor has it that King Fahad's favorite youngest son prevailed in this disagreement. In the meantime, the Royals have stolen this hospital from Sheikh Khalid for a mere 22 million riyals, money that went to the ex-employees. For all these reasons, A.R., Sultan, and the other family members have very mixed emotions about opening another hospital. They could change their minds at any time. At the moment, though, I do not believe their interest is there for a new Al-Salama."

For just a moment, I felt that now familiar deep hollowness in my chest, that numbness that all was lost. Than just as quickly, I experienced a sensation that a huge weight had been lifted from my shoulders. It was as though a sense of freedom had come quickly over me. I realized that I would soon be going back home to be with my family again. All of the endless frustrations in dealing with the Palace and KFSHRC representatives would soon be no more. Perhaps in my sub-conscience, I knew all along that there would not be a new Al-Salama Hospital. Unlike many others, I was extremely fortunate to have a round-trip ticket back to the greatest country in the world.

We both decided that my services heading up the DMT would no longer be required after mid-October 2000. A couple of the other DMT members would probably be needed until the first of the year. If the family got serious about another hospital, Dr. Rayes knew how to reach me.

I like so many of the other employees, had given my total dedication to the hospital and had affection for it that was very strong. Perhaps one should not become so attached to one's work. Even now, I often reflect on the time I was employed by the Bin Mahfouz family and the aftermath of the hospital takeover. The Royal Decree that forced the take over of the Al-Salama Hospital was a sad demise of a magnificent private hospital owned by a unique individual that was built to serve the health care needs of middle and upper middle class Saudi and other Middle Eastern patients and their families. It clearly demonstrates what can happen in a monarchy where point of law is lacking and when strategic collaboration with those in power turns into reverse privatization.

Afterword

As of summer 2005, the hospital remains under the control of the Royal Family. KFSHRC's venture into the private business sector has had very mixed results. My sense is that they lack the mindset, initiative, and experience to function in a competitive marketplace. Without the funding of the Royal Commission, the hospital will be unable to survive. The outpatient volume is reported to be only about one-fifth of what it was under Al-Salama. The inpatient census is now about the same as when the Al-Salama Hospital existed, but very few of the patients are private. Most are members of the Royal family, MOH referred patients, and special sponsorship patients. The KFSHRC, Jeddah employee count and payroll is more than twice as much as what it was before. Rumors have it that the King's youngest son is disillusioned by the hospital's poor financial performance, which has not represented the type of profitable business that he was originally led to believe existed.

In March 2005, I received a letter from a Washington D.C. attorney who represents Sheikh Khalid and the Bin Mahfouz family. The letter mentioned that secondary sources had indicated that this book was about to be published. The letter was polite but had a subtle warning referring me to the Bin Mahfouz family website, www.binmahfouz.info. After reviewing the website, I could understand how Sheikh Khalid and the Bin Mahfouz family might be a bit paranoid about publications such as this. The vast majority of the publications referred to on the website were written after 9/11 and inferr that the family was significantly involved in funding certain questionable charities that were fronting Al Qaeda activities. Some of the articles even claim that Sheikh Khalid was a brother-in-law of Osama Bin Laden, which is completely false. Although obviously not privy to many of the family's dealings, as the CEO of one of their largest investments, I saw absolutely no evidence that such allegations were valid. I am sure this is why the attorney sublty mentioned in his letter that Sheikh Khalid had taken aggressive steps to vindicate his reputatiion against numerous publications where such accusations have been reported. Yes, rumors were heard, but I saw no evidence.

After responding to the attorney, he did provide me some additional information that was quite helpful in filling in some gaps where I did not have first hand information. I also reminded the attorney of what I had written in the Prologue; sometimes the truth and the perception of truth are not always the same.

Regarding the present political situation of the country, many Saudis want an elected parliament, an independent court system, and basic rights for women in a society in which they can't even drive. Such changes as establishing a point of law within the monarchy would help avoid situations similar to what happened to the Al-Salama Hospital. Thousands of Saudis have been educated in the West and admire the American system. At the same time, most want Washington to stay on the sidelines regarding affairs in their own country. Saudi officials insist that the ruling family is committed to reform, but at a pace that suits the traditional and highly devout Saudi society. It is a fact that the ruling Saud family has been buoyed by recent victories against Islamic militants and an unexpected economic boom fueled by record oil prices. The monarchy has gained some breathing room but, according to some, that will not last for long. In the end, there has to be real reform. It appears, unfortunately, that the House of Saud is slowly closing the door on political dissent, not opening it. A recent law prohibits government employees, including many academics and journalists, from signing petitions or publicly criticizing the regime. According to one of the Kingdom's leading moderate Islamic activists, reform has been intermittent and people are disappointed. The monarchy must find ways for people to participate in the society and to have a voice. After all is said and done, the debate over true reform has to be resolved by the Saudis themselves, without outside influences, especially from the United States.

About the Author

Gordon Utgard has some thirty years of experience in the health care industry, nine being in International markets. He has served in the CEO capacity at five hospitals and one health plan. He created a proprietorship business in early 1997 to support the Blue Cross and Blue Shield Association's development of a worldwide hospital network. This business, Utgard Associates, was also the entity that contracted with the Al- Salama Hospital in Jeddah, Saudi Arabia, to provide the hospital's CEO, which this book is about. Gordon holds a BA degree in Economics/Finance from Baylor University and a Masters of Health Care Administration from Trinity University in San Antonio, Texas. He is a fellow in the American College of Health Care Executives and is a Lead Faculty Member in the school of Graduate and Professional Studies at LeTourneau University in Dallas, Texas. Gordon has served as a Director on several Boards and has presented at several domestic and international seminars. He is also a Rotarian. Gordon is married and has one son and one daughter. He is currently serving as the CEO of a specialty hospital in West Texas.

ISBN 1412065b5-8